MARGARET SCHLAUCH

DOVER PUBLICATIONS, INC. NEW YORK

the

gift

of

language

FORMERLY ENTITLED "THE GIFT OF TONGUES"

Preface

Almost everyone who talks must have wondered at one time or another why he used certain words for certain things. Children, whose ignorance is often so wise, have frequently baffled their parents by the penetrating question: "Mother, why do we say 'table'?" And mother is necessarily forced to evade this question, along with innumerable others. Bilingual persons usually speculate at least tentatively on the relations between the two languages they know. With three or more languages, they begin to wonder about more complicated questions in making comparisons.

An American or an Englishman who knows German is aware that there is some likeness between the words "deep" and *tief,* and he asks himself what it may be. A person with a classical training who learns Russian wonders whether the adjective *vernyi* or верный, meaning "true," is connected with the Latin *verus,* meaning the same thing. A missionary priest learning Cakchiquel in order to work in Guatemala might be struck by the fact that Hebrew *ishshah* or "woman," corresponds fairly closely to the native *ishok,* expressing the same idea. He might be tempted to regard this as evidence that his prospective Indian converts are descended from the lost tribes of Israel, but upon further study he will probably conclude that the correspondence is purely accidental.

A mother teaching her child to talk notices that he has trouble with some sounds while others come quite readily. While she patiently drills him in the "right" pronunciation (that is, the accepted one), she may say to herself: "What makes John drop the *s* in 'story' and say ' 'tory'?" A foreigner learning English shows some psychological difficulties in handling our idiom; we ask him to explain why it is so hard for him to omit the article in using such words as "truth" and "beauty," and he finds that he can't explain except by saying that in his own language one says "the truth" and "the beauty."

v

These are all linguistic speculations—that is, they deal with technical problems of language. They are sometimes very entertaining to the speculator. But the mere thought of reading or studying on the subject usually fills him with horror. What! Learn anything about linguistics! Why, that is surely the dullest of all subjects! Its disciples are supposed to be grim and chilly individuals with never an atom of humanity in their dispositions. Entertainment must be entirely absent from this recondite field. Romance may be expected to lurk in physics, chemistry, biology or mathematics; but in linguistics—never!

Still, with so much curiosity about the subject evident among people in general, the romance must after all be lurking somewhere. The speculation implies at least a possibility of intellectual adventure. Perhaps a book like this can give the answers to some of the questions popularly current about language, without at the same time marshaling a host of unnecessary facts in a forbidding formal array. There are ambitious textbooks and reference books in abundance which could be consulted by inquiring amateurs, but it is doubtful whether the inquirer's ardor could escape dampening in the process. To a trained eye these same volumes may appear to be repositories of the most exciting information, but a non-linguist sees in them nothing but a mass of irrelevant and uninspiring facts. He groans and turns away—to look for romance rather in the latest text expounding the sublimities of mathematics.

The educated reader with an unprofessional, merely casual interest in language has not yet, I believe, received the kind of book he deserves. He is entitled to the information he wants, expressed in language he can understand. The overdiluted and superficial accounts which often pass as popularizations give him too little and leave him justly dissatisfied. The heavily incomprehensible volumes which specialists sometimes produce under the illusion that they are being popular leave him, on the other hand, completely mystified. But surely there must be a middle ground for this much-abused general reader!

This book represents an attempt to reach the general reader and to find the middle ground. There is no wish to repeat

Preface vii

(less well) the extremely competent general introductions to linguistics designed for more advanced students, such as the volumes by Graff, Bloomfield, Gray and Sturtevant, to which grateful recognition will be made in the notes. But the author does hope to answer some of the simpler questions clearly, and at the same time to show some of the fascination of a much maligned subject of study. Afterwards the reader can consult more detailed works with pleasure and profit.

There is a pure joy to be derived from the perception of clear relationships where none was observed before. This exciting experience is for many persons a reward in itself. Linguistic studies yield it abundantly. But there is an even more practical reward to be gained too. If you learn that a certain type of relationship is apt to appear in a language of one given family, then you are quite justified in looking for something like it elsewhere; and you will probably find it. As a result the effort in learning the second will be much easier than the first. What is known as a "gift for languages" is largely an ability to see these likenesses quickly. To see them is to remember more readily the words that exemplify them. Memorizing new words is only difficult when you can't see any sense to them—any relationship to something already known. Some relationships become plain when we observe the difference between our own pronunciation when we are being careful or bookish, and at other times when we are careless. For example: notice consciously what happens to your pronunciation of "Give me" when you are tired. It tends to become "Gimme." The [v]-sound has been changed until it becomes identical with the next one, [m].[1] The resulting [m] may be spoken a bit prolonged, as an indication that it is now taking the place of two different sounds. This "doubled" sound (if you will) is the result of a process known as assimilation, or the changing of two unlike things until they become more alike.

[1] It is customary in employing characters of the phonetic alphabet to use enclosing brackets. See chapter 2, note 1. Ordinary letters are often ambiguous in our spelling.

But if assimilation happens today, in our own rapid speech, it must have happened many times before, in the speech of other peoples. And it did. You observe, for example, that Italian words with a "double letter," as it is popularly called, show clear signs of assimilation from an earlier stage when there were two different letters representing two quite different sounds. It is easy to guess what sounds were there originally, before the change took place. If you encounter the word *otto,* meaning "eight," a little experimenting will lead you to surmise that it was once *octo,* and is connected somehow with our word "octave." Likewise *notte* shows connections with Latin *nocte* and English "nocturnal," *massimo* with "maximum," and so on. Once this sort of thing has been pointed out it seems ridiculously clear and obvious, and it facilitates the learning of a whole series of similar words. Yet the relationship has to be pointed out in the first place.

There is a practical use for all linguistic principles. They clarify what was once obscure and they also make learning new languages very much simpler. The practical aids which linguistic study gives should not be scorned by the exponent of science for its own sake. In this book there will be constant reference to the everyday helps to be used in learning languages. There will be exercises and suggestions for further experiment, designed for those who wish to apply the principles concretely. The notes will tell of additional books to be read in each field. From these initial studies the roads lead out endlessly into other terrains of research: psychology, sociology, anthropology, music, physics. . . . It is a presumptuous thing, no doubt, to attempt so brief and undetailed a survey as this of a vast field where so many great scholars have labored. A wish for brevity and simplicity may have led to inaccuracies or false impressions in the survey. Yet it is to be hoped that the two chief purposes may be served in some measure, no matter what the faults may be. These purposes are: a revelation of some of the poetry and romance in language studies, and an exposition of some of the more practical benefits which may be derived by teachers and learners from these same studies.

CONTENTS

1. Language as Communication

EXPRESSION IN TALKING

Suppose you are about to step across a crowded street without looking about you with due caution. An automobile is careening towards you in conspicuous contempt of traffic regulations. If you continue in your blind carelessness, you are sure to be knocked over, possibly killed. But a quick-eyed stranger, let us say a monolingual Hungarian, sees what is about to happen to you. Shrill with horror, he shouts something at you in the Magyar tongue. You get something of his message without understanding a single word, draw back suddenly, and are saved. Somewhat breathless and also more than a little sheepish at your recent oblivion of surroundings, you stammer your thanks. If in your sudden retreat you have stepped on your savior's foot, you add some words of apology. He on his side smiles, disclaims any reason for your gratitude, and graciously accepts your apology in the appropriate Hungarian formula. Neither of you has understood a word of the other's speech, and yet the interchange has so far been quite clear and eminently agreeable to both participants. It was facilitated, of course, by the simplicity of the situation and the urgency of the first cry. Ideas have been exchanged; there has been communication in the sense that these ideas have been successfully made *common* knowledge to the two people concerned.

Again, suppose you are walking through the park of a seaport town frequented by sailors of many nations. On one of the benches a visiting naval lad is declaring to one of the town's nymphs, in facile, well-practiced phrases, that she is the most

1

beautiful feminine creature that he has ever had the privilege of discoursing with on a park bench. He utters his protestations with the deepest conviction, no matter how many times he has used the time-honored vows before. He may be speaking Swedish, however, whereas the temporary object of his eternal vows may be limited to self-expression in an obscure local Indian dialect of the Pacific coast of Central America. Only a few words of most elementary significance are common to the two of them. Nevertheless, she unerringly comprehends the general import of his remarks, and with appropriate giggles and slaps—repulses not seriously intended—she may assure him that she knows how many times he has used these protestations before. He, for his part, is sure to increase the ardor and conviction of his wooing, employing oaths of sincerity at which (so they say) Jove has been laughing these thousands of years as he has heard their polyglot expression from all parts of the globe. The entire dialogue may be brought to a conclusion entirely satisfying to both parties without having one complete sentence in it actually intelligible to the party listening. And an eavesdropper ignorant of both tongues might also be aware of its import and its happy conclusion.

In both of these situations the pitch, intensity, and tone of voice, the qualities which we generally call "expression" in talking, have conveyed the entire message. "Look out! Danger ahead!" can be understood in any language if the speaker dramatizes the warning sufficiently. It is also rather easy to convey the hyperbolic proposition, "You are the most beautiful girl I have ever met," across any conceivable barriers of speech. A tone of flattering raillery and caress is reported to be unmistakable from the Arctic to the Antarctic.

GESTURE

But variations in quality and volume of voice are not the only methods of carrying messages across a linguistic divide. Gesture is another aid very closely associated with tonal expression. You ask a stranger in a strange city how to find a certain public building. If his reply is to be, "Sorry; I don't know," you will be aware of it before he has so much as opened his mouth, if he merely raises his shoulders and eyebrows, draws down the corners of his mouth, throws his hands out with the palms facing you, and frowns slightly. The extended palms appear to mean: "I put my entire knowledge at your disposal, concealing nothing, but unfortunately the information you require is not there"; the frown says: "I am concentrating on your inquiry—in vain, alas!"; the elevated shoulders and deflected mouth add: "I feel quite disconcerted and physically ill at ease to think that I should fail you in your need, O stranger."

We use these non-linguistic means of conveying ideas, all of us, as an accompaniment to speech. A cry, a tonal inflection, a gesture, are means of communication far more universal than language as we understand it. They are in fact universal enough to be conveyed to animals as well as other human beings. When a man snaps his finger at a trained dog and points to the ground beside him, he is using gestures to substitute for an entire sentence: "Come here, Brownie, and sit beside me." Animals can also understand quite complicated commands by means of tone and voice inflection alone, without the aid of gesture.

We have, then, various ways of communicating with one another and with the lower animals, quite apart from a mutual understanding of the separate speech symbols which we call words. Communication of messages is far more general than an understanding of the languages used by human beings throughout the world. To understand a language, you must always attach the same meaning to a highly conventionalized group of sounds. An enormous number of these groups of sounds—words—in any language have an abstract meaning which could not possibly be conveyed by any gesture, even the most eloquent. There is a great gap between the cry "Look out! Danger!" and the statement "I regret what I did last year. Had I known this fact, then I should have done otherwise." Certainly no conceivable gestures could convey the import of the following terrifying sentence from Immanuel Kant:

But, although extension, impenetrability, cohesion, and motion—in short, everything which outer senses can give us—neither are nor contain thoughts, feeling, desire or resolution, these never being objects of outer intuition, nevertheless the something which underlies the outer appearances and which so affects our sense that it obtains the representations of space, matter, shape, etc., may yet, when viewed as noumenon (or better, as transcendental object), be at the same time the subject of our thoughts (*Critique of Pure Reason*).

Spoken language, as contrasted with gesture, is a highly symbolical method of expression adapted to abstract concepts. But because of the cries, gestures, grunts and similar elemental expressions which form a considerable part of its accompaniment, we are justified in asking ourselves whether it is not closely connected with the means of expression and communication employed by some of the lower animals.

SPEECH OF ANIMALS

It was formerly assumed (with typical human conceit) that man, as a special and separately created being, had received the gift of language ready-made from his Creator. Just as woman was supposed to have appeared suddenly, by a swift if unaccountable exit from Adam's side, so speech was supposed to have begun abruptly on the day when Adam named the animals and other creatures under God's tutelage. Many religions contain a myth about the origin of speech at a given moment under divine instruction. It seemed sacrilegious to suppose, in these days of early speculation, that the infinitely flexible instrument of human expression, which more than anything else makes us men, could have any kinship with the grunts and cries of the lower animals. Some writers, particularly those of a theological bent, deny the kinship today. But when Darwin and his followers pointed out the biological kinship of man with those same lower animals, students of language re-examined their attitude. It became the intellectual fashion, indeed, to look for "evolution" in all matters concerning living things. The sounds made by animals were regarded with a new and salutary respect, since they seemed to offer the proximate simple explanation of the origin of human speech. Presumably grunts and cries merely became standardized and increased in number—and behold! the result was human speech: the result of a clear and steady development or "evolution."

Today we are inclined to think that the relationship of man's speech to animal cries is far more complicated than that. Mere numerical increase in the number of cries will not account for the appearance of abstract, highly conventionalized meanings. Moreover, the shift from the one level (haphazard expression) to the higher one (standardized meaning) may not have been the result exclusively of an infinite series of gradual adjustments, the kind of slow process implied in the term "evolution." It is not impossible to imagine sudden spurts of progress such as occur in other cultural arts.

We shall never know just how or where language first developed, because no records of speech survive from that very distant epoch. A number of scholars have devoted themselves hopefully to the observation and recording of the sounds made by chimpanzees. About the turn of the century, R. L. Garner went so far as to claim that these sounds should be dignified by the name of language. He also claimed that he had learned the meaningful sound-symbols used by his primate subjects, and had communicated with them in what might be called elementary conversations. Others denied this claim entirely, or restricted it to a few general correlations between sound and meaning. Two German students reported that the expression of fear was connected with a high sound like English *ee*, lament by a deep one resembling English *oo,* and joy by a series of repeated *ah's.* Another scholar recorded sounds with musical notations—since pitch might be an essen-

tial element here—and obtained what appeared to be meaningful sound-symbols such as *gak, nghak, gah, gha, kah, ko-ko,*
and so on. There seemed also to be a general association of
some of these sounds with certain emotional situations.

But the curious thing is that despite the well-known ability
of apes at imitation, and the evidence that they can reason
their way through fairly complicated situations, all of these
responses of theirs are too fluid and vague to constitute
language. The sounds which some have called ape-words or
the speech of the chimpanzee do not form symbols which can
be repeated and recognized, always with the same meaning attached to them. In other words, although an ape can ape (imitate gestures), he can not reproduce sound stimuli consistently
enough to establish the beginnings of language. Robert M.
Yerkes suggests in his *The Great Apes* that these animals might,
however, be trained to a gesture language such as deaf-mutes
employ.

Origin of Human Speech

The great question is: what was there in man's physical equipment and his mode of living in the earliest times which permitted him to make use of vocal stimuli and auditory impressions for speaking? It is one of the most fascinating mysteries
of early human development. We shall never know the details of that progress forward towards humanity from the lower
animals. But we can be quite sure that the physiological equipment and the beginnings of sociological organization were
very intimately associated in making possible the great stride.
Each element must have been both cause and effect; and whatever tended to advance the one no doubt advanced the other
also. We no longer assume that the relation between speaking man and the unspeaking primates is a simple one—a matter of straight "evolution"—but neither do we any longer in-
voke miracles to explain the great differentiation. We can
even go so far as to surmise some of the non-miraculous factors which caused it. If language means communication,

probably communal activity played an important part in shaping it.

SIGNALS FOR WORDS

Returning to the human level, as we know it, we find some very elemental signals persisting and helping us in the task of reaching other human beings quickly despite linguistic barriers. In fact, we are very little aware how many signals we receive and comprehend in our daily living apart from spoken words. Emotional sounds and gestures are of surprisingly wide range. We express not only fear, desire, and approval but many other states too when we click the tongue against the roof of the mouth (mild disapproval or reproach), hiss (strong disapproval), cut short a yawn (boredom or sleepiness corrected by regard for other people's feelings), expel the breath with a whistling sound (surprise), inhale with a somewhat osculatory effect. (This last is self-explanatory.) The list could be greatly extended.

Civilized humans who live in cities are constantly receiving complicated signals and interpreting them correctly without the use of words. A red light, a green light, or the gestures of a traffic policeman—all these are the equivalents of imperative or permissive sentences. A bell which rings a certain number of times will announce to students a change of classes, to workers a shift in jobs, to persons on a party wire of a telephone the summons to a conversation with a friend. The bells on shipboard are highly conventionalized signals marking the passage of a day of maritime work. A trumpet call in the Tuileries garden of Paris warns visitors that they must depart. The dirge of a funeral and the chimes of a wedding tell a whole story without words. A green line painted on the ceiling of the New York subway station at Forty-second Street conveys the message: "Follow me, all you who would shuttle over to the West Side trains." The red line, pointing contrariwise, guides the tense and hurrying throngs eastward. Here the symbolism of signs and warnings is almost as elaborate as that in Dante's Hell (to which the place is said to have further similarities), but we who are accustomed to it follow the stylized guides without conscious reflection. A red flag seen in one context means: "Danger! Keep away!" In another connection it may convey a whole political platform, to which the spectator responds with either heated distaste or heated approval, according to his own complicated theories and beliefs. The heat he evinces when he sees the symbol indicates that it has at least been successful in making him conscious of a whole series of theses without the agency of words.

People who live in cities, then, make use of a large number of conventional signals, gestures and acts. Their response to these is quite like that of "primitive" Indians—to whom they may otherwise feel themselves entirely superior—when using an elaborate language of gestures. A dog responding to the snap of fingers, deaf-mutes conversing with their hands, Indians using signs, and New Yorkers intently pursuing a green line, are all behaving in precisely the same way, and to the seeing eye they are also showing their close kinship within the animal realm.

IMITATIVE WORDS

Some spoken words can easily be recognized as concrete signals, hardly more abstract than the flashing of a red light to indicate danger (because that very destructive element, fire, is also red?). Words that imitate the sound or act they are to designate are called onomatopoetic (from the Greek *onoma*, a name, and *poiein*, to make; that is, "name-making"). Such words exist in every language. Many people assume, without further thought, that the languages of peoples remote from the doubtful blessings of European culture are necessarily made up almost exclusively of such imitative words. Conversely, it is commonly thought that the languages of so-called civilized peoples contain a very small number of these words in proportion to the general vocabulary. Actually, the relative number is very small in all languages, whether "backward" or "advanced." In English we have words like "whippoorwill," "peewee," "bumblebee," "humming bird," "murmur," "ding-dong," "bow-wow." Many of them, it will be observed, refer to birds, animals, and insects which are designated by an attempt to reproduce the sound they make. Latin gives us an excellent example of onomatopoeia in the sibilant *susurrus,* meaning "whisper."

We must beware, however, of supposing that a word which we imagine to be imitative is necessarily "primitive" or that it was created by an act of imitation. Sometimes it has reached the form which we imagine to be onomatopoetic by a long development, beginning from entirely different sounds which would appear to us to be far less descriptive. Thus the German word for "anger," spelled *Zorn* and pronounced [tsɔrn], seems to suggest a disagreeable emotion by the hissing explosion of the initial sound; but when we examine its history we discover that it has developed from a milder pronunciation like the one preserved in the English "torn." (The words are actually related; in German, a sister language of English, anger is conceived to be the thing that *tears* at one's vitals.) Still farther back the word is discovered to have existed in a form beginning with a *d,* with a root something like *der-n.* In its more primitive state, therefore, nothing appears of the violent *ts*-sound which presumably gives the German *Zorn* its descriptive emotional effect.

Again, the English words "twitch," "witch," and "itch" end in a sound *tsh,* which may be imagined to be descriptive in one way or another; and yet in all of these words the sound was developed from a very different one, namely, *k,* which is made at the back of the throat instead of being hissed between the tongue and the palate. The Russian language is full of sounds which appeal to many listeners as exceedingly tender and caressing. There are those who find this quality in the word *zhenshchina* for "woman" (the *zh* being pronounced like the French *j* in *jardin*); and no doubt when properly spoken, in appropriate circumstances, it conveys the desired effect. Its origin, however, shows a less tender set of consonants. The word comes from an older form which we can reconstruct as *guen-stina*. (The first syllable is cognate with Greek γυνή [*gunē*], meaning "woman," and also with English "queen" and "quean"—which were formerly undifferentiated.) It would be easy to imagine that the long-drawn-out sound at the beginning of "thin" was descriptive of a state of being—long and narrow—but comparative study shows us that the word originally began with a simple *t* which cannot be prolonged at all. "Thin" is in fact first cousin to the Latin *tenuis*, which has kept the more primitive initial sound.

MEANING AND THE SPEAKER

What happens in the mind of a person using words is a complicated process, about which something more will be said later. It is at least clear after a moment's reflection that the person who talks is not only affecting the listener but also affecting himself, insofar as talking may clarify his own ideas, strengthen his own convictions, or bring to the surface doubts hitherto unnoticed. The words he uses serve to bring back former experiences associated with them, more or less vividly.

MEANING AND THE LISTENER

If we look at the effect of speech on the listener alone, the procedure is more patent. One receives a signal and acts upon it. The signal differs from the red lights, bells, flags, and gestures we have been discussing in that it is made by the tongue, the teeth, the vibration of vocal cords, or a combination of these. The advantages of these organs of speech are obvious. The emitting of sounds is a process capable of wide variety, and it can be accomplished very rapidly. Perhaps at some future time humanity will develop a method even more rapid, varied, and precise for the communication of ideas; but so far we know of none more efficient than speech.

Try to conceive of a human race without language and you realize at once what it has meant to us. There could be no accumulation of the more abstract types of wisdom from one generation to another without the use of spoken syllables and later their recording in written characters. Only skills involving muscular dexterity could have been passed on: improvements in pottery-making, weaving, and building of the simplest sort. Speech is not entirely divorced from skill in handicrafts, as a matter of fact. It has been pointed out that control over organs of speech and increasing complexity and subtlety in their use have developed concomitantly with increasing skill in the use of the hand. Speech and work together have made us men. Neither is conceivable without the other.

If, however, this complementary development had not occurred, yielding us the amazingly intricate and efficient and beautiful instrument known as language, it is difficult to imagine what our history might have been. A race of speechless men is really a contradiction in terms. Our dependence on the written word alone is incalculable. The spoken word, which made possible Greek drama and oratory, Roman law courts, medieval preaching, and the political debates of the French Revolution (to name but a few examples), has conditioned our whole culture as human beings.

LANGUAGE AND COMMUNITY LIFE

Language as communication implies community of living. A symbol is not a symbol—that is to say, it is not effective—unless it is understood in approximately the same way by a group of people living and working together. Students of peoples in remote parts of the earth have described in detail the overwhelming importance of the clan as a whole in shaping the life of an individual. Especially the major events of his career have a public significance far outweighing his private feelings in these matters. There is reason to believe, indeed, that the first person pronoun (singular) was a comparatively late development in some languages. This is vivid grammatical testimony to the relative unimportance of the individual as opposed to the tribe. It seems to imply that in such tribes men could conceive of themselves only as parts of a larger social whole. In such cases it was not possible to say "I do this," but something like "People do so-and-so by means of me, John." Perhaps it is for this reason that the pronoun "we" is rather awkwardly expressed in some languages, since it means "you in addition to the insignificant me." For instance, in Nahuatl (descended from old Aztec), the word for "we" differs from *tehua*, meaning "thou," only in having an *n* at the end of it. Here the first personal idea seems to be subordinated to the second if affixing means subordination.

Apart from grammar, we know from other sources about some of the occasions and ceremonies which would tend to make an individual feel unimportant in earlier forms of society. He would find himself quite submerged in a number of group activities calling for expression through language. For instance, songs and chants used while work is performed tend to merge a man's ego in social activity. Tribal dances accompanied by song are also said to reduce a person's awareness of himself. In this respect they differ from our own social dancing in couples, where a heightened sense of personal qualities and allurements is the gratification desired. It is perhaps unfortunate that modern urban men, working so often in silent isolation and amusing themselves in an individualistic manner, are prevented from enjoying this salutary experience. If it is language that has made us men, we forget at our own cost that language is impossible without communal living.

Besides work and dance, it would appear that language was employed at an early date for two closely associated functions: praying and invoking curses. Blessings were important too. We are perhaps less apt to remember them because the rites which generally accompanied imprecations, such as the stabbing and melting of waxen images, seem more vivid to our imaginations. In any event, it is clear that these spoken formulas represent an attempt to control nature through words. It was felt that if you expressed the desire "Send us rain" or

"Kill my enemy" or "May my child prosper" in the right way, the wished-for consummation would surely result.

MAGIC IN LANGUAGE

From time immemorial men have thought that there is some mysterious essential connection between a thing and the spoken name for it. You could use the name of your enemy, not only to designate him either passionately or dispassionately, but also to exercise a baleful influence over him. Something about him could be affected for good or ill whenever you pronounced the appropriate syllables. To say "Curse and destroy that warrior over there, whose name I don't know," was considered to have little or no effect. The warrior would continue on his way, happily insensible of your hatred. But to say "Curse and destroy Chief Cross-Eye; strike him even as I strike this image of him" was supposed to have a most deleterious effect on his health and spirits, even on his life. Chief Cross-Eye might confidently be expected to show serious damage within a very short time. Not only people, but plants, animals, forces of nature, gods, demons, in fact all creatures could be affected for good or ill by solemn pronunciation of their names in the proper context.

Such a close identification of name and object was a form of sympathetic magic, as it is called. Things alike in appearance were supposed to influence one another. Even today these ideas prevail among us more than the sophisticated reader may suppose. Children have sayings and beliefs which stem from the primeval jungle: "Step on a crack; break your mother's back"; touch wood to ward off bad luck; touch a toad and you'll get warts; wash your hands in the fresh rain water gathered in a hollow tree stump and you'll get rid of them. Even adults do some things and avoid others for the same reasons. A friendly pair walking down a city street will scrupulously avoid passing on opposite sides of a lamppost out of a dimly sensed apprehension that the physical separation will become a permanent spiritual one, and the friendship may turn to enmity.

If the objects about us are thus bound together to each other and to us, it is no wonder that words too should be felt by many people to have a similar powerful magical connection with things. A child named for a famous ancestor is in some societies considered to stand in very close relation to his progenitor's soul, or even to be a reincarnation of it. Giving the name is here tantamount to conferring a whole defunct personality on a living person. In other groups, on the other hand, if the ancestor is still alive, transfer of his name will cause him to die in the near future, since his spirit will be consumed by the younger growing lad to whom it is transferred with the name.

If this organic connection exists between things and the terms for them, it becomes extremely important to apply friendly epithets to beings one would like to placate. Calling them friendly will actually help to make them so. Invisible beings who might be too dangerous should not be named at all, but only alluded to by elaborate indirection. Substitute phrases are used for the Nameless One; then these phrases themselves become too dangerous to handle, and are avoided like a lit charge of dynamite. Substitutes for the substitutes succeed one another, so that some parts of a people's vocabulary become almost unintelligible through timorous circumlocution. It all springs from fear of word magic. A special vocabulary is sometimes developed by the women of a tribe, which the men do not dare to use. Words are used in twisted meanings in order to deceive evil spirits. A woman will say to her child, with false zeal: "You poor, squint-eyed, rickety, miserable changeling!" The words will discourage any lurking demon from stealing such a misbegotten creature; but at the same time there is some danger that the child will become exactly what the words say he is. Verbal magic again! To prevent them from working so effectively, the mother will make some secret sign, such as crossing her fingers, which will check the sympathetic magic of language from operating directly on her child. In games children still cross their fingers to indicate that they are saying the reverse of what they mean, and that the fib "doesn't count."

EXAMPLES OF MAGIC IN LANGUAGE

Here are some examples of charms, prayers, and imprecations which illustrate the potency of words. They are not very ancient, having been recorded in recent historical times, but they do suggest the atmosphere which probably surrounded language at an early date.

First, a Roman inscription, illiterate but highly effective, which expresses someone's lively desire to cause the death of another man. The words fairly tumble over one another in an access of eager hatred: *"Molo Porcelo molomedico interficite, eum occidite, enicate profucate Porcellu et Malisilla usore ipsius!"* Translated, this means: "Please kill Molus Porcellus the mule-doctor; bump him off, croak him, kill him, that guy Porcellus—and (for good measure) his wife Malisilla too!"

Just as intense is the imprecation which Schulze-Jena heard pronounced by a Quiché Indian in Guatemala: "Today I call on you, you cross of evil, and tell you this thing: So-and-so, a man who has money, he scorns me, and it gnaws at my vitals that he scorns me! Did I want anything from him? Did I want any of his money? Let him have it and welcome! But today I bewitch him. . . . Let him feel it now! Mountain of witchcraft, cross of evil, I call on you. . . . I call on a rocky cliff, I call on an abyss, on the hollow tree, on the clump grass, on the thorn bush, on the wind and the clouds, so that he may see and know: I am a master of witchcraft!" The effect of the repetitions is quite horrific in Quiché, for the phrase "I call on" is rendered each time as *k-in-ch'ab-ēkh,* a word rich in guttural sounds.

In a poem written in ancient Scandinavia during the Viking

Age we find further lurid passages of this sort. Skirnir, the messenger of the god Frey, utters the following curse on Gerth, a giantess who has been impudent enough to reject the god's wooing:

> I strike thee, maid,   with my magic staff,
>   To tame thee to work my will;
> There shalt thou go   where never again
>   The sons of men shall see thee.
>
> On the eagle's hill   shalt thou ever sit,
>   And gaze on the gates of Hel;
> More loathsome to thee   than the bright-hued snake
>   To men, shall thy meat become. . . .

Survivals of Word Magic

But we do not need to go to Rome, Guatemala, or ancient Scandinavia in order to get a sense of the supernatural power attributed to the spoken word. This particular form of sympathetic magic, like the others mentioned, can be detected in the people around us. Listen sharply to children at play in the streets of New York and you may hear a dialogue like this:

"What's your name?"

"Puddin' Tane!—Ask me again and I'll tell you the same!"

"What's your number?"

"Cucumber!"

The second youngster is unwittingly repeating a time-honored device for preventing an enemy from using the right name, or "number," even, to curse him by. Even so Odysseus replied falsely that his name was "No Man" when the blinded Polyphemus asked him; and Sigurd the Volsung replied to the dying question of the dragon Fafnir: "The Noble Hart is my name, and I wander abroad a motherless man. I had no father as others have, and ever I live alone." The scribe who recorded this in the *Poetic Edda,* the great collection of early Scandinavian verse about gods and heroes, added this note in prose: "Sigurd concealed his name because it was believed in olden times that the word of a dying man might have great power if he cursed his foe *by his name*."

Among adults, certain words are avoided out of a mixture of motives. Cumbersome and intentionally vague expressions are often substituted for the simple words "death" and "die." Here the reason is partly, no doubt, a courteous desire to avoid reference to topics presumed to be distasteful to the listener. Deeper still, however, are vestiges of fear that Death may respond too readily to the sound of his own name, and visit the heedless persons who use it. Hence the elaborate and (to the rational observer) cowardly-seeming phrases like "passed on" or "gone west" or "gone to their reward" for people who have died. Disease, too, is talked about by means of periphrases which betray personal apprehension as well as a sense of conversational etiquette. Magic awe is strongest where there is a minimum of scientific training, of course. A woman who believes in the baleful power of the evil eye will also tremble at the sound of certain words of ill omen, believing that they can induce plague without the mediation of any germs known to the laboratory. Simple folk in various parts of the world who have vague or inaccurate ideas about paternity believe that mere phrases may bring about pregnancy in a woman; among them one is consequently apt to find cautious or veiled references to conception and gestation, as well as to wounds, blood, and death.

This brief excursion into topics of magic and folklore has perhaps enabled us to sense more vividly the aura of wonder and fear which most probably surrounded the use of words by early men. Despite their airy structure and evanescent nature, these meaningful sequences of sound must have been treated somewhat as were fingernails and spittle and shorn hair, which might be put to baleful use by an enemy. Utterance of the words gave power to the speaker; they were feared somewhat even by the most eager listener. They could be used along with other symbolic acts, it was believed, to control crops and weather and the animals of the chase. They could aid in

winning victory and in defeating death. They might arouse
the dead and call spirits from the vasty deep. When chanted
together they could induce a sense of profound well-being,
of submergence and identification with the group. They could
also shorten labor and speed a long march. They could extend men's memories, and enable sons to learn from their
fathers what had happened before their time. When everything in the world was subject to magic, words were a most
efficient instrument of magic.

In a metaphoric sense they are instruments of magic still.

Before telling more about them, it will be necessary
to explain a few quite simple physiological facts about
the way in which we make those purposeful sounds which
go to make up words. Then it will be possible to explain
what happens to words in the processes of change and development to which they are constantly being subjected while
we talk.

2. Sounds and Alphabets

1. SOUNDS

The Consonants

If you stop to become aware how you make the sounds which flow from you when you are talking, you are already half way to an understanding of the changes in any language at any time or place. The very nature of talking involves a lack of perfect perception on the part of the listener. He hears words from a different personal background, with a different set of experiences which color his reception of both the physical sounds and their meanings. And his attention may be distracted, too. In any event his thoughts are apt to be a step or so ahead of the words vibrating in the air at the moment, so that he does not take them in precisely as pronounced. Nor does the speaker actually hear his own words as he really says them, since he too is constantly thinking ahead as he speaks. There results a lack of complete coincidence between sounds intended and sounds made, a series of slight maladjustments and readjustments which inevitably cause change.

During the course of centuries the changes become very great. Slowly or more rapidly, as the case may be, a language will be so transformed that the older written records are unintelligible to the descendants of those who wrote them. Such changes are by no means arbitrary. If we know the physiological basis of sound production, we can actually reason back to the nature of the older sounds, and perhaps in some instances even foretell what our present sounds are about to become. Reasoning of this sort underlies much of the science of comparative linguistics. Although evanescent, speech can be captured and analyzed.

It is not necessary to go into an elaborate study of *phonetics,* or the scientific analysis of sounds used in speech, to discover the main physical principles of sound change. A few general descriptions and a few definitions of terms are quite sufficient for our purpose. The rest is really a matter of observation and common sense.

Look at someone talking, and you will see that the most obvious movements are made by his lips. A number of sounds are made by them, either alone or in combination with other organs of speech. The technical name given to such sounds is *labials.* Examples are [p] and [b],[1] both made by blowing the lips apart. Partly because their formation is clearly visible, children learn to make labials easily.

Watch more closely for sounds from just inside the lips, and you will find that they are made by using the teeth in conjunction with the tongue. These are called *dentals.* In making English dentals the tongue does not usually strike at the teeth directly, but at a point on the hard ridge just behind them. The effect is slightly different, but not greatly so. In either event the sound is called a dental. Examples are [t] and [d].

Deeper in the throat and therefore more difficult to observe are the sounds made by elevating the back part of the tongue towards the back of the roof of the mouth (the "soft palate"); [k] and [g] are among the sounds made at this point. It has been suggested that many children find these more difficult to manage than the dentals, since they can catch glimpses of the tongue at work on the teeth, but not of its activity at the back where *gutturals* are made. Hence they tend to substitute dentals when trying to learn gutturals. They say "Tum to papa" for "Come to papa." The [p] gives no trouble at all at this early stage.

In between a [t] and a deep [k] it is possible to make a higher

1 It is customary to enclose letters which represent phonetic values within square brackets.

sound, resembling a [k] but formed by the tongue up on the bony roof of the mouth. It resembles a [k] with a *y* (as in "yes") following it. In English we hear it if the word "key" is pronounced very high in the mouth; also in certain dialects where a gliding sound follows all *k*'s as if the word "yes" were about to follow. An example is the local Southern American pronunciation of "car" as something like [kʲar]. (The symbol [j] is used for the sound of *y* in English "yes.") For accuracy it is customary to use a separate letter for this high or *palatal* sound. It is possible to write [c] or [k̓] or [kʲ] to express it. Probably [c] is the best symbol since it indicates that the sound really comes from a different position in the mouth than [k]. A corresponding palatal exists for [g] when it is raised as if one were about to say a "yes" after it. This may be written as [j'] or [g̓] or [gʲ].

We now have a whole series of sounds beginning with the lips and retreating to the back of the throat. Here they are:

Labial	[p]	[b]
Dental	[t]	[d]
Palatal	[c]	[j']
Guttural	[k]	[g]

Put your finger on your throat, at the eloquently named "Adam's apple" (or larynx), and say these sounds in pairs, as they appear above. You will notice that the sounds indicated at the left are expelled without any vibration of the vocal cords. They lack voice. For this reason they are called *voice-le* . The ones at the right, on the other hand, are produced by means of vibrations in the vocal cords. They are consequently called *voiced* sounds.

Strange as it may seem, there is much more effort required to make a voiceless sound than a voiced one. The air must come out in a clear current, caught only at the lips or teeth or on the roof of the mouth, as the case may be. But if you are tired or inertly relaxed, you will tend to make all of your sounds vibrate through the vocal cords. You may say "dib of the dongue" for a neat sharp "tip of the tongue." This is a very important tendency in language. Laziness of one sort or another explains many changes in speech down through the ages. The drift towards voicing the voiceless consonants has been very strong at certain times in languages we all know.

Whether voiceless or voiced, the sounds so far listed are alike in one respect: they are quickly made and quickly finished. If you try to prolong a *p*-sound you simply become red in the face as if you were very angry. So it is customary to refer to all of these [p, b, t, d, k, g] as *stop* sounds, because they are stopped quickly and cannot be prolonged.

There is a double set of sounds corresponding to the ones already listed, and made in approximately the same positions, which we shall call *continuants* (others say *spirants*) because they do lend themselves to prolongation. The voiceless ones in English are the labial [f] and the dental which we write "th" but which phoneticians write with the Greek character *theta* [θ]. Other languages have in addition the voiceless prolonged palatal sound (as in German *ich*), written phonetically [ç], and the corresponding guttural (as in German *Nacht*), which is written with the Greek character *chi* [χ]. The voiced sounds are in English the familiar labial [v] and the voiced dental "th" as in "this" (written [đ] to keep it distinct from the voiced sound in "think"). The two deeper sounds are the palatal [ĵ] (made by voicing ç), and [γ] (a deep and prolonged sound made by voicing and prolonging [χ]). This last is to be found frequently in Dutch. English tongues find it alien and therefore difficult, but with a little practice it can be achieved.

To summarize: we now have an important set of consonants which appear entirely or in part in any language you may study. They are:

	Stops		Continuants		
	VOICELESS	VOICED	VOICELESS	VOICED	NASALS
Labial	p	b	f	v	m
Dental	t	d	θ	đ	n
Palatal	c	ǵ	ç	ĵ	ɲ
Guttural	k	g	χ	γ	ŋ

The column of *nasals* which appears at the right needs little explanation. These sounds are made on all of the four positions—labial, dental, palatal, and guttural—but they are produced by sending the air through the nose instead of the mouth. In descending order they are: labial [m], dental [n], palatal [ɲ] (as in Spanish *ñ*, represented in our English word "canyon"), and guttural [ŋ], which is the final sound of our word "sing." Nearly always when we write *ng* we are trying to indicate this single nasal sound, formed by elevating the tongue towards the back of the mouth's roof, and expelling the air through the nose. Most of the time there is no actual [g] pronounced after the [ŋ]. These sounds are all prolonged. They too are voiced continuants.

The most important remaining consonants can be briefly described. They include the hissing or sibilant sounds: [s] (voiceless) and [z] (voiced), made on the hard palate. If the tongue is turned backwards while the voiceless hiss is produced, the result is the sound we indicate in spelling by "sh" —written [ʃ] by phoneticians. By voicing this you get [ʒ], sometimes transcribed *zh* in foreign names. It is a common sound in French and Russian. It exists medially in English words like "pleasure." Too much alcohol tends to make people convert all *s*- and *z*-sounds into [ʃ] and [ʒ] respectively, because the position is more relaxed and requires less concentrated effort on the part of ill-controlled muscles. Only a person in a state of complete sobriety should attempt to read a line of verse like "The weary shepherd sits and whets the sounding shears," from Thomson's *The Seasons*. The phrase "Please pass the salt" is apt to become "Pleazhe pash the shalt." In English [ʃ] is often found combined with a preceding [t], as in the word "catch" [kætʃ]. Some writers on phonetics use ž for [ʒ], š for [ʃ] and č for [tʃ]. Another combination is [dʒ] as in the word "judge" [dʒʌdʒ].

THE LIQUIDS

The sounds represented by our ordinary characters *l* and *r* need little comment. The *l*-sound may be made either on the teeth or behind them. In English it is always voiced, but it is quite possible to expel your breath from the same tongue position without vibrating your vocal cords. If you do so you get what is known as a "voiceless *l*" (written [l̥]). It exists in Welsh, where it is written *ll* as in names like Lloyd. The Spaniards heard it from the Aztecs when they invaded Mexico. Since they had no such sound in their own language, they compromised by writing it "tl." Words like *coatl* meaning "snake" or names like Quetzalcoatl ("Bird-Snake") are pronounced with a voiceless [l̥] at the end.

There is another liquid sound rather akin to [l] which may be pronounced in several different ways. We write it *r* in English, but we do not trill it as other peoples do. Our untrilled pronunciation is indicated by the symbol [ɹ]. In some languages it is trilled so deep in the throat that it is practically the same as the guttural continuant [ɣ]. Like [l], it can be pronounced unvoiced. You will hear it so, in final position in the French pronunciation of the word *théâtre*. Because the [l] and [r] are formed in a similar position close together, it is easy to substitute one for the other in rapid speech. You may find yourself saying "prease" for "please." Speakers of Chinese whose native dialect has no [r] corresponding to ours, usually replace it by an [l] in speaking English, making "bring" into "bling" and "very" into "vely." A curious characteristic of these liquid consonants, which they share with the nasals, is that they sometimes function as vowels. In the word "table," for instance, there are two distinct syllables: "ta-ble." It is the [l] which permits us to pronounce the combination [bl] as if it contained a regular vowel sound. (The "final *e*" of this word is a meaningless orthographic flourish.) Likewise "seven" can be pronounced "se-vn" in two syllables. In final position [l] and [r] are easily lost. We frequently drop the final sound of "well" in informal speech, and final *r*-sounds are not heard in standard British speech unless the next word begins with a vowel; nor are they always audible even then. Thus "car" is [ka:]. (The colon indicates that the preceding vowel is long.)

Because they can function in two possible ways, both as vowels and consonants, the sounds [l, r, m, n] are vocalic consonants. To indicate in phonetics that any one of these is being used as a vowel, a short vertical mark is placed under it, thus: [se-vn̩] for "seven." Some writers use a dot, as in [l̩].

THE SEMI-VOWELS

There is a palatal sound in English somewhat like a vowel glide which is represented by the *y* in words like "yes" and "yarn." The phonetic character is [j] as pronounced in the German *ja*. The sound represented by [w] requires little comment, at least for English-speaking readers. It is made through pursed, rounded lips, and is voiced. In emphatic exclamations we sometimes pronounce it unvoiced. This variation of [w] was formerly more common in English than it is now, and was indicated by the spelling "wh." The phonetic character is [ʍ]. In some dialects of English today the voiceless [ʍ] is seldom heard except under some emotional stress, as when we exclaim "What!" with amazement or distaste. As for [h], it represents an expulsion of air through a somewhat contracted space between the vocal cords.

Since [j] and [w] closely resemble two vowels, [i] and [u] respectively, they are sometimes called semi-vowels.

USES OF PHONETIC CHARACTERS

Most of the sounds discussed so far are represented phonetically by symbols already familiar in ordinary print. The unusual special symbols introduced so far have been: [ɹ, θ, ç, χ, đ, ǵ, γ, ɲ, ŋ, ʃ, ʒ, ʍ, ɹ, l̩]. These are made necessary in scientific work because it is awkward or ambiguous to use two symbols for one sound, or one symbol for several sounds. For instance, the sound we wish to indicate when we write "th" is not really a stop [t] followed by a separate voiceless aspiration or breathing [h]; it is an entirely different one: a continuant made between the teeth. Again, in ordinary spelling the letter *c* may stand for a *k* or an *s* in pronunciation. This doubtful spelling of ours is a great handicap. Merely to avoid confusion it is worth while to use the few extra symbols listed above in linguistic discussion. If our orthography made use of them as a regular thing, our language would be much easier for children and foreigners trying to write it correctly. A little practice in rewriting words in the scientific alphabet will bring home to you as never before what we really say in talking—which is, for English, perceptibly different from what we write.

SUMMARY TABLE OF CONSONANTS

	Stops				Continuants			
	VOICELESS	VOICED	VOICELESS	VOICED	NASALS	LIQUIDS	SIBI-LANTS	SEMI-VOWELS
Labial	ɲ	b	f	v	m			w
Dental	t	d	θ	đ	n	l	s z	
Palatal	c	ǵ	ç	ĵ	ɲ	ɹ, r	ʃ ʒ	j
Guttural	k	g	χ	γ	ŋ			

It is a common convention to refer to the sounds discussed above as consonants. The word means "sounding with" something else. Presumably none of these sounds could make a syllable in a word by itself, but would have to be combined with a vowel to "sound with" it. This was the traditional test for distinguishing vowels from consonants. There is no such rigid separation between the two in practice. Several sounds like [l] and [r], as we have seen, can be employed either way.

Languages vary greatly in the richness and variety of the consonants they use. Some manage very nicely with what might appear to us as a poor, monotonous assortment. Spanish missionaries in Mexico noticed and commented on the absence of the sounds represented in Castilian by the letters *b, d, f, r, s, j* [b, d, f, r, s, χ] in the Aztec language. The dictionaries present a rather monotonous appearance because of this lack. Russian, on the other hand, is heavily endowed with consonants, and makes use of combinations and modifications of them which present some difficulties for our tongues. Among other innovations (from our point of view), Russians have made a new and additional set of consonants out of most of our plain ones by shifting them towards the palate. They possess not only [l, r, t, d], and so on, but also a second series of consonants made as if these were about to be followed by the glide-sound [ʲ]: [lʲ, rʲ, tʲ, dʲ] or [l', r', t', d']. It makes a real difference in meaning whether one says [stal] or [stalʲ], since the former means "he stood" and the latter "steel." When modifications like the presence or absence of that small palatal glide make a difference in meaning in a language, we say that we are dealing with two quite different units of sound or *phonemes;* but when —as in English—it is felt that such minor variations of a given sound are unessential to its meaningful use, we say that only one phoneme is represented by it. We recognize but one *l*-sound in English for practical purposes; hence it is for us a single phoneme.

THE VOWELS

A description of the vowel sounds familiar to us in English is much more complicated than an account of the consonants. Here our orthography is even more confused. The conventional symbols, the traditional *a, e, i, o, u,* are so inconsistently employed that they must drive foreign students to despair. In every one of the following words the letter *a* has a different phonetic value from each of the others: "play," "arm," "any," "cat," "amuse," "awful." Inconsistency could hardly go farther.

There are many historical reasons for this anarchic condition. One of the most important ones is the great respect with which succeeding writers and printers treated the spelling first established by Caxton in the fifteenth century. The first presses, under his direction, made use of a final *-e,* no longer pronounced even in his day, to show that the preceding vowel was spoken long, as in "take." Therefore we still write scores of unpronounced final *-e's* to the mystification of all foreigners. Furthermore, English spelling has been disorganized by large numbers of loan words from many other languages. Some observers regard the archaic spelling of words like "knight" and "cough" as an endearing example of the Anglo-Saxon love of tradition. The causes must be explainable, but they do baffle the casual observer and render his way more thorny when he is trying to learn "correct" orthography.

In the phonetic alphabet vowels are treated with more scrupulous care. In general the values given to the five vowel letters are those accepted in Italian, Spanish, or German, where the spelling relates more consistently to sounds than in English. If you know one of these languages you will have no further difficulty in recognizing the values in phonetic transcriptions. For approximate English equivalents these words will help:

[i] as in the word "machine"
[e] " " " " "they"
[ɑ] " " " " "father"
[o] " " " " "so" (spoken as a single vowel)
[u] " " " " "rule"

Each of these may be prolonged. When it is long, a vowel is written with a colon after it: [mi:] for "me." Note that the vowels are arranged as the consonants were, beginning with the ones made high in the front of the mouth, with the tip of the tongue, and retreating to the low or back sounds. Notice, too, that as you pronounce the series in order, your lips change from a parallel to a rounded formation. Thus [u] is called a *rounded vowel,* and [i] is *unrounded.* Between [e] and [ɑ] we have a "lowered *e*" written [ɛ], which you can hear in positions where an [r] follows (or used to follow). The vowel in "there" [ðɛ:(ɹ)]is lower than the one in"they."(In French the two sounds are spelled *é* and *è* respectively.) There are a few additional symbols needed to account for the other chief vowel sounds in English:

[a] as the first part of [ai] (the diphthong of "I")
[æ] as in the word "cat"
[ʊ] " " " " "good" (a short sound)
[ɔ:] " " " " "awe"
[ʌ] " " " " "up"
[ɪ] " " " " "pin" (short)
[ə] " the final sound of "Cuba" (unaccented, short) [kjubə]

Other languages contain still further sounds, unrepresented in English. They will be explained in the course of discussion when reference is made to them.

DIPHTHONGS

When two vowels come together in a word they may be pronounced with the same expulsion of the breath or with two separate expulsions. In the former instance you have a *diphthong* (from Greek *di-phthongos,* or "sounded twice") in a single syllable: "gray" [gɹei] is an illustration. But when two vowels come together they may be in two separate syllables, as in the word "re-enter." Here you can detect the slight separation caused by the fresh impulse given to the expelled air on the second *e*: [ɹi'entə]. Vowels thus separated are not diphthongs.

If you prolong a vowel beyond the length of time usual in normal speech, you will find it difficult to keep the sound pure. As in singing, the longer you make the quantity the more you are apt to modify the quality also. In English we generally assume that we pronounce a long clear [i:] in such words as "me" [mi:], but one can quite frequently hear an off-glide [ʲ] at the end of the sound: [mi:ʲ]. The tongue appears to become restless at the prolonged maintenance of a single position, and shifts slightly towards the end. Such a tendency repeatedly causes "long" vowels to become diphthongs. Actually, we don't say "go" with a pure long vowel sound, but with a final rounding of the lips which gives [gou] as a result. Likewise the word "they" contains a diphthong rather than the simple long [e:]. Most persons say [ðei]. In Cockney speech, diphthongs even become *triphthongs* through excessive prolongation. The effect is supposed to be intrinsically humorous: at least it is so treated by novelists and playwrights, who themselves usually belong to a different class. They indicate the Cockney version of "now" as "naow" [næɒʊ].

The Russian language, unlike English, has no "long" vowels; at least, none prolonged as we treat them in accented final position. Probably this is one reason why accented vowels have remained comparatively stable in Russian for many centuries.

A tendency opposite to lengthening, namely *curtailment,* can also be noticed in the treatment of vowel sounds. Just as over-long vowels tend to become diphthongs, so diphthongs in rapid speech tend to become simple vowels (usually, but not always, long). Many of us say "my" [maɪ] without the second element, in other words as [ma·], although on being challenged we usually deny the clipping vehemently. (The raised dot means a semi-long vowel.) Lengthen the simplified sound a bit, and you have something like the Southern American pronunciation of the word. The second part of the diphthong in "now" [nɑʊ] often disappears, giving an abbreviated [nɑ·], occasionally even [næ·]. The effect is distinctly colloquial, not to say vulgar, especially when the vowel is nasalized by sending part of the air through the nose. Because the speech habits of the majority of educated persons do not permit such simplification of the diphthong, [næ·] for "now" is considered a mark of low social standing. In the end, though, it may become the accepted pronunciation, if the tendency to simplify existent diphthongs in English becomes widely prevalent. The tendency has prevailed before now; it may do so again. Even the nasality is not vulgar *per se.* The same effects in certain French and Polish words are classically correct.

ACCENT

When sounds are put together in words, especially in long ones, some new elements appear in the situation. It would be very hard to pronounce a long word such as "circumstantially" in a dead even manner, without varying the stress and level of musical pitch. Instead we are accustomed to emphasize one or two syllables quite sharply, giving them more energy of emission than the others get, and we permit the voice to rise and fall in a musical melody while we speak.

Accent or *stress* (indicated by placing the symbol ['] before the syllable to be emphasized) may be important in determining the meaning of a word. "I shall re-'cord the 'rec-ord" shows that nouns and verbs expressing the same idea are at times distinguished only by the shift in accent—nothing more. Many pairs of words show this grammatical function of accent in English. Think of Shakespeare's

> "Now am I cabined, cribbed, con-'fined" (*Macbeth*)

and his

> "Shall in these 'confines with a monarch's voice
> Cry 'Havoc!' and let slip the dogs of war."
>
> (*Julius Caesar*)

Sometimes we tend to shift accent on words to show emphasis. The usage is limited in English. It is exemplified in the variant pronunciation of " 'absolutely" as "abso-'lutely" and of " 'positively" as "posi-'tively." Neither of these variants is considered "good" or accepted English. The principle they exemplify is important, however, in other languages, where shifted accent indicates a change in meaning connected with emotional stress.

Now that we have surveyed the most important symbols, you can see how a passage in transcription looks when compared with conventional spelling:

The phonetic alphabet is useful because it's clear. If you are learning new languages, and you wish to keep in mind the actual sounds by means of a system of characters scientifically ar-

[ðə fo'netɪk 'ælfəbet ɪz 'jusfʊl
bɪ'kɔːz ɪts 'kliːə(ɹ). ɪf ju ɑ(ɹ)
'ləː(ɹ)nɪŋ njuː 'læŋgwɪdʒz, æn ju
wɪʃ tə kiːp ɪn maɪnd ðə 'æktjʊəl
saʊndz baɪ miːnz əv ə 'sɪstəm əv
'kæɹɪktəz saɪən'tɪfɪklɪ ə'ɹeɪnʒd,ɪt

ranged, it will help you. The phonetic alphabet is even more useful for a foreigner about to study English, since our spelling is most confusing. It's a good thing for such a person to master a phonetic transcription of each word he learns, at least until he's accustomed to our strange orthography.

wɪl help ju. ðə fo'netɪk 'ælfabet ɪz i: vn mɔ:(ɹ)'jusfʊl fɔ(ɹ)ə'faɹɪnə ə'bɑʊt tə 'stʌdɪ 'ɪŋglɪʃ, sɪns ɑʊə(ɹ) 'spelɪŋ ɪz moʊst kn'fjuzɪŋ. ɪts ə gʊd θɪŋ fɔ(ɹ) sʌtʃ ə 'pə:(ɹ)sn tə 'mæstə(ɹ)ə fo'netɪk tɹæn'skɹɪp ʃn̩ əv i:tʃ wə:(ɹ)d hi: lə:(ɹ)nz, æt li:st ʌn'tɪl hi:z ə'kʌtmd tə ɑʊə stɹenʒ ɔ(ɹ) 'θɑgɹɪfɪ.]

Symbols in parentheses are pronounced by some speakers and not by others. There are of course many variations according to local dialects.

INTONATION

Musical *intonation,* the melody of a sentence, can serve the purpose of modifying meanings in a manner which requires special mention. It is ignored in ordinary phonetic transcriptions. Commands and questions can be detected by melody as much as by word order. In some languages the melody alone distinguishes between such sentences as "You are reading" and "Are you reading?" Furthermore, some languages make a permanent distinction of meaning between certain syllables spoken with a high pitch and exactly the same syllables spoken low. It might be a matter of life and death to distinguish

between 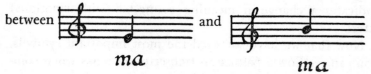 and

In such cases the musical pitch has semantic value; that is, it changes the whole *meaning* of a syllable. In languages like Chinese and Mende (an African dialect) there are a number of clearly distinguishable pitches with semantic connotations. Writers who wish to indicate their musical value in phonetic transcription use subscript numbers, each number in ascending order standing for notes in an ascending scale. The Mende language, as studied by Ethel Aginsky, uses tonal patterns to differentiate among words which would otherwise be homonyms, such as

$$kpu_4 lo_2 \text{ meaning "woodcock"}$$
$$kpu_4 lo_4 \quad \text{" "swelling"}$$
$$kpu_2 lo_2 \quad \text{" "container"}$$

An approximation of the relative intervals may be obtained in musical notation:

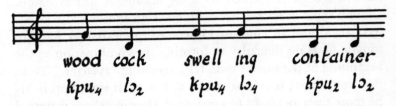

The only analogous situation arises in English when our intonation of the same word varies to show a change in emotional attitude corresponding to differing grammatical functions in an unspoken sentence. You can say "Helen!" with a peremptory expression implying command, or "He—len . . ." with a reproachful down-glide on the first syllable, or "Helen?" with an inquiring upward inflexion. The printed page cannot indicate these differences satisfactorily, but musical notation would afford an impression of the differences:

To show how much the intonation implies, we have only to expand the three forms of address into the sentences they stand for. According to context, they may mean: "Helen! Come here!" or "Helen . . . How *could* you do it?" or "Helen! What are you doing?" The music of the word may imply a whole predication about Helen's charm or misbehavior or dilatoriness. When you are learning a foreign language, it is worth while to identify and practice the typical sentence pattern of intonation that goes with it. The melody will rise to your ears above the current of a general conversation that is as yet unintelligible to you. Using it yourself will help you to achieve what is popularly called a good "accent" quite as much as the proper formation of the individual sounds in a word.

SPEECH HABITS IN LANGUAGES

Each language is marked by some dominant speech habits. Certain types of sounds are avoided, both individually (as we have seen) and in clusters. Others are preferred. A Russian tongue finds no difficulty in forming the combination at the beginning of the word ['mstʲi-telʲ], meaning "avenger." To us the group [mst] is at least mildly awkward. It would probably be more than awkward to a native of Hawaii, whose maternal tongue favors open syllables ending in vowels, and eschews the grouping of heavy consonant sounds together without intervening vowels. The Polynesian languages, besides, are conspicuously inclined to the use of identical syllables in repetition, as in *hula-hula* and "Waikiki." This particular configuration of sounds in a word is known as *reduplication*. We have comparatively little of it in English. Words like "mama" and "papa" and "tomtom" are obvious examples. Reduplication is one of many devices conspicuously employed in some languages and avoided in others.

It must not be thought, however, that the tendencies and preferences of languages for certain patterns of sound are fixed and unchanging things. And it is really inaccurate to talk of a language itself as "preferring" one type of configuration over another. We mean that the people who actually speak the language have themselves eliminated one type or built up another. It is always dangerous to talk about a language as a living entity apart from those who speak it. The changes in speech are made by speakers, not by disembodied forces or tendencies in the language. Our task is to find out when and, if possible, why the changes occurred.

The historical development of consonant clusters in Russian is a case in point. They were not always there. From its earlier history we know that the first three sounds of ['mstʲi-telʲ] did not always form a single group. Originally a vowel existed between the [m] and the [s], as we can surmise, in fact, from the cognate simple word [mʲestʲ] meaning "revenge." Though we may feel now that difficult consonant groups are "typically Russian" and in some mysterious way express the "Slavic soul," there is nothing essentially soulful or sempiternal about them. The lack of accent simply caused loss of the first vowel in what was once a trisyllabic form [*mes-'ti-telʲ].[1] Thus a long development in many individual words was necessary to produce the groupings now felt to be characteristic of Russian, Czechish, and other Slavic tongues.

In the same way, the use in other languages of vowels as the most common endings for words may have arisen out of an earlier situation in which consonants were the most usual final sounds, but were later slurred and finally lost. Italian, with its characteristic vowel endings, developed from Latin, which used final consonants more freely. "He doesn't like my mother" was in Latin "*Meam matrem non amat*," or more colloquially "*Illam meam matrem non amat*"; in Italian we have "*Non ama la mia madre*." The final [t]'s and [m]'s were lost, and the resulting sentence became as a result more "liquid" and musical to our ears, because more vocalic.

2. SYSTEMS OF WRITING: ALPHABETS

PICTURE WRITING

Now that we have reviewed the sounds most commonly used in speech, together with the conditions of accent and pitch affecting them, it will be interesting to look at some of the devices which have been employed throughout history to record them in writing. We must remember that written records have been very recent in man's cultural history. For many

---

1 An asterisk before a word indicates that it is written in what we presume to be an earlier form, deduced from existing forms but nowhere recorded.

ages languages have been developing, expanding, merging, changing, and disappearing in all parts of the world without leaving any trace behind. Many are as if they had never been, because the lost tribes who spoke them had no method of putting them down for future ages. Writing is, in relation to the whole of man's history, a comparatively modern invention.

The first attempts to express ideas graphically belong to the history of art. The entire picture of an act corresponds in a way to a sentence. We have all heard the anecdote so famous in the chronicles of journalism about an editor anxious to explain the nature of "news" to a young reporter. He did so epigrammatically: "Dog bites man; that's not news; man bites dog—that's news!" The humorous inversion can be expressed quite clearly in pictures. A medieval scribe did in fact once draw a picture presenting such a comical situation graphically. At the bottom of a page on one of the manuscripts formerly displayed at the Bodleian Library, Oxford, a visitor could have seen a lively little sketch showing a bold huntsman setting out to chase a timorous hare; next to it he was shown the hare suddenly reversing the chase and pursuing the man, who is forced to climb a tree with all the symptoms of comical distress plainly visible on his face. The humor of the inversion emerges without words. It corresponds quite clearly to a grammatical inversion of sentence parts (subject and verb).

Early history, that is, straight narrative, can be recorded in a sequence of pictures which yield their meaning to later students with a fair degree of clarity. We know most of the important events in the lives of certain royal personages who lived in Mexico before the Spaniards because they left such picture chronicles. Herbert J. Spinden has been able to decipher the career of a princess named Six Monkey living in the Toltec region, from the pictured accounts of her in one of the pre-Conquest codices. She was, it seems, much sought in marriage. One of her suitors, named One House, received a rebuff when he came hopefully bearing gifts. The picture units give meanings equivalent to the following English sentences: "A suitor,

One House, brings presents to Nine Wind and Ten Eagle, the parents of Six Monkey, living at Cloud-Belching Mountain, but Six Monkey turns her back on him."

Reproduced from Herbert G. Spinden's "Indian Manuscripts of Southern Mexico," *Smithsonian Institution Reports* 1935, p. 436.

The wooer's discomfiture is eloquently expressed, as is the maiden's rebuff, by means of posture.

Such ideas as wooing, fighting, and rejecting—"turning one's back" on someone—can be depicted unambiguously by this method. The separate groups of figures expressing one simple idea each are called *pictographs*.

HIEROGLYPHS

It is easy to make such units a bit more conventional and to generalize the ideas they represent. Stylizing of pictures is the first step to conventional writing. In the Egyptian hieroglyphs or sacred carvings this stage is still apparent. A figure of a man leaning on a staff is used to represent   the idea "old man"; but it is also used for the related   ideas "age, old; lean upon." At this point the picture may be called an *ideograph*. A more symbolic one, which is nevertheless still an ideograph rather than a letter, is the figure   indicating water and liquid, or any action connected with water. The general term *hieroglyphs*, "sacred characters," is used because such ideographic writing originated with a priestly caste.

Now it happens that Old Egyptian was very rich in homonyms, or words (largely monosyllables) identical in sound with other words, like our own pair "road" and "rode," or "bee" and "be." Therefore it was possible for an ideograph to do duty not only for the word pictured, but for all its homonyms too. For example, the word *kha* meant "lotus" and was represented by the picture of this flower itself; but it also meant the numeral 1000. The word *djēba* meant "finger," but also the numeral 10,000. Therefore the conventional way of writing "32,000 cattle was an ox plus three fingers plus two lotuses. Notice that the idea is expressed "oxen: 32,000" instead of "32,000 oxen." The limiting image comes first in Egyptian. The principle employed is the one familiar to us in the drawing room game of charades.

LETTERS

In some cases, however, a symbol in Egyptian served as a true letter: that is, it represented the same *sound* wherever it appeared, regardless of sense. An example is the symbol which originally meant *ra* or "mouth" only; but in time came to be employed for [r] in any context. Another example is , a rectangle first used to picture a pool or tank in a garden and later the sound *sh* [ʃ]. Its phonetic value appears in the word or *shm* [ʃm]. (Vowels were never written.) The lower part of the hieroglyph is still pictorial, but the upper is purely phonetic. The glyph does *not* mean that the pool walked! Instead it *spells* the word meaning "to go," without reference to the idea of "pool."

There is an enormous advantage, obviously, in the use of

letters which represent single sounds rather than general ideas or even syllables. Early Greek and Hebrew were both based on some Semitic alphabet which had this virtue of efficiency. Some of these letters show that they too were once word-pictures. In fact, there is reason to suppose that some of them were directly connected with Egyptian hieroglyphs. Here is a table of a few corresponding symbols, showing hieroglyphs parallel with forms of a very early Semitic alphabet (the Sinaitic script found in an inscription of 1500 B.C.), the characters of the Moabite Stone (another early Semitic inscription), Hebrew letters as written and printed today, and Greek characters at various stages. In some cases the name given to the letter in one of the Semitic languages was also the name of an object having the same initial sound.

EGYPTIAN HIEROGLYPH	OBJECT	SINAI SCRIPT	MOABITE STONE	HEBREW LETTER	HEBREW WORD	GREEK LETTER
𓃾 𐤀	ox-head			𐤀	aleph (ox)	Λ A alpha
	house				beth (house)	beta
	water				mem	mu

ALPHABETS

When a simple relationship of one sound to one character has been established, the alphabet has become phonetic. Writing becomes easier and there is much less ambiguity as to its intent. Still, even those systems which have broken away from picture writing and developed a sound-to-symbol correspondence often fall short of strict accuracy in recording sounds. Originally Hebrew, like Egyptian, ignored the vowels and put down only consonants, thus leaving a reader to guess at the sounds connecting them. English, as we have seen, is notoriously inaccurate in representing sounds because its spelling is archaic. The ancient Sanskrit alphabet, on the other hand, offers a refreshing example of orderly and accurate correlation, the symbols having been systematically arranged by native grammarians. No more than one sound is associated with each. A student of Sanskrit is also learning elementary phonetics painlessly, because the order makes him aware of the lips, teeth, base of the teeth, palate, and velum as organs of articulation. He also learns to contrast aspirated and unaspirated consonants.

क k	ख k^h	ग g	घ g^h	ङ η
च c	छ c^h	ज j	झ j^h	ञ $\tilde{n}$
ट $\underset{.}{t}$	ठ $\underset{.}{t}^h$	ड $\underset{.}{d}$	ढ $\underset{.}{d}^h$	ण $\underset{.}{n}$
त t	थ t^h	द d	ध d^h	न n
प p	फ p^h	ब b	भ b^h	म m

The consonants of the third row were pronounced with the tongue turned backwards. This modification is indicated by a dot below the phonetic sign. The arrangement contrasts very favorably with our own senseless order: "a, b, c, d ... ," which has no relation to the placement of speech organs.

The alphabets developed at various historical times in Europe all stand in direct or indirect relation to the Greek (either the classical letters or their earlier forms). Latin modified *P* to *R*, Σ to *S*, Δ to *D*, but kept other letters like *B, E, O* practically unchanged. The Romans made use of *Q*, a Semitic character for a deep guttural; and they used *H* for a new purpose (simple aspiration). They had no use for symbols like θ, Φ, Ψ. But the general relationship between the two sets of characters is fairly obvious.

Modern Russian letters are also based on the alphabet of the Greeks, with some additional symbols to represent sounds not present in the Hellenic dialects, for which the Greeks naturally had no characters. The following letters coincide nearly enough to reveal their relationship at a glance. Phonetic values are indicated in brackets; the ancient Greek letters appear in capitals and the modern Greek equivalents appear in cursive type:

Ancient Greek	A	B	Γ	Δ	E	K	Λ	M	Π	P	Φ
	[a]	[b]	[g]	[d]	[e]	[k]	[l]	[m]	[p]	[r]	[pʰ]
Modern Greek	α	β	γ	δ	ε	κ	λ	μ	π	ρ	φ
	[a]	[v]	[g]	[d]	[ɛ]	[k]	[l]	[m]	[p]	[r]	[f]
Russian Alphabet	А, а	В, в	Г, г	Д, д	Е, е	К, к	Л, л	М, м	П, п	Р, р	Ф ф
	[a]	[v]	[g]	[d]	[ʲe]	[k]	[l]	[m]	[p]	[r]	[f]

Other languages besides Russian are indebted to the Greek alphabet for their written characters. In fact, wherever writing was introduced to a European people together with Eastern Christianity, it took the form of the Cyrillic alphabet (modified from the Greek), which the apostles Cyril and Methodius originated for writing down the Old Bulgarian language in connection with their missionary work. The Cyrillic characters in their turn were modified somewhat as they were adapted to Russian, Bulgarian, and Serbian respectively. Roman Christianity, on the other hand, brought with it the use of the Latin alphabet to peoples who had up to that time had practically no contact with the spoken Latin language.

RUNES

In northern Europe from the third century onwards, the early Germanic tribes made use of an alphabet called *runes*. The word is connected with a root meaning "whispering, mystery, secrecy" (German *raunen*), and it had connotations of magic. Since not many persons in the early tribes knew the significance of these mysterious characters scratched on staves, armor, horns, and obituary stones, they were regarded with superstitious awe. Magic powers were supposed to attend upon them.

The origin of these thorny and angular characters has been disputed with verbosity. The Greek capital, Greek cursive, Thracian, Etruscan, North Italic, and combined Latin and Greek alphabets have been proposed as their source. The order of the letters was as follows in the ninth and tenth centuries, after several of the earlier series had been lost:

ᚠᚢᚦᚨᚱᚲᚷᚹ : ᚺᚾᛁᛃᛇᛈᛉᛊ : ᛏᛒᛖᛗᛚᛜᛞ

f u þ a r k g w   h n i j ɛ p z s   t b e u l ŋ g o d

Reproduced from Holger Pedersen's *Linguistic Science in the Nineteenth Century*, p. 234.

Thus the runic ABC was known as "futhark" in Scandinavia. As in the Semitic alphabet, the letters also stood for things. In the Old English series [f] stood for *feoh* or "money"; [u] for *úr* or "aurochs"; [θ] for "thorn," a word that has changed very little in pronunciation from that time to this. There is a poem in Old English of King Alfred's time or a bit later which gives a short verse describing each letter-word, in order to facilitate memorizing. (Children still learn the alphabet this way, I believe.) The first three verses are:

> Money gives comfort   to all men's moods,
> But each who possesses   should give to others,
> If from God he would have   a goodly fate.
>
> The aurochs is bold   and antlered above,
> An animal fierce;   he fights with his horns,
> That moor-dweller famous;   he's a mighty brute.
>
> Thorn is most sharp   to the touch of man,
> Its assault is evil   and angrily harsh
> To any man's hand   that rests upon it.

RUNIC MAGIC

Alphabets have been surrounded with an atmosphere of magic quite as much as the spoken words. We can find some illuminating suggestions in the stories that have come down to us from early Germanic literature. These tell of the supernatural power of runes. Everyone knows the story of Sigurd the Dragon-Slayer, who fearlessly climbed a mountain surrounded by fire and awoke a sleeping Valkyrie with a kiss. The lady in question, Brynhild, was a daughter of the gods and therefore skilled in all sorts of magic wisdom, including the lore of runes. This knowledge of hers must have impressed the bold hero even more than her beauty, for we read that, with a self-restraint most extraordinary in such a romantic situation, Sigurd asked Brynhild first of all (after the initial kiss) to teach him the magic powers inherent in runes. Not a whit disconcerted by the request, Brynhild obligingly instructed him in several eminently practical applications of runic magic:

> Ale-runes learn,   that with lies the wife
>   Of another betray not thy trust;
> On the horn thou shalt write,   and the backs of thy hands,
>   And Need shalt mark on thy nails. . . .
>
> Birth-runes learn,   if help thou wilt lend,
>   The babe from the mother to bring;
> On thy palms shalt write them,   and round thy joints,
>   And ask the fates to aid.
>
> Wave-runes learn,   if well thou wouldst shelter
>   The sail-steeds out on the sea;
> On the stem shalt thou write,   and the steering blade,
>   And burn them into the oars. . . .
>
> Branch-runes learn,   if a healer wouldst be,
>   And cure for wounds wouldst work;
> On the bark shalt thou write,   and on trees that be
>   With boughs to the eastward bent.

The Icelandic hero Egil, son of Skallagrim, who lived early in the tenth century, knew how to cure sickness by means of runes. Once when he was visiting in Vermaland he found that his host's daughter was suffering from a malady which had been made much worse when an unskilled person had cut the wrong letters on whalebone and put them in her bed. Egil shook his head disapprovingly over such blundering leech-craft; then he "scored runes and laid them under the bolster in the resting-place where she rested. It seemed to her as if she wakened out of sleep, and she said that she was then healed." Distinctly, this must have been an art worth knowing.

ALPHABETS AND THE DECORATIVE ARTS

One more use of the runes deserves our attention. They were commonly scratched on metal objects of war and peace to indicate the name of the artisan who had done the work. One of the oldest inscriptions we have was put on a golden horn discovered at Gallehus in Jutland, Denmark. It forms a band of lettering above the ornamentation of animals' and men's figures.

ekhlewagastir ⋮ holtijar ⋮ horna ⋮ tawido ⋮

Reproduced from Wolfgang Krause's *Runeninschriften im älteren Futhark,* p. 596.

It means: "I Hlewagastir of the Holtings made this horn." The words show a very early stage of Germanic. They are eloquent of the worker's pride in his creation. Later, the name of the sword-smith alone was often scratched on the weapon in runes or Latin characters. Here the runic signature resembled something like a modern trade-mark.

The importance attached to work on early armor brings us to an interesting question: How far have alphabets been shaped by the medium in which the writers worked? Technology and script were very closely related in the beginning. When stone was the material to receive images from the chisel's blows, writing resembled sculptured relief. When brushes and paint succeeded, the lines became flowing and better adapted to become the stylized abstract symbols of alphabets proper. This occurred in the Coptic script which was used by the brush-and-paper writers in Egypt under Roman domination. Angular characters resulted when wood carving was the medium of expression, as with the runes. Angles and strokes were also favored for stone inscriptions proper, whether in runes or Ogham (the pre-Latin alphabet of ancient Ireland), when the technique was elementary. The cuneiform or wedge-shaped characters of the Assyrians, Babylonians, and Hittites were likewise adapted to stone and clay tablets.

TECHNOLOGY AND ALPHABETS

The techniques of writing were determined for centuries to come by the tools which were at hand in the first stages. And the mental processes themselves may conceivably have been retarded or accelerated as the medium of writing down favored or hindered rapid, efficient notation. The physical basis, in the shape of tool and medium, has reacted upon those using it and has been subjected to further changes by the inventors' descendants. Improvements have occurred as a result of general technological advance: the invention of paper, the adaptation of animals' skins to parchment, the refining of instruments used for carving. The impetus towards such invention has come repeatedly through the stimulus of trade and contact with other peoples, or the diversification of economic relations at home. Merchants have more than once taken over and made more efficient the script formerly limited to priests. We can trace the spread of alphabets over ancient trade routes; we can see alphabets within a given country, like Egypt, being modified as they spread beyond the confines of a privileged hierarchic caste.

But culture is conservative, too, in its forms, and old practices are carried on long after a better medium has been discovered. Chinese characters, which were first shaped by brushes dipped in ink, are reproduced in all their traditional complexity by the modern printing presses, which might have been expected to favor the introduction of a simpler phonetic system. The first books printed in England faithfully reproduced all the disadvantageous effects of fourteenth-century handwriting, with its heavy down-strokes of the pen. The result was the early "black-letter" type, which non-German readers find tiring to the eye. In Germany something very like it is still favored by some presses despite the greater clarity of the rounded roman font. The will to improvement must be present besides the physical equipment, it seems. Sometimes a political revolution is needed to get rid of an ancient and cumbersome alphabet and replace it with a modified phonetic system. Russian was simplified after 1917 by the elimination of some useless characters. But even the French Revolution, it may be observed, did not succeed in modernizing the medieval French orthography, although it did perform the great service of introducing the decimal system of measurements.

A few words in English reveal entertainingly the conservatism of our terminology for an art which, though itself conservative, has been transformed many times in history. The word "write" originally meant "to scratch, to cut," and is cognate with German *Ritze,* although we have long since given up cutting runes on metal. "Book" is a variant of "beech," the name of a tree on which runes were often carved. "Read" preserves almost the same form it had when it meant "to guess, decipher," although our printed words are now comprehensible to the entire literate public, and the magical obscurity which separated them from the uninitiated has been quite dissipated. "Pen," like French *plume,* really means "feather," although quills were abandoned some time ago. We say "paper," from *papyrus,* although our own sheets have nothing to do with the Egyptian reed of that name.

Foreign languages reveal something of the same cultural lag in the vocabulary of writing. Spanish *lápiz,* meaning "pencil," shows its origin from a word for "stone" (compare English "lapidary"), although ordinary lead pencils have long since replaced the chisel, stone, or slate instruments in Spain. In Nahuatl (modern Aztec) the verbs for "write" (*cuilóa*), "carve" (*tetlacuilóa*), and "paint" (*tlecuicuilóa*) all contain the same root. If the shapes of our letters have been retained long after technological advances should have improved them, the vocabulary of script has remained still more conservative in the ideas it expresses. History shows many instances of this aversion to change where cultural matters are concerned. Even when people have learned the truly revolutionary art of making books by a printing press, they avoid recognizing the change in their vocabularies. They go on talking about "cutting" words as if they were runes in the bark of a venerable beech tree. The earlier sense is forgotten slowly.

If in many cases writing began as the invention of a class of priests, it was permitted to make its greatest step forward when it was taken out of the temples into the bustling turmoil of the market place. It was trade that spread the new art abroad. The ubiquitous merchants of the ancient Mediterranean carried far and wide the knowledge of the tiny pregnant characters, easily scribbled on papyrus, which could serve not only to reckon bills of sale and shipments, but also to commemorate the dead, convey love-messages, and set down enduringly for later ages the splendors of literature. No longer was it necessary for the epics of great poets to be memorized entire by the rhapsodes who chanted them. From that time to this, pieces of paper have served to extend still further the living record vouchsafed us by the development of oral speech. Now that we can set down comprehensible signs for all sounds made by all peoples, we are in a position to level the barriers which formerly stood between cultures of different speech—if we should but choose to do so.

3. Family Relationships Among Languages

FAMILIES OF LANGUAGES

In happier times, it was possible to cross the length and breadth of Europe by train in so few days that the journey could still be conveniently measured by hours. Paris to Berlin, fifteen hours; Berlin to Moscow, forty hours; Berlin to Milan, twenty hours. In certain parts of that complex and explosive continent, it was necessary to change one's official language three or four times in the course of a pilgrimage which in the United States would appear to be, in length, a mere uneventful hop. You could cross the English Channel and find yourself greeted within a couple of hours by the slow even courtesy of a Dutch immigration officer; a few more hours and a Belgian would appear at the door of your compartment and, in French idiom sounding somehow un-French, make the same routine demands with a courtesy of a different tang. Then eastwards, you could encounter the clipped precision of German official-dom, followed by softer accents emanating from the speakers of a series of Western Slavonic national languages. And to the south there lay, also easily accessible, the varied music of Mediterranean Romance languages, maintaining a certain insidious charm even as spoken by the stampers of passports and openers of trunks. The landscape might not change perceptibly at the political borders, but there would be a stir in your compartment, a coming and going of people, new phrases to be caught on the wing as travelers passed by in the corridor; and as you sat in your corner eagerly experiencing the linguistic kaleidoscope of the continent, you would strain to catch the first sounds of the new idiom as fresh companions settled themselves about you. The Dutch commercial travelers condoling or congratulating with one another in measured tones on the current market would give place to a group of French *permissionaires* exchanging rapid chaff on the exploits of their leave, in an esoteric professional jargon of considerable gayety; their still-warm places might be occupied by a domestic group on the German border, *Vati* and *Mutti* complete with *Brüderlein* and *Schwesterlein* who were sure to be the silent, well-behaved recipients of a series of solicitous imperatives. Cries from the station platforms might echo in your mind in rich polyglot confusion at the end of such a long journey eastwards: *"Cigarren! Cigaretten!"*—*"Paris-Soir! Figaro!"*—*"Abfahrt!"*—*"Het is al tien uur."*—*"A la aduana . . ."* *"Agua mineral, chocolade . . ."* *"Priïdjóte, pozháluista!"*

Certainly these differences in tongue would be bewildering in the extreme to any traveler, until instruction and experience could bring order out of the chaos of aural impressions. But an enthusiast who set out to acquire some smattering of the languages in a series of countries to be so traversed would soon begin to observe some curious parallelisms in the words learnt to designate the same object. For two or even more languages he would find repeated similarities, remote but still perceptible, not only in individual words but in the manner in which these words were put together in sentences. Naïve observers explain these similarities by talking of a vague "mixture" or "corruption." When they come across a sentence in Dutch like *"Ik heb het gekoopt voor mijnen zoon"* they are pleased and surprised to observe how much it resembles English "I have bought it for my son" or German *"Ich habe es für meinen Sohn gekauft."* And so they inform you gleefully, with all the assurance of a non-linguist: "Dutch is a funny language; it's a mixture of English and corrupt German."

A Hollander would of course protest vehemently that Dutch is no more corrupt, funny, or mixed than any other national speech in Europe, and he would be quite right. There is another way of explaining its gratifying resemblance to things we already know.

Let us take a single sentence and follow its land-changes, its mutations, over a fairly wide territory—as territories are reckoned in Europe.

Suppose you begin a trip in Sweden, and you find yourself seated with a mother who is anxiously supervising the box lunch of several small children. She turns solicitously to one of them and says, "Did you get any cookies (or apples, or candies)?" And the child replies: "Yes, Mother, I have three." In Swedish that would be, *"Ja, moder, jag har tre."* In Norway, to the west, or Denmark, to the south, it would be almost the same: *"Já, mor, jeg har tre."*

The slight differences in vowel sound and in sentence melody do not disguise the fact that we are listening to the same words. A moment's reflection will suggest the right explanation. We are not confronted by a borrowing or "mixture" in any case. The three Scandinavian languages mentioned are equally ancient. At one time they were identical, for all practical purposes. A traveler in olden times (let us say the ninth century) could traverse the whole length of Norway or Sweden and pass to the southern extremity of Denmark without any change in his speech. Everywhere he would hear children say: *"Ja, módir, ek hefi þrjá."* (The last word was pronounced [θrjaː].) The changes and differences developed during centuries, rather rapidly in Denmark, more slowly in Sweden. As a result, we now have diversity where once there was unity. Three national languages, equally venerable, have replaced Old Scandinavian. They are extremely close relatives, but none could claim parental precedence over the others. If any branch of Scandinavian could exact respect on the grounds of conservatism (that is, fidelity to the parent, the Old Scandinavian) it would be modern Icelandic, spoken in the distant island which Norwegians settled in the ninth century. Here children still say: *"Já, módir, ek hefi þrjá."* The values of the vowels have changed slightly; that is all.

When the train crosses from Denmark into Germany, a greater change becomes apparent. Here the maternal inquiry elicits the answer, *"Ja, Mutter, ich habe drei."* In Holland or the Flemish-speaking parts of Belgium, tow-headed lads murmur,[1] *"Ja, moeder (or moer) ik heb drie."* The cleavage is greater, but the separate words still look distinctly familiar. We can even group the versions of our little sentence to show where two or more languages show particular likeness:

ICELANDIC:	*Já, móđir, ek hefi þrjá.*	
SWEDISH:	*Ja, moder, jag har tre.*	
DANISH:	*Ja, mor, jeg har tre.*	
NORWEGIAN:	*Ja, mor, jeg har tre.*	
GERMAN:	*Ja, Mutter, ich habe drei.*	
DUTCH:	*Ja, moeder, ik heb drie.*	
FLEMISH:	*Ja, moeder, ik heb drie.*	
ENGLISH:	Yes, mother, I have three.	

German stands somewhat apart because its consonants show certain peculiarities: it alone has a [t] between vowels (that is, intervocalic) in the word for mother. Still, it is clear that we are still dealing with variations on the same theme.

Just as the Scandinavian examples revealed close kinship among themselves, so all of those in the extended list show some degree of relationship with one another. Sentences betraying the close linguistic ties within this same group could be multiplied indefinitely. Such being the case, we are justified in speaking of a "family" of languages, borrowing a metaphor from the realm of human relations.

PARENT GERMANIC

Detailed comparisons of this sort indicate that all the members of this Germanic group go back to a single parent language, now lost, spoken as a unity somewhere between the first century B.C. and the first A.D. We call this lost parent language Primitive Germanic. Its modern descendants are grouped into what is known as the Germanic family of European languages.

English is one of them. The precise geographical location of Primitive Germanic is not known. We can surmise the nature of its sounds (*phonology*) and inflections (*morphology*) with what is probably fair accuracy, however, because of some early literature and inscriptions dating back to a time when the separate descendants had as yet separated very little from one another. The runic inscription on the Gallebus horn (p. 44) belongs to this early period. It was Old Scandinavian, but it might almost have been composed in an early form of any of the others mentioned.

By comparative study it has been established which sounds in the quoted words are most faithful to the original language. We know that English has preserved the initial consonant of the word "three" [θ] as spoken in Primitive Germanic; but that Icelandic, Flemish, and Dutch have kept the consonant at the end of the first person pronoun singular (*ik*), which has been lost in English and transformed in the others. Back of the multiplicity of extant forms we can feel our way to the existence of the single speech called parent Germanic.

ROMANCE LANGUAGES

But now let us continue the journey south. In Belgium our anxious Flemish mother may be replaced by a fellow-country-woman who speaks French. Her child will say something strikingly different from anything heard so far. "*Oui, mère* (or *maman*), *j'en ai trois.*" As the train goes southwards towards that fertile cradle of cultures, the Mediterranean basin, it may be routed towards the Pyrenees, or across the Alps into Italy. If it should cross the Iberian peninsula you would hear in Spain: "*Si madre, (yo) tengo tres;* and in Portugal: "*Sim, mãe, tenho tres.*" But if it should take you across the barrier which Hannibal—even Hannibal—found all but impassible, down the steep slopes to the smiling Lombard plains, you would hear: "*Si, madre, ce n'ho tre.*" And even across the Adriatic, on the far side of the Balkan peninsula, hardy descendants of the Roman army and Roman colonists will be saying in Rumanian: *"Da, mama mea, eu am trei."*

The similarities are apparent:

FRENCH: *Oui, ma mère, j'en ai trois.*
SPANISH: *Sí, madre, (yo) tengo tres.*
PORTUGUESE: *Sim, mãe, tenho tres.*
ITALIAN: *Si, madre, ce n'ho tre.*
RUMANIAN: *Da, mama mea, eu am trei.*

The situation is comparable to the one which diverted and possibly mystified you in Germanic territory. You have been traversing lands where the people communicate with one another in tongues clearly descended from a single parent. This time the parent language was a form of Latin: not the solemn speech, stilted and formal, which was reserved for polite literature and speeches in the forum, but the popular or "vulgar" Latin spoken by common people throughout the length and breadth of the Roman territory. Plain soldiers, tavern keepers, itinerant merchants, freedmen, small traders, naturalized citizens of all the polyglot Roman provinces, must have used this form of discourse as an international *lingua franca*. In this idiom they bought and sold, exchanged jokes, flirted, lamented, and consoled with one another. We know from late written documents and inscriptions (especially those on the humbler tombstones of poor folk) just how ungrammatical, rapid, informal, and even slangy this Latin was, compared with the intricate and highly mannered periods of a Cicero. People had become impatient with the many case endings required in classical Latin, and were reducing them to two or three. Even these were treated with playful carelessness. The verb was handled in a different way—a more vivid one—to show changes in tense; and the word order was simplified. Moreover, slang words triumphed completely over traditional ones in some provinces. Ordinary people in Gaul (perhaps emulating the jargon of the army) stopped referring to the human head as *caput,* and substituted *testa* or "pot," from which comes modern French *tête*. It is as if all persons speaking English should have fallen into the way of saying "my bean" for the same object, so that it became the accepted word, while "head" was lost entirely.

The popular Roman speech differed from one province to another because popular locutions do tend always to be regional, and because the Romans came in contact with widely differing types of native speech. Thus the pronunciation and even the grammar were affected by the underlying populations. In one place the Latin word *habēre* continued to be used for "to have"; in the Spanish peninsula, however, it so happened that *tenēre,* meaning "to hold," came to be used in its place in the more general sense of "to have." That is why our imaginary Spanish child says *tengo* instead of any form of the classical *habēre*. The number "three," on the other hand, varies only slightly in the series of Romance sentences quoted. The numbers have remained fairly stable in the various daughter languages perpetuated from vulgar Latin. One of the factors tending to preserve a similarity in them throughout the ages has been their similar experience in developing a strong stress accent during the transition to the Middle Ages. This new accentuation caused similar losses in unaccented syllables in a given word in all Mediterranean areas. There were differences, of course, in the forms that emerged; but certainly not enough to make the results unrecognizably alien to one another.

The neo-Latin languages (if the expression may be permitted) give us another example, therefore, of a family which bears its signs of consanguinity very legibly on the external aspect of each of its members. In Roman times, Latin itself could claim cousins (in the ancient *Italic* group) which have since been lost.

THE SLAVIC FAMILY

And here is one further example of language relationship which may metaphorically be called close consanguinity. In eastern Europe a sharp-eared traveler on an international train will also have an opportunity to detect fundamental similarity behind the changing visages of national speech. A far-flung territory is occupied by peoples speaking *Slavic* languages and dialects. It would be possible to pursue the transformation of our key sentence addressed to an imaginary Slavic mother to the east as follows:

CZECH: *Ano, matko, mám tři.*
POLISH: *Tak, matko, mam trzy.*
RUSSIAN: *Da, matʲ, u menʲá tri.*

When our international train crosses into the Soviet Union, it will pass through various sections of Russia showing distinct dialect colorings. Ukrainian, for instance, shows enough differentiation to be dignified as a national language, with an official spelling of its own. Even an untutored eye, however, can see how close it is to the official language of Great Russia, the classical medium of literature known to the world as "Russian." In the Balkan states, South Slavic languages show these perceptible nuances of our chosen theme. For instance, the Bulgarian version of it would be: "*Da, maika, imom tri.*"

Once again, we are justified in assuming that centuries ago there was a single language from which these cousins descended. About the seventh century it was probably still fairly unified. In the ninth century a southern dialect of this early Slavic (Old Bulgarian) was written down in a translation of the Bible made by Saints Cyril and Methodius. The text helps us to get quite a clear picture of parent Slavic, just as runic inscriptions bring us close to Primitive Germanic, and unofficial documents of the Roman Empire tell us much about Vulgar Latin.

INDO-EUROPEAN, PARENT OF PARENTS

Slavic, Romance, and Germanic represent three families of languages spoken in Europe today. But surely it must be clear that similarities link these families to one another besides linking the smaller subdivisions within each given family. In *all* the national languages surveyed so far, it will be noticed, the word for "mother" began with the labial nasal [m]; in a considerable number a dental [t], [đ], or [d] appeared in the middle of the word after the first vowel. Likewise in *all* of the languages listed, "three" began with a dental [t], [d], or [θ], followed by an [r]. Why is this?

Clearly, at a still earlier period than the days of early (prehistoric) Germanic and Slavonic, and of Vulgar Latin, there must have been a more ancient and inclusive unity which embraced all three.

The same procedure, if pursued farther, would have revealed to us other major families belonging to the same larger embracing unity in Europe and parts of Asia. These are:

Celtic, including Irish, Highland Scottish, Welsh, and Breton. (In modern Irish, "mother" is *mathair* and "three" is *tri.*)

Baltic, including Lettish, Lithuanian, and an extinct dialect once spoken in the territory of modern Prussia (Old Prussian). The word for "mother" is *motina,* not closely related to the cognates already cited. *Tris* for "three" is, on the other hand, an obvious cognate.

Hellenic, including modern Greek dialects, some of which go back to very ancient times. (An ancient Greek dialect, Attic, spoken in the city of Athens, produced a body of literature of enduring splendor. Its word for "mother" was *matếr* and for "three," *treîs.* This is the classical language studied in school.)

Albanian, the national language of Albania, with no close relatives outside its own borders. Here "three" is *tre;* but the word for "mother" is not related to the forms in the above languages. A new form, *nona,* has replaced the Indo-European term preserved elsewhere.

Armenian, spoken in Armenia (between Europe and Asia Minor), is, like Albanian, a language with many diverse elements borrowed from outside, but it has an independent history traceable back to the fifth or sixth century A.D. Its word for "mother," *mair*, is easily recognizable as a cognate of the others given; not so, however, is *erek* for "three."

Even in Asia there are languages with venerable histories and rich literary heritage which can be recognized as members of the same linguistic clan:

Indian, including Hindustani, Bengali, Marathi, and Hindi. These dialects are descended from Old Indian, preserved to us in a classical literary form (Sanskrit) which dates back to the fifteenth century B.C. or even several hundred years earlier. Sanskrit, despite its great antiquity, still shows close generic resemblance to its modern European cousins. Its word for "mother" was *mātṛ* and for "three," *tri.*

Iranian, very closely related to Sanskrit, was spoken in the Persian highlands while Indian was spreading over the interior of India. It produced an early literature in the form of Zoroastrian hymns. Since those ancient times Persian has been subjected to large foreign infiltration, notably Arabic, but its structure still reveals its kinship with the other groups listed.

Hittite, a language spoken by people frequently mentioned in the Bible, is now extinct. Cuneiform inscriptions give us enough material to reveal its fundamental character. Some sort of relationship it surely must have had with the members of the broad family of families now being surveyed, but the precise nature of that relationship is still under discussion.

Tocharian, now extinct, is represented by some fragmentary texts (probably antedating the tenth century), which were discovered in eastern Turkestan in a Buddhist monastery. The material is too scanty to permit of definitive analysis, but it shows relationship to the above subsidiary groups.

Our railroad trip beginning with Germanic territory has taken us far afield, even to the shores of the Indus River in Asia. Even so, and despite the most baffling diversities, skilled comparison of key words has been able to establish that the miniature families surveyed do undoubtedly belong to the same large, inclusive family already postulated to account for likenesses observed among Germanic, Slavonic, and Romance (from Old Italic).

Back of the smaller families lay a single family; attached to this single family it is almost certain there must have been a single language. We call the whole family by the name "Indo-European," a term generally preferred today to "Indo-Germanic" or "Aryan," both of which could easily be misunderstood. That is to say, every language mentioned so far is an Indo-European language, no matter what smaller group it may belong to.

HOMELAND OF INDO-EUROPEAN

But if they are all related thus, we must assume that a single definite language, parent Indo-European, gave rise to all of them. This is probably true. Some time before 2000 B.C., in some part of the world, a group which was essentially a single community spoke this single parent language. Later, dialect forms of this tribal language were carried into many different countries, from Iceland to India—by emigration, by conquest, by peaceful transfer. We do not know how this occurred in every case, but the expansion had already begun in earliest historical times.

Where the parent language was spoken, and by whom, is something of a mystery. By studying words that are common to a number of the family groups listed above we can, to be sure, get some idea of the culture these people had before their language was spread over a wide area and differentiated by the divisions, migrations, or conquests of a half-dozen millennia ago. We can surmise that they probably lived in a temperate climate because a number of the descended languages have similar words for spring, summer, autumn, and winter. There are common words indicating a developed (though still simple) agriculture: terms having to do with the plow, spade, sickle, and mill; with carting, sowing, and mowing. For instance, the word for plow is *arðr* in Icelandic, *áratron* in Greek, *arātrum* in Latin, *arathar* in Irish, *árklas* in Lithuanian, *araur* in Armenian. The names of certain plants and animals are supposed to offer some guidance. Parent Indo-European had terms for dogs, cows, sheep, bulls, goats, pigs, and horses; also for wild animals such as the bear, the wolf, and the fox. Hermann Hirt, author of an elaborate discussion of the subject, considers the common words for "eel" in several languages as very important. If the original speakers of Indo-European knew this fish, they could not have lived originally near the Black Sea, where it is not found. Another important word is the old term for the beech tree in the various languages. The words *Buche* in German, *fāgus* in Latin, *Bachenis* Forest in a Celtic place-name, and *phēgós* (φηγός) in Greek (where it had been transferred, however, to the oak tree), indicate that the beech was a tree known at the time of the parent language. The forms just quoted could all have come from a single root. Now the eastern boundary for the presence of this European tree is a line drawn roughly from Königsberg to the Crimea. Therefore Hirt argues that the parent language must have developed to the west of such a line.

North central Germany, Lithuania, the Danube Valley, and Southern Russia (near the Black Sea) have been suggested in turn as the original homeland of the parent language. India, once regarded as the cradle of our general Indo-European speech, has been relinquished in favor of European territories answering to the geographical clues of the joint vocabularies. Of these it may be said that probability favors those districts in which there are many physical traces of early mankind, such as burial mounds, skeletons, fragments of pottery, signs of human habitation. The Danube Valley is particularly rich in these, and also Germany and Southern Russia. Lithuania can boast an extraordinarily archaic language, similar in many ways to ancient Sanskrit, but its territory is poor in archaeological remains, those mute witnesses to the daily living of people like ourselves who "flourished" (if that is the proper word) in prehistoric times. Lithuania may have been settled early in the age that saw the spread of Indo-European, but it is less likely than other districts to have seen its first development.

No matter where Indo-European developed out of still earlier linguistic stages now hopelessly lost, it is important to remember that we know absolutely nothing about the physical appearance of its first speakers. They have long since been leveled with the dust; we cannot say whether their skin was light or dark, their vanished hair shadowy or bright. Among the broad-skulled and long-skulled and medium-skulled remains of prehistoric man, we cannot tell which—if any—moved their bony jaws in olden times to the sounds and rhythms of the Indo-European parent language. Although most of the contemporary peoples of Europe may be descendants, in part, of members of our postulated Indo-European community, still it is not safe to assume that this community was itself racially homogeneous.

In any event we cannot be sure about what happened in those early ages. It is instructive to think of the mutations of history in the era since writing began. Whole peoples have suffered extinction as nations in past centuries, yet they may perpetuate and hand on the language of the conquerors when the latter in their turn are destroyed or absorbed. A West Indian Negro today can often be found speaking with the faultless accents and intonation of choice classical English; if you closed your eyes you would think he had been nurtured on the playing fields of Eton or by the Cam. He speaks standard English *as his native tongue;* he is aware of nothing alien about it as it leaves his lips; there is no psychological strain involved in employing this particular instrument merely because his ancestors in Africa used a very different one long ago. No doubt flawless Latin was spoken in the streets of Rome by naturalized provincials of many races, showing wide variety in the hues of their epidermises. In somewhat the same way all of us, for that matter, may be using variations of a borrowed instrument. So completely separate are the questions of language and race.

Most scholars would, to be sure, look to one or another of

the contemporary peoples of Europe or India or even Persia to find lineal descendants of those who first spoke Indo-European. Yet two well-known authorities, Sigmund Feist (a German) and Vendryès (a Frenchman), have argued that even the Germans of today—who usually claim that honor—do not have the blood of the parent tribe in their veins even though they speak an Indo-European language (which some may choose to call "Aryan"). Feist and Vendryès point out that German (like Dutch, English, and Scandinavian) shows a very great change from the parent speech which lies back of the other Indo-European offshoots. The Germanic family has changed many of the supposed original sounds. Where Latin had *piscis,* Germanic substituted a form like *fisk* (English "fish"); where Latin and Greek had *patēr,* Germanic showed something like English "father." Thus this one particular group looks quite different from its Romance, Slavonic, Hellenic and other cousins because of an unusually complete shift of consonants (see chapter 7, note 4). According to Feist and Vendryès, the reason is that the Primitive Germanic tribesmen were an alien race trying to learn to pronounce an Indo-European or "Aryan" language. They had trouble with sounds like [p] and [t], and so distorted them to [f] and [θ]. If this theory is sound, the Germans of today would be a non-"Aryan" race (granting that the phrase means anything), speaking an "Aryan" language imposed upon them by conquerors in prehistoric times! The whole question is very speculative. It may be pointed out that if Germanic tribesmen had trouble with [p] and [t] in primitive times, at least their descendants soon made good the loss by developing new [p] and [t] sounds out of Indo-European [b] and [d].

At the moment, however, what interests us most is the evidence of underlying unity, not of divergence, in the Indo-European family. As we shall see, the divergences turn out to be fairly regular when they are closely examined. Because they are more or less predictable by an advanced student, they do not disturb seriously his impressions of the underlying unity which justifies him in regarding the whole majestic array of tongues as a close-knit family. The more acutely one observes the principles of correspondence and divergence, the easier it becomes to learn a new member within the widely scattered group.

Cursory as this review has been, it has probably indicated the approach and even something of the methods used in the study of comparative linguistics.

Comparisons of a similar sort have established family relationships for the rest of the world. For the languages less familiar to us speakers of English a briefer survey will suffice.

THE FINNO-UGRIC FAMILY

Within Europe itself there are several languages which are completely alien to those of the Indo-European confraternity. A visitor in Finland, for instance, will look at posters and newspapers and remark with a puzzled air: "How strange! Not a word looks or sounds familiar! Why, in most countries you can guess something here and there, at least phrases—but not this; it's *outlandish*." The same remark will be heard from tourists in Hungary, Estonia, and (on rare occasions, I suppose) from visitors among the Laplanders in the far north of western Russia and Scandinavia. The term "outlandish" is here justified in its literal sense. The languages here spoken did come from an "outer land" centuries ago. They reached Europe by migration from the Volga and the slopes of the Ural Mountains, both from the Asiatic and the hither side. The Magyar (Hungarian) speech was transferred in a series of incursions lasting down into the Middle Ages, which were fraught with considerable terror for the turbulent inhabitants already more or less established on the fringes of the Roman Empire.

Finnish, Estonian, Lappish, and Magyar are members of the *Finno-Ugric family*. It also includes minor languages and dialects spoken in restricted areas, such as Carelian, Mordvian, Cheremiss, and the Permian languages (Zyrian and Votiak) which were carried to the northern Urals from the Volga region. Mordvian and Cheremiss are still spoken in scattered communities of the Volga basin. It is thought that Lappish is a Finno-Ugric language imposed by conquest on a people who originally spoke a quite different tongue. The Lapps, indeed, may be the physical survivors of one of the primeval races inhabiting Europe long before history began.

FINNO-UGRIC, NENETS, AND PARENT URALIC

In north central Siberia a number of small scattered tribes speak variations of a language referred to in most textbooks as Samoyedic. The term is an unflattering one, and did not originate with the tribesmen themselves. It is a Russian word used in Tsarist times and seems to mean "self-eaters" or cannibals. (It comes apparently from two common Indo-European roots: *samo-* cognate with English "same," and *¹ed,* cognate with English "edible," from Latin *edere,* meaning "to eat.") According to the *Soviet Encyclopedia* these people refer to their own nation and language as Nenets—a term preferable, therefore, to the contemptuous epithet hitherto current.

Finno-Ugric and Nenets ("Samoyed") together form a supergroup showing remote but still perceptible similarities among themselves. There is one trait of sound patterns common to almost all, which in particular impresses even a beginner in Finno-Ugric linguistics. It is known by the pretty term "vowel harmony." To Finno-Ugric ears, the vowels of single words are like notes in a musical chord. To combine front, back, and mid-tongue vowels in the same word indiscriminately is as bad as striking a group of notes on the piano by bringing down the flat of your hand forcefully on the white keys. In constructing a word, when the first syllable happens to contain a front vowel (*e, i, ä, ö, ü*),[1] then all following syllables must also contain front ones; and if the first syllable contains a back vowel

---

[1] ä = [ɛ]; ö = [ɛ'], a sound formed by rounding the lips while pronouncing [ɛ]; ü = [y]. For [ɛ] see chapter 2, p. 13; ö and ü are familiar to students of German.

(*a, o, u*) then all suffixed syllables must likewise contain one. You can have words like *äpä, küsöb, vesi, mato,* and *muna,* but not *veso.* Vowel harmony existed, apparently, in early Finno-Ugric, but Magyar shows exceptions and the Permian group and Lappish no longer observe it. A very practical result of this craving for vocalic similarity is the necessity to vary vowels in regular suffixes (inflectional endings). There must be two forms to choose from, according to the root vowel of the word. In Magyar, for instance, *marad-unk* means "we remain," but *el-ünk* means "we live." The vowel of the suffix alternates between [u] (after a back vowel) and [y], written *ü*, (after a front one).

Here again we are justified in assuming a single parent language, a common ancestor of Nenets and Finno-Ugric, which we may call parent Uralic. This broad term may be used for all the ramified descendants, just as Indo-European was applied to all the languages descended from it. The geographical location of this lost ancestral Uralic speech is not known. Some of its characteristics can be deduced by reasoning back from extant dialects, as in the case of Indo-European. It has been claimed that a still more ancient kinship existed between Uralic and Altaic (a group centered in the region of the Altai Mountains in Central Asia) and even Japanese, but most specialists regard these speculations as unconvincing.

BASQUE

One more language of an "outlandish" character remains in Europe: Basque, which is spoken by a small but closely knit group in the French and Spanish Pyrenees. The vocabulary and grammatical structure are as alien to Indo-European as can be imagined. Hence the legends (current about Finnish too, by the way) to the effect that the devil himself was foiled in an attempt to learn this language, and his tutor (unlike Faust) emerged safe from the bargain to teach it, with his soul still his own. According to some writers, it is possible that Basque represents the sole surviving fragment of a common speech spoken by Neolithic tribesmen scattered over Europe, long before Indo-European or Finno-Ugric had entered the continent by migration or conquest. Possibly the same type of speech extended into the British Isles and across the Spanish peninsula into Northern Africa in these prehistoric times. The arguments in support of this possibility have to do with similarities in culture and physique among the prehistoric peoples concerned. They are not based primarily on linguistic evidence.

SEMITIC LANGUAGES

This brings us to another linguistic family which has had cultural contacts with Indo-European at various points in its history: namely, the Semitic group. The name for it is taken from Genesis 1:10, in which the names of the three sons of Noah are given as Sem (or Shem), Cham (or Ham), and Japheth. It was believed that the numerous folk speaking Semitic languages owed their physical existence to the first son, to whom descendants of remarkable fecundity would appear to have been attributed. In ancient historical times, branches of Semitic were spoken in the city-states of Babylonia and Assyria in Mesopotamia. (An earlier language, Sumerian, was superseded by this spread of East Semitic.) To the West, Phoenician and Hebrew and Aramaic (including Syriac) occupied territory in Asia Minor which extended to the eastern shores of the Mediterranean. Hebrew was destined to play a memorable part, long after the end of political independence for Palestine, because of the incalculable influence of its Biblical literature. South of Palestine, and extending far west across the north of Africa, at one time even including Spain, there lay an imposing concatenation of peoples using Arabic, which with the rise of Islam became a world language of prime importance. It is still one of the first claimants for the attention of students desiring to broaden their studies beyond the more proximate Indo-European subgroups. Finally, the dialects of Ethiopian in Abyssinia, though close to Arabic in many features, constitute a separate division in the group of south-west Semitic languages.

One striking feature in grammatical structure is common to all the Semitic languages, and that is a marked preference for verbal roots using three consonant sounds. These consonants remain clearly recognizable no matter what vowels appear or disappear between them, or what prefixes and suffixes may be added. The characteristic core of the word, stripped of its mutations, is called the "triliteral root." A student learns, for example, that variations of the idea "to kill" cluster around the unpronounceable abstraction [qtl],[2] which has no independent existence but which can be detected in these related forms meaning "they killed:"

	HEBREW	ARAMAIC	ARABIC	ETHIOPIAN
Imperfect	yiqṭəlū	yiqṭəlūn	yaqtulu	yəqattəlū
Perfect	qāṭəlū	qəṭal (ū)	qatalū	qatalu

Nouns related to verbs show the same three-pillared structure of consonants. In Hebrew the present-tense root form meaning "reigning as king" is [moːleːχ]; "to be or become king" is [mɔːlaχ]; "to make one king" is [mɔlaχ]; "a king" is [meleχ], plural [mələχiːm]; and "kingdom" is [malǝχuːs]. The consonantal abstraction of the root is [mlχ].[3] These examples are sufficient to clarify a persistent and very easily recognized trait in Semitic.

HAMITIC LANGUAGES

Contiguous with parts of Semitic territory and rather similar to Semitic in structure are the languages of the Hamitic group. They were named from the second son of that early navigator, Noah. Ancient Egyptian (known historically since 4000 B.C.)

---

[2] The phonetic symbol [q] stands for a consonant resembling [k], but spoken much deeper in the throat.

[3] It may be noticed in passing that in certain of the Semitic languages a consonant is modified in pronunciation if it comes after a vowel. In Hebrew and Aramaic, for instance, an older [k] became [χ] in such a position. An earlier form of the verbal root [m¹χ] appears in the word [malkaː], "queen."

belonged to it, and produced in turn the Coptic or neo-Egyptian language which continued to be spoken down to the seventeenth century of our era. This Hamitic tongue has one of the longest careers so far as records are concerned. Akin to it are surviving dialects of Berber, spoken in scattered communities across the north of Africa as far as the Canary Islands, and also the Cushite languages bordering the Red Sea: Bedja, Somali, Saho, and Afar.

There is good reason to suppose that Hamitic and Semitic are themselves differentiations of an original linguistic unity called Hamito-Semitic by specialists. For one thing, Old Egyptian shows a marked preference for triliteral consonant roots, as a glance at its grammar will show, even though biliteral consonant roots are also common. Moreover, there are a few phonological traits common to the combined group, and one or two grammatical usages which appear to come from a common source. The peoples concerned have been neighbors from time immemorial. It is not unlikely that the idioms now spoken by them had a single origin. There has been quite enough time during and before recorded history for the multiple ramifications to occur.

SUDANESE AND BANTU GROUPS

The rest of Africa is occupied almost entirely by two large groups, somewhat loosely defined: the Sudanese (generally southwest of the Hamitic belt) and Bantu (south of Sudanese). Though the field of African Negro languages has been comparatively neglected, the study of these two major groups has already revealed evidence of common origin from a single language before the cleavage into these two major divisions. Research is hampered, of course, by an almost complete absence of written texts before modern times. (The study of Indo-European reveals clearly how illuminating and decisive an ancient text can be in determining family relationships among languages.) Even today, however, Bantu and Sudanese agree in classifying nouns grammatically according to the class of objects they represent, each class being marked off by an affixed syllable to designate it. Parent Bantu, for instance, probably had a prefix *mu-*, usually reserved for human beings. An example is *mu-na* ("child") in the Duzala dialect. Other prefixes were *ba-*, *gu-*, *mi-*. Sudanese uses such class prefixes for nouns too. Bantu and Sudanese also inflect their verbs to show *aspects* of action rather than the time relations which we consider so very important. A Bantu verb shows completeness, negation, emphasis, continuity, and other relations, but not very many temporal ones. *Na-pula* means "I desire" in Duala, and *na-puli*, "I desired"; other inflexions are: *na-si-pula*, "I desire not"; *na-pulise*, "I cause to desire"; *na-pulana*, "I desire because of something." Phonology and vocabulary mark off Bantu as distinct from its northern neighbor in Sudan, but it may well be that underlying similarities will be increasingly revealed in this domain too.

ALTAIC LANGUAGES

Returning to the Balkans and the Near East we find another huge family of languages represented by one, Turkish, spoken within the very portals of Europe. The broad term for Turkish and its relatives is Altaic. It includes three main divisions: Turkic, Mongol, and Tunguz. These extend from the southeast of Europe (Istanbul) through the Volga district and Turkey, through Azerbaijan, Anatolia, and the Caucasian districts, to Mongolia and the Tunguz-Manchu region around the Yenisei River. Among the Turkic subdivisions are the groups in the east or Altai region (including Yakut); the Central Asian groups; the western ones (including Tatar in the Volga district and Kirghiz); and the southern (Turcoman, Anatolian, Caucasian Turkic dialects, etc.).

The Mongolian subdivision centers in Mongolia, showing little diffusion outside the political boundaries of the country. Tunguz is spoken east of the Yenisei River, while Manchu, a close relative, is limited to the valleys of the Khurkha and Sungari rivers. It is being replaced by Chinese.

A common trait which links these widely sundered languages is the principle of vowel harmony, which also marks Finno-Ugric, as we have seen. There are other characters of a general phonological nature which can be found in all of them. An example of the vowel harmony is a pair of compounds from the Osmanli dialect (spoken in the Balkans):

> *öl-dür-mä-yälim*, "let us not kill."
> *otur-ma-yalïm*, "let us not stay seated."

Notice that in the first word, the first syllable began with a front vowel, so that all the following vowels—including those of the first person plural suffix—had to be fronted. In some, this front quality is indicated by two dots over the vowel. The second group began with [o], a back vowel, and as a consequence the following syllables also show lowered vowels. Even the [i] is lowered to [ï], and the [l] preceding it is lowered from its front position. (The sign [ł] represents an *l*-sound made with the back of the tongue instead of the tip.) These subtle gradations of sound within the phrasal unit are practiced automatically by the vast numbers of people who speak Turkic-Mongolian-Tunguz as well as those who employ Finno-Ugric, making a very imposing total in all.

SINO-TIBETAN LANGUAGES

In the Far East there is another inclusive group employed by an imposing section of humanity, namely the Sino-Tibetan languages. The subdivisions are Chinese, Tai, and Tibeto-Burman, covering a belt from China on the east to the Tibetan highlands of India, and dipping down into Siam. The characteristic word-form in all these languages is an uninflected monosyllable which shows its role in the sentence by position only. Yet there are traces of dissyllabic roots and inflectional forms which must have been common in the parent language. To a very limited degree English may be compared to Sino-Tibetan languages, since we too depend on word order to show relationships in the sentence; but of course we use many other devices as well.

Musical pitch is an important feature of all these languages. It may change the meaning of a word, since many syllables otherwise complete homonyms (that is, identical) are distinguished by high or low pitch alone. It is as if we distinguished between "sea" and "see" by giving one a high and the other a low tone. There is evidence that originally high pitch accompanied syllables beginning with a voiceless consonant, so that *tai* would necessarily be spoken—or, rather, intoned—higher than *dai;* but many intricate sound changes throughout the centuries have obscured this neat correlation.

MALAY-POLYNESIAN GROUPS

The Malay-Polynesian belt, including peoples in the Dutch East Indies, Philippines, Malay Peninsula, Madagascar, Hawaii, and small Pacific archipelagos, reveals the close connection of its members with one another to the most casual observation. They make use of roots of two syllables and employ a variety of prefixes, suffixes, and infixes; yet their nouns are innocent of inflection to show gender and number. In Hawaiian, original consonants have been slurred away in so many positions that the language has become a tissue of vowels held together by a minimum of consonants in initial and intervocalic positions.

AMERICAN INDIAN FAMILIES

Across the Pacific we come once more to the two American continents where a pair of Indo-European languages, English and Spanish (together with Portuguese) dominate official life. They have displaced but not yet eliminated completely an enormously diversified series of Indian languages, extending from the Arctic to the Antarctic. Some families of these have been carefully studied, but the variety is so great that we are in no position to make hypotheses concerning underlying unities. Specialists differ widely in their estimates of the numbers of groups showing so little similarity at present as to appear to be independent. Emigration, conquest, cultural interpenetration, and merging have done much to confuse the picture. The reader will recognize the names of some of the larger groups in North America, such as the Algonquian, Iroquoian, Muskogean, Siouan, and Uto-Aztecan. Eskimo, which is spoken in the north of Canada, is now considered to be a relative of Nenets (Samoyedic) in the Uralic group which includes Finno-Ugric.

AUSTRALIAN, CAUCASIAN, AND DRAVIDIAN
FAMILIES. KOREAN AND JAPANESE

In this rapid encirclement of the globe several important linguistic territories have been omitted, either because they have been too little charted for even the most summary description, or because they were too unified or too limited to illustrate ramified family relationships. The native languages of Australia are, for instance, a treasure-house of unexplored mystery. The region of the Caucasus mountains presents a bewildering complexity of diversified tongues spoken by fairly small groups, neighbors to one another, many of which are mutually unintelligible. Of these, one, Georgian, achieved literary expression at a comparatively early date (fourth century A.D.), but others have remained practically unknown outside their own territory. (Now that they are being recorded in print there will be a basis for comparative study.) In India, the Dravidian dialects represent a large but shrinking language group which antedated the conquering Indo-European Sanskrit in the Indus valley, and has retreated before it. India, the Malay peninsula, and the Siamese territory include linguistic patches or "islands" designated as Austro-Asiatic, grouped together on the basis of parallelisms in vocabulary and word-formation.[4] Korean and Japanese, both languages associated with high cultures, resemble each other in vocabulary and general

---

[4] Father Wilhelm Schmidt has tried to prove their generic relation to Malay-Polynesian. This hypothesis is described by Przyluski as "grandiose—but fragile." See bibliographical note at the end of this chapter.

grammatical forms, but the relations of the two are not entirely clarified despite arguments to prove their kinship. Both have impersonal verbs and uninflected nouns; both depend largely on word order to indicate relationships within the sentence.

There is much work still to be done in charting the unknown or little known territories of human speech. If we can judge from experience in the past, we may expect that further relationships may be discovered by the comparative method, and that groups hitherto thought to be isolated will have relatives discovered for them, sometimes in lands quite far away. Indo-European linguistics was launched on its triumphant way by the discovery of a most distant émigré member of the family in India. The agreeable experience of perceiving unity beneath diversity has rewarded linguists so often that they have some justification for expecting it to be repeated in the future.

SINGLE OR MULTIPLE ORIGIN OF SPEECH?

Already the question has often been asked: "Do we know enough to decide whether all languages, the world over, had a single origin? Is *every* language related to every other?"

It is a fascinating question. The mere possibility of unified origin for all human speech appeals strongly to the imagination. Here indeed would be a most gratifying satisfaction for our natural desire to simplify our understanding of the universe about us by reducing the number of categories under which we conceive of it. There is also something aesthetically grandiose about the thought that the vast symphony of all languages and dialects was elaborated, so to speak, from a single theme.

In the early days of linguistic science, the presuppositions were naturally in favor of monogenesis of speech, because the story of the Garden of Eden, whether understood literally or not, exerted a strong influence on investigators. Then under the spell of Darwinism there was a reaction to a belief in polygenesis, likewise often expressed in dogmatic terms. Analogies were drawn and misapplied in linguistic science, for which Darwin himself should not be blamed. The chief exponent of linguistic polygenesis was Friedrich Müller, who assumed that the "speech" of animals must have developed gradually into human speech, so gradually indeed that man must have been a diversified type long before the evolution was completed, "and herewith," he argued, "we may be said to have an *a priori* postulate, from the point of view of the history of evolution, of the derivation of human speech (as an ideational and conceptional language based on sounds) from several mutually independent sources."

Today most authors are extremely cautious when they touch upon the unrecoverable epoch when speech originated. They usually avoid committing themselves on the question as to whether this happened once or several times in various parts of the world. In any case, they say, the answer is unimportant, even irrelevant, for the solution of problems significant for us today.

Nevertheless a few individual writers are willing to commit themselves. Alfredo Trombetti, for instance, has presented a lengthy, ambitious argument for monogenesis, fortified with many concrete illustrations. On the basis of extremely wide and detailed study, Trombetti builds up a scheme including wider and wider groups and families of languages, making use of surviving similarities in numerals, pronominal forms, and the like. Such structural words are apt to be conservative of their form, and they are not readily borrowed from one language by another in most cases. He records similarities between numerals in Sudanese-Bantu and Munda-Khmer of the Austro-Asiatic group; between pronouns in Hamitic-Semitic, Dravidian, Munda, and Polynesian; between numerals in Indo-Chinese and Uralic (he says "Ural-Altaic"); between verbs in Dakota (American Indian) and Georgian (in the Caucasian territory). He observes that the greatest similarities are to be found between groups most widely separated on the periphery of a huge circle having its center in India. Therefore he deduces that India was the home and starting point for all races as well as all languages. It is true that Trombetti produces some astonishing parallelisms. But one becomes suspicious of them when one reflects upon the great mobility of language: its proneness to change and transformation. After observing the behavior of vowels and consonants over the very short span of recorded history, one begins to suspect that two words that look alike now are probably unrelated for that very reason—unless they belong to two subgroups in demonstrably close generic relation, and also mean approximately the same thing. English "book" and German *Buch* are indeed cognates, but it is quite accidental that Quiché *buj* or *vuj* (also pronounced [buχ], but with a loose *b*) means the same thing. We know too little about the early history of the languages outside of Indo-European and Hamito-Semitic to commit ourselves too far on the matter of ultimate relationships. For one thing, change operates very slowly in some groups and with almost dizzying rapidity in others. We must allow for this in estimating the value of Trombetti's parallels. The question about a single origin for the diverse tongues of mankind must be tabled until we know more of their earlier forms; and that may be—forever.

4. Treasury of Words

Consider for a moment this rather absurd sentence: "Notwith-standing such a likelihood, I should rather work beside you; but only if you know it is because I trust you. Moreover I can do very well without you; but nevertheless I choose to keep you." I admit that the emotions prompting so tangled a statement would have to be very intricate indeed; but the words were chosen for reasons other than their rhetorical effect when placed in juxtaposition.

The words which concern us at the moment are not the leading ones, the subjects and verbs which make the core of this impassioned statement. Instead let us examine these:

notwithstanding	only
such	because
rather	without
moreover	nevertheless
likelihood	beside

They belong to the small counters of our sentences which we employ without regard, very much as we might be careless of small change valued at no more than a tenth of a cent. Some of them are among the most difficult words to define. And yet a sentence lacking in these tiny units is lacking in all nuance; it is bald, abrupt, and ungracious. When you are learning to speak a foreign language you find the process full of unease until you have learned the little verbal qualifiers like "nevertheless" and "notwithstanding" which temper and shade the import of a sentence. Some linguistic gourmets would prefer to begin travel in a new country equipped with words like "undoubtedly" and "moreover" than with equivalents of "champagne" and "pâté de foie gras."

There is something curious about both "nevertheless" and "notwithstanding." When you look at them closely you perceive that they are made up of complete, unmodified words put together unchanged, and yet each group is pronounced as a unit so far as accent is concerned. "Never-the-less" upon examination means "not at all lessened by that consideration" since "the" in this expression is still used, as in olden times, in a neuter pronominal sense. "Notwithstanding" means "not standing against it," since here too an older meaning is preserved: namely "with" in the sense of "opposed, against." But aside from these slight archaisms, the meanings of the component parts are easy to detect. The words are put together out of elements already familiar to us. They are not modified, either, except insofar as a slight slurring due to the telescoping within one stress unit has made them less readily isolated as separate units.

The elements of a word like "nevertheless" are, then, undisguised because they are merely juxtaposed.

The other words are less readily broken down. "Beside" is clearly "by the side of." The word "because" is surely pronounced and thought of as a unit; yet a moment's reflection will show that it is made up of two parts: a form of "by" plus the separate, familiar word "cause." Thus what appears to be a single conjunction turns out to be a petrified phrase. The French equivalent is also a phrase: *par-ce-que* corresponds to "for this thing, that . . ." and Russian *po-tomu-shto*, to exactly the same thing. Yet the Frenchman and the Russian are as little conscious of the separate parts as we are when they use the expressions. The same is true of our words "with-out" and "more-over." As for "rather" and "only," the compounding has been disguised in them, so that more is required than a moment's reflection to provide the clue. "Rather" is really a comparative degree of the simple adverb "rathe" (now lost), meaning "soon, early." Tennyson employed the obsolete positive form, somewhat self-consciously, in *Lancelot and Elaine* when he was describing the deplorable insomnia of his heartbroken Lily Maid of Astolat:

> Till *rathe* she rose, half-cheated in the thought
> She needs must bid farewell to sweet Lavaine.

When we say "I'd rather do this than that" expressing preference, we are actually saying "Since I have (like all mortals) limited time, I'd *sooner* do this. . . ." In the same way the French say *plutôt;* whereas the Germans say "dearer" (*Ich möchte lieber . . .*) and the Russians, "better" (*luchshe*).

"Only" is unrecognizable for a slightly different reason. Neither part of the word is completely archaic, but each has been shortened from its original form. At an earlier date the word was "one" plus "like." Now the latter element, "like," came from an old English noun *līc,* the basic meaning of which was "image, form, shape" and even "body, corpse." It was used in many ways to create new words. As an adjective, our "like" got its meaning of "resembling" from the phrase "in the *like*-ness of . . ." So "only" really means "one image." And "lonely," by the way, is a shortened from of "all one image." To concretize it, think of a damsel peering hopefully into a mirror on All Hallow's Eve, hoping to glimpse the *like*ness of her future lover—and to her chagrin, seeing only her own countenance staring back at her! "Likelihood" is made up of the same word twice: first in its stressed form "like," then unstressed as "-li-"; and finally a suffix meaning "state of being" (originally "office, function, employment") to make a noun of it. In adverbs, our suffix "-ly" is also derived from the weak form of the word for "image, shape." Finally, the word "such" contains a very much concealed form of *līc.* Originally the word was a phrase *swā līc,* or "so-like." This gave forms like *swilch, swich,* finally "such." The Scots form was *swilk.* Here the *-lk* was all that was left of *līc.* Even the vowel had vanished.

PUTTING WORDS TOGETHER

English has many words and phrases with abstract functions like "like" itself, which have been put together from words originally concrete in meaning. When we hear "on the other hand" we don't visualize a hand, because the significance has become abstract; it now has to do with a nice balancing of pro's and con's. But it arose from the real world of objects, in which concrete things like tools or weapons must be arranged for the convenience of right-handed or left-handed people. Another vivid phrase is "in spite of." [1] To say "I accomplished this in spite of obstacles" implies that those obstacles felt pain and resentment at your scornful success. A nice bit of magic thinking—only presumably you don't mean it to be such.

In various ways these forms illustrate how words are compounded. Two or more elements are simply put side by side, and in time they are regarded as one. It is true that in words derived from phrases the elements show some kind of grammatical relationship; the preposition is an abstract little word that "introduces" or "controls" the noun object, as we were taught in school; but even the preposition itself can sometimes be traced to a more vivid expression such as "like" meaning "image." It is useful to remember that some of our most abstract words were put together out of very pictorial elements.

COMPOUNDING IN OTHER LANGUAGES

Outside of English we find examples of the same transparent process. German *zurück,* "backwards, in reverse," uses a part of the human body (*Rücken,* "back")—as indeed "*back*wards" does in English—to indicate general direction. *Kopfüber,* literally "head-over," like English "headlong," compresses a

---

[1] *Cf.* the Dutch phrase *het spijt mij,* which merely means "I regret it." The original meaning of "spite" (from Vulgar Latin) was "scorn, contempt." Dutch has weakened the implication.

whole process into a single adverb. The German *überhaupt* and Danish *overhovet* (both meaning "over-head") also use the human head to express a logical relation. In French, the phrase *à côté de* means "by the ribs or the side of" someone. In Irish, "before" is expressed by *cheana,* a variant of the word *cenn,* "head"; "when" is *an uair,* literally, "the hour"; "behind" is *ar cúl,* "at the back"; "above" is *os cionn* or "above the head"; and "against" is *i n-aġaid,* literally "in the face of, against the countenance of." Hebrew *li-pʰnéi,* "before," also meant "in the face of" (*pnei* being "face" or "surface").[2]

These concrete terms make free use of the parts of the human body, often availing themselves of those spatial relations closest to us in order to express general temporal relations. Perhaps the most obvious example of such use of concrete for abstract—for English readers, at least—is to be found in the dialect or jargon known as Pidgin English used for communication between white persons and Chinese. The word "Pidgin" is supposed to be a corruption of "business." It is reputed to give some impression of Chinese ways of indicating relations, at the same time making use of English vocabulary. According to an anonymous *Voyage to the East Indies in 1747 and 1748* this "business" English was already in use in the eighteenth century. The author records such sentences as "I moiki grandi chin-chin for he," meaning "I saluted him, made my compliments to him." Here is a passage recorded in the latter nineteenth century. It is called "The Little Wife," and recounts the domestic tempests incident in the life of a Chinese with two wives.

Supposey one Chinaman hab catchee waifo—by'mby maskee [however] he gettee nother piece waifo. He [i.e., she] numpa [number] one waifo talkee [is called] "largo waifo" China-fashion, numpa two he talkee *"likki* waifo." Allo t'his pidgin [business] belongey [pertains to] olo custom. Supposey numpa one waifo floggee likki waifo, likki waifo no can do [can do nothing], must

2 On the change of [p] to [pʰ], later [f], see chapter 3, note 3.

catchee floggee all-same supposey t'hat numpa one waifo belongey
he mata [mother]. T'hat plopa [proper] pidgin for he.

One-time one Chinee má-chin [merchant] he belongey two piece
waifo. Numpa one waifo he velly likki, numpa two he one piece
velly largo woman, all same she catchee too muchee floggee,
numpa one flog t'hat other waifo allo tim. Numpa two no can do
one ting.

There is no need to follow the domestic difficulties of our
unfortunate Chinese further. It will be noticed that comparatively specialized, concrete words are used to express general,
abstract English terms: *supposey,* for "if," *belongey* for any
relationship implying dependence (grammatical or otherwise),
one-piece for the indefinite "a, an," and *numpa one* for "first,
primary, superior." In a glossary compiled by Charles W. Leland for his book of Pidgin English selections there are further
examples of native compounding with English elements. Since
joss is the native word for "God," "religion" is *joss-pidgin* or
"God-business," "priest" is rendered *joss-pidgin-man;* "bishop"
is *top-side piecee Heaven pidgin man.*

This is supposed to be very funny, and it gives English audi-
tors a pleasant feeling of superiority when they listen to it. As
a matter of fact, Jespersen has pointed out that the English
settlers in Pacific regions have themselves been largely respon-
sible for the perversions and over-simplifications of their standard tongue which they have passed on to Eastern natives. They
assumed that infantile constructions were as much as "infantile" intelligences could grasp, and hence arrested their own
servants permanently at the initial stages (difficult for anyone)
of learning a new type of language which puts words together
in an entirely novel manner. The result, as Jespersen puts it,
is a consequence "partly of the difficulties always inherent in
learning a totally different language," and partly of "the linguistic behavior of the English-speaking people themselves."

But aside from the historical reasons for Pidgin English
(which might yield an interesting chapter on language relations under imperialistic conditions), it is worth our while to

ask: Is there anything inherently absurd in its methods of expression? If an abstract English word like "if" (formerly *gif*) turns out upon analysis to have had the more concrete sense of "given over, granted" in earlier times, perhaps we have been speaking modified Pidgin all our lives. "Gi'n [for "given"] "a body meet a body comin' through the rye" instead of "If a person encounter another person . . ." is pretty near to Pidgin, as compared to standard London English. You can translate any English sentence into Pidgin (or something like it) if you look up the etymology of the abstract words. Here are some results:

"If the hypothesis be correct . . ."

"You give me that-thing-laid-down, then it reaches out straight along with others . . ."

"Since the solution is incorrect . . ."

"Following after later, that thing loosened up not reaches out straight along . . ."

"The substance of your deductions is contradictory . . ."

"Standing under fellow you lead out, he talks back . . ."

"The result of our speculations may be subsumed . . ."

"That thing jumping back from our looking on, perhaps we take him under, so . . ."

Like the character in Molière who discovered to his amazement that he had been speaking prose all his life, we may be forced to confess that our most learned jargon is, upon analysis, tantamount to a recently modified Pidgin!

COMPOUND WORDS

All this is by way of introduction to the general question: How is a vocabulary, the word-treasury or *thesaurus* of a language, built up? It is clear that many words in any dictionary turn out, like our own "nevertheless," to be put together out of elements already familiar in simple form. Compounding, then, is one of the most conspicuous methods of creating new words out of old. It often produces a result with far more inclusive meaning and ambitious scope than might have been expected from the simple elements composing it. In language, indeed, it often turns out that the whole is much greater than the sum of its parts; but for a detailed account of the way this happens we shall have to wait for the next chapter, dealing with the reasons for semantic change (or change in meaning).

Two Types of Compounds

A rough division may be made in the compounds known to us in English. On the one hand we have what may be called *phrasal* compounds, words like "nevertheless" or "beforehand" which are groups of words still completely distinguishable; and *fused* compounds, like "likelihood" in which one or more elements exist which no longer have the status of separate words, if indeed they ever did, in English.

Phrasal Compounds

The English language, especially in America, is still extremely prolific in the creation of phrasal compounds. Of course it is a delicate matter to decide when two separate words in conjunction are to be regarded as a new, compounded entity. Sometimes accent alone will tell. We say "This is a 'hot 'house" when we mean that an ordinary abode is too warm; but "This is a 'hothouse" when we refer to a glassed-in nursery for plants. Accent also tends to differentiate a slang phrasal compound from the same words used conventionally. Compare "I wish you good night" with the slang ejaculation "Good night!" At an earlier period in English it was possible to make many new nouns by forming a phrasal unit of an adverb and a verb form. Thus arose words like "output, outpouring, uprising, income, upkeep, outgo." More recently we have been making wider use of another type: namely, verb plus adverb suffix. We don't say "a downsitting strike" but "a 'sit-down 'strike," or simply "a 'sit-down." Other examples are:

touch-down

wash-out

lay-out (*cf.* outlay)

hold-up (*cf.* uphold)

make-up (i.e., cosmetics)

kick-back

check-off

write-in (vote)

throw-away (i.e., handbill)

set-up (*cf.* upset)

lock-out

look-out (*cf.* outlook)

hand-out

fade-out (i.e., end of a cinema)

push-over

walk-away

pay-off

shut-in (i.e., invalid)

A number of these vivid locutions have to do with sports, labor struggles, politics; in short, fields of human endeavor involving conspicuous activity. They are largely, though not exclusively, made up of the Germanic elements in English. Latin and French words appear seldom in such a list. Compounds of such elements in German words appear in reverse order, the adverb first followed by the verb: *Abfahrt, Aufruhr, Zuflucht, Mitleid,* and so on.

FUSED COMPOUNDS

Fused compounds are not so readily broken down into independent elements as are the hyphenated forms written above. "Unlock the door!" contains a verb with two parts fused. Few persons stop to think that "un-" is a prefix meaning "not" when he hears the command; but when he hears the phrase "It's a lock-out!" he may still be aware of the separate sense of "out," even visualizing the turning of a key on one side of the door, and the group of men standing outside on the other, excluded from the factory in which they had worked.

When words are fused in English and related languages the parts are commonly designated as root, prefix, and suffix. In "unlocked" the root is the simple verb "lock." The syllable, "un-," negating the root idea, is the prefix, and the ending "-ed," showing that the action was accomplished in past time, is a suffix with a grammatical function. A limited number of native English prefixes and suffixes are still active, as we say, and can be used in making entirely new words. A few examples of Anglo-Saxon prefixes are "off-" (in "offprint, off-size"), "under-" (in the recent "underprivileged," genteel term for "poor"), "over" ("overplay, overact, overemphasize"), "mis-" ("miscast, misfit"). Among suffixes still used afresh there are: "-dom" ("stardom, nazidom, moviedom"), "-ful" ("vitamin-ful"), "-ish" meaning "approximately" ("sixtyish, five-o'-clockish, whitish"), "-ster" ("roadster, punster"). The ending "-er" is very prolific; it appears in words designating tools or instruments like "masher, slicer, clipper, creamer." The adverbial suffix "-ly," a weakened form of *līce* ("in the shape of") can be added to almost any adjective.

COMPOUNDS TAKEN FROM LATIN

In general, however, our English vocabulary has been enriched far more by loans from without than by new formations made from within. Some of the most interesting compounds in the English language were originally not English at all, but Latin words taken over centuries ago, either directly from the classical tongue or indirectly through French. They have been ours so long that we no longer feel them to be alien. On the other hand few besides scholars can perceive that they are made up of parts, since we do not recognize those parts. Hence we are unaware of the vivid metaphors which the compounds originally implied. Often the significance has changed greatly since the word was put together. It would be absurd to try to keep words always close to the original or etymological meaning of their component parts. Inevitably the original sense is lost and new ones are acquired throughout the ages. Nevertheless an examination of those same compound parts will show some very interesting principles involved in the formation. It will also reveal some striking figures of speech which underlie the original compounding. There are hosts of examples, but only a few of the livelier ones of Latin origin need be cited here. In referring to Latin verbs two forms of each will be given: the infinitive and perfect (passive) participle.

The word *cadere, casus,* meaning to fall, was the name of a very physical act. It was the equivalent of tumbling on one's nose. In "accident" we have a slight change in the root. The combination was literally a term for "falling *on*" to something; later something which be*fell* (notice the same type of combination in English); and still later in philosophical language it meant the extraneous qualities of things as distinct from their essential nature. A far cry from the original "fall," indeed! "Decadence" is a falling *off*, "incidence" a falling *in,* and "coincidence" a falling *in with* something else. The much-used word "case"—used to cover all sorts of things like cases of beer, cases at law, and cases of fire—meant anything that happened or befell.

Capere, captus also designated a physical act: to take or seize. "Participation" is a taking part; "concept" is a thing taken *with* something else (into the intelligence, presumably); "perception" a thing taken *through* (the five senses, no doubt); and a "precept" something taken *before* something else. "Deception," which in French means "disappointment," means literally the act of taking *away*. One can imagine the child whose lollypop has just been *taken away*. He is deceived—in both senses.

Caput was the Roman term for "head." *Capitis* meant "of the head." In compounds the root appears as *-cipit-*. A pre*cipit*ate person is headlong; pre*cipit*ation of a chemical solution means that certain parts of it fall headlong to the bottom. A "chapter" of a book, from Latin *capitulum* through Old French, is really a "little head"—presumably of a Hydra-headed monster. *Caput* itself became *chief*, later *chef*, in French (with palatalized [c]); a verb using the prefix *ad-* gave *achever*, English "achieve," literally "to bring to a head." The latter phrase made up of English words is used when we refer to pimples, boils, or other unpleasant situations, and "achieve" in boasting of gratifying success, but the literal sense is close in both compoundings.

Cernere, cretus referred primarily to sifting, in either a literal or metaphorical sense. A person skilled at making any kind of necessary divisions and distinctions, as between that which gains social approval and that which does not, was called discerning, discreet, possessed of discernment. He was described by the same term used for one who could separate chaff from wheat. The prefix *dis-* gave to the compound the important nuance "to sift *out from*." Our words "certain, ascertain, certify" come from slightly changed forms of the same root. "Skill," it may be noted, comes from a Scandinavian word meaning divisions; "skillful" thus corresponds to "discerning" so far as meaning goes.

Fundere, fusus meant "to pour." If a blush "suffuses" a lady's cheek it is poured *under* it (*sub* being assimilated to *suf-*); a "transfusion" is poured *across* and an "infusion" (whether of tea, salts, vigor, or new ideas) is poured *into* something (or somebody).

*Hendere, *hensus,[3] a lost Latin verb, now preserved only in compounds, must have meant originally to grasp—as did *capere. Comprehendere,* giving us "to comprehend," meant to grasp a thing (later an idea) *before*hand and *with* something else; to "apprehend" was to grasp *towards* something. Thus is a criminal apprehended by a policeman; but thus too is a woman prone to worrying said to be "full of apprehensions."

The verb *ire,* "to go," appears often with the root form *it-*, taken from the participle. Thus "transition" and "ambition" mean a going *across* and a going *about,* respectively. An ambitious person is one who keeps running hither and yon, intent upon getting himself ahead. "To perish," with a French modification of the root, meant to go *through (per)* to the bitter end. It is easy to see the sense of *ob-* (a Latin prefix meaning "across, in opposite direction") in "obituary." The person of whom it is written has gone across—a veiled reference to the simple fact of dying.

Plicare, plicatus designated the act of folding material or paper. A "complicated" affair is consequently something

---

[3] On the asterisk, see chapter 2, note 2.

folded in *with* others and thus difficult to straighten out; an *"im-plication"* is a thought folded artfully *in* with others; a "suppli-cation" comes from a person folded *under*—hence, we sup-pose, kneeling to the authority of another. Shakespeare re-stated the thought in vigorous English when he spoke of court suppliants who "crook the pregnant hinges of the knee That thrift may follow fawning." To "apply" oneself to a task is to bend down *to* it—fold oneself over it—with zeal, or, if you will, with application! "Pliant, comply, pliers" represent modifi-cations of the root, with loss of the consonant *c* [k]. The sim-ple form in English is "to ply." Another form resulted from a compounding of the root with a prefix meaning "two, twice." To "duplicate" thus refers literally and physically to the act of folding *twice,* as we do with paper when copies are made. But "duplicity" refers to a moral characteristic analogous to the paper folded over so that you can't see what lies underneath. In dealing with our brother man we have always preferred the type that lies open, unfolded, uncomplicated, and undupli-cated (that is, not guilty of duplicity). The opposite of "du-plicity" is "simplicity" or a state of being folded only once—which is as good as saying not at all. *Sancta simplicitas* means "holy innocence." A thing lying quite open and exposed gives an impression of guilelessness.

Pōnere, positus is another verb designating a physical act of placement. A "composition" of music or painting or any of the arts appears etymologically as a mere placing *together* of com-ponent parts (the connotation of design and aesthetic intent appearing later); a "proposition" is something put *forward;* a "deposition" is a statement of fact put *down* before someone acting as judge, for instance, by a witness in a law suit. An "exponent" and an "exposure" have to do with laying or plac-ing something *out*. "Repose" is a word derived from the use of two separate Latin verbs of similar sound: *ponere, positus* and **pausare*. It is a state sought not only by putting oneself *back* (*re-ponere*), that is, reclining, but also by pausing from work (*re-pausare*).

Putāre, putātus takes us back (like *cernere*) to the simple hardworking days of the Roman Republic—to habits so ardently praised and studiously avoided by the wealthy and luxurious writers of the Empire. It meant "to prune, to trim" vines or trees; also "to reckon, consider, think." (Both vines and thoughts must be disciplined and cut into a semblance of order.) To "amputate" is to cut *around* on both sides; to "compute" is to trim (estimate?) *with* something else; to "dispute" is to cut *apart* or *away* from another person. In some words like "putative, repute, reputation," however, the sense of cutting has been quite overshadowed by the more abstract one of thinking.

Sedēre, sessus referred to the humble act of sitting down. Its physical sense appears in our word "sedentary." A "session" of Congress is merely its sitting; in fact we can use both terms in English. The "sediment" is what sits at the bottom of a liquid. To "reside" is to sit *back,* presumably at one's ease. To "possess" (originally **pot-sedēre*) was to "sit down potently" on something: to squat. To "supersede" someone is to move up and sit *ahead* of him. One can imagine a Roman senator doing it with an arrogant confidence, happy that his ambition ("running around") has been achieved ("come to a head").

Sequi, secūtus meant following after a thing or person wanted for some urgent reason by the follower. A "sequence" is a series of objects following one after another. A "consequence" is that which follows along *with* another event—the result being implied ("folded in"!) within the nature of the deed itself. To "execute" (*ex-secūtus*) is to follow *out* a decree, whether it is an order to hang someone or merely to apply a law to specific, less dreadful cases. To "persecute" is to follow something *through* (in an unpleasant sense). The Bible and early Christian history gave it a particularly ominous connotation; of the typical waverer it was said: "yet hath he not root in himself, but dureth for a while: for when tribulation or *persecution* ariseth because of the word, by and by he is offended." In disguised (pre-French) form *sequitor* and *sequita* appear in "suitor" and "suite." The former is one who follows after a thing he desires; or, to use another disguised form of our same root, he *pursues* it; whether it be a pension or a woman's favor. A "suite" is a series of rooms or other objects following one another in order.

Solvere, solūtus was once limited to the act of loosening an object from anything that bound it. "Soluble, solvent" still show this clearly, as does "dissolve" in the sense of loosening the constituent parts of something in a liquid. To "solve" a problem, however, and to reach a "solution," refer to the loosening up of mental obstacles which at first glance presented an insuperable barrier—possibly like logs jammed in a stream. The component parts become loose and fluid to the comprehension. (We have already detected the root meanings of "component" and "comprehension.") The "resolution" of a discord is a loosening of its elements *back* into harmonious relation. Other "resolutions" (decisions, formal parliamentary statements) are similarly conceived. An "absolute" is something loosened or released from limiting relationships. That is why it can be a term in philosophy—denoting a condition actually inconceivable to us who are bound in by relativities—and also a description of certain types of government unhampered by parliaments or such limitations. When we say, unreflectingly, that a thing is "absolutely certain" we mean without regard for any "if's" and "but's" which might constrict its application.

Specere, spectus, "to look at," offers us many derivatives. An "aspect" is something you look *at,* as is a "specimen" (in a narrower sense); a "circumspect" person is a cautious soul who is always looking *around* himself for hidden dangers; a "retrospect"—poignant word!—is a looking *backwards.* "There is no greater pain," says Dante's Francesca da Rimini in Hell, "than to remember past felicity when one lies in misery." She is reporting the love of Paolo and herself—in *retro*-spect, looking back to the time when they were on earth. "Speculation" means simply the ability or act of looking closely at something. Its basic meaning appears in Macbeth's horrified question to the

ghost of Banquo: "Hast thou no speculation in those eyes?"
An unwise "speculator" in the stock market has obviously not
looked closely enough at proposed investments. "Respect"
means a looking *back at.* A "despicable" person is one you look
down on. An "introspective" one is given to looking *within*
himself. *Speculum,* a Latin word for mirror, was widely used
in the Middle Ages to give titles to encyclopedic surveys of human knowledge. The book was like a mirror which "reflected"
(that is, *bent back* the rays of) any particular science. Thus
reading the *Speculum Historiale* meant looking at the "Mirror
of History"; the *Speculum Naturale* was the "Mirror of Nature"; *Speculum Meditantis,* the edifying mirror of a man
thinking. The English "Mirror for Magistrates" carried out
this tradition of titles. A "specious" argument is one that appears sound only to the casual looking or glance; analysis (a
Greek word which, like "solution," means "loosening up") reveals its inner weakness. In Greek, a cognate form *skepsis*
(with interchange of the *k* and *p*) means "doubt"—looking mis-
trustingly at something. Hence our "skeptical," which is descriptive of one who looks too closely on the event.

Surgere, surrectus, meaning "to arise," was itself a compound made up of *subs-* ("under") and *regere* ("to control").
The "surge" of the sea refers to that which rises (and falls); so
does "the surge and thunder of the *Odyssey*," metaphorically.
An "insurgent" is one engaged in the act of rising *into* a state
of rebellion; "insurrection" is the rebellion itself. "Resurrec-
tion" is an arising *again*—this time in a very special sense, limited usually to a restoration of life to the body after death.

Tangere, tactus gives us two words, "tangible" and "tactile"
which are still applied primarily to the physical sense of touch.
A "tangent" in geometry, though it too has to do with touching, refers to incorporeal lines and circumferences brought
into such relationship at a single point. They are said to be in
"contact"—or to be touching *with* each other. In the unreal
world of Euclid it is startling to find so physical an expression.
A "contingency" is an event touching *with* another. "Attain"

shows a modified form of *tangere* combined with the assimilated prefix *ad-*, "to." (The diphthong [ai] in this Old French word is due to the softening of the [g] to a sound like [j].) To attain is to touch *to* something. A similar idea underlies the modern French way of saying "He has attained the age of sixty": *Il a touché 60 ans.*

Tendere, tentus (also *tensus*), "to stretch," evokes the concrete image of a man about to shoot an arrow from the stretched string of a bow. But it is also said that his body and his thoughts are stretched—"tense"—as he concentrates on the act. He gives it his "attention," or stretches his thoughts and energy *towards* what he is doing. "Tension" is a quality of strain in physical matters (as when we speak of "surface tension" of liquids) or emotional atmosphere. An "intention" is something you are stretched *into* doing; in other words you are "intent" on it. When you "contend," therefore, you must be stretched *with* your struggle. A "tendency" is something merely stretched out, or running through, the course of events, but a "tendentious" article is one stretched out with a deliberate purpose: with an intention, we might say, at the risk of overworking the same useful root.

Vidēre, vīsus meant "to see," just as *specere* meant "to look at," both with the physical eye. The ordinary significance is still to be found in "visible" and "vista." In "vision" we have the literal meaning if we speak of a man's eyesight; but there is a transferred significance if we speak of the visions vouchsafed to a saint or mystic. A "visage" is the part of a person (or thing) you look at. A "provident" person is one who sees or looks out *for* himself in the future, and "providence" is the ability to look *ahead*. "Providence" can in fact be applied in the loftiest sense to the quality of divinity which enables it to foresee. ("Foresee" is a close parallel to "provide," so far as the compounded parts are concerned.) Since the way in which a person looked at another was supposed from earliest times to have magic effects, many words compounded by special prefixes with the root *vid, vīs* will be found to have an ominous meaning probably due to a belief in the evil eye. *Invidēre* in Latin meant "to look into," apparently rather askance than directly. It developed a connotation of hatred as a result, and yielded (by way of French) our English word "envy." The same unpleasant flavor exists in "invidious." An invidious distinction or discrimination is made by one who looks askance. Curiously enough, the same sort of compounds are used in Russian to designate envy (the noun is *zavist*^j and the verb *za-vid-ovat*^j, with the Indo-European root preserved as in Latin). Shakespeare's Sebastian in *Twelfth Night* says that Olivia's eyes have "o'erlooked" him when he means "bewitched." Here an English verb is used to convey a similar belief in magic influences.

SOME COMPOUNDS IN OTHER LANGUAGES

These Latin etymologies give us an insight into the processes of making fused compounds. Humor and superstition and sharp observation have been at work in the formation of them. A few examples from German and Russian will show the same procedures, and reveal some of the same lively pictures which come to the surface upon analysis. In many instances, as a matter of fact, it is most likely that the compounds in these modern vernaculars were consciously put together in imitation of already existent ones in the classical languages, Latin and Greek.

When a German wants to say that something is independent, he says *unabhängig,* which, precisely as in the Latin, means "not hanging down from" something else. The Russian uses the same elements to construct an equivalent adjective *ne-za'visi-myi,* derived from *za-viset*^j, "to hang from." Referring to "circumstances" (which, in the English-Latin loan word, are "things standing *around*"), the German constructs an identical picture with his *Umstände,* the Russian too with his *obsto'ja-tel*^j*stva,* for the German root *-stand-* means exactly what it does in English, and so does Russian *-stoi-*. German *begreifen* and Russian *no-ni'mat*^j mean, as did Latin *comprehendere,* a taking hold of something. "Evolution" presents the picture of something turning or rolling *out* before our eyes; German *Entwick-*

lung compounds similar elements in the same way; Russian *raz'vitie* also means "untwist, unwind." "Superficial" is an adjective literally applied to things constructed or made *on top;* so with German *oberflächig* and Russian *po'verkhnostnyi.*

COMPOUNDS AND ABSTRACT MEANINGS

This exercise in breaking down abstract compounds, both native and foreign, could be extended indefinitely. It would simply be a heaping up of evidence to the effect that our own language, and languages nearest akin to us, have possessed the ability to augment their treasury of words from within. William James pointed out some time ago, with humorous intent, what might have resulted to the English tongue if we had continued to compound words purely out of the Anglo-Saxon (Germanic) elements of English, instead of using loans from the classical languages. He presented the following quotation from Herbert Spencer as an example of our use of learned Latin compounds:

Evolution is an integration of matter and concomitant dissipation of motion; during which the matter passes from an indefinite homogeneity to a definite, coherent heterogeneity; and during which the retained motion undergoes a parallel transformation.

This, James suggested, would appear as a barbarous tissue of concrete compounds if we excluded our present scientific loan words:

Evolution is a change from a nohowish untalkaboutable all-alikeness to a somehowish and in general talkaboutable not-all-alikeness by continuous sticktogetherations and somethingelseifications.

He might have added: "of stuff"—since the key word "matter" is not included in his Germanicized version.

German philosophical language does in fact avail itself of a number of refreshingly concrete terms for very special abstract thoughts. Some of them were coined in conscious answer to the needs of such intellection, just as the medieval schoolmen consciously created terms like "essence" and "substance" to fill a linguistic gap in philosophical terminology. It is instructive to take a few sentences from Hegel's *Phenomenology of Mind* and place it beside an extremely literal English version which attempts to use native roots for compound words as German is still able to do. This literal version may sound outlandish, but it will bring home to us just what was lost in our language, for good or ill, when we began wholesale borrowing instead of original compounding.

Die Vollständigkeit der Formen des nicht realen Bewusstseins wird sich durch die Notwendigkeit des Fortganges und Zusammenhanges selbst ergeben. Um dies begreiflich zu machen, kann im allgemeinen zum Voraus bemerkt werden, dass die Darstellung des nicht wahrhaften Bewusstseins in seiner Unwahrheit, nicht eine bloss *negative* Bewegung ist. Eine solche einseitige Ansicht hat das natürliche Bewusstsein überhaupt von ihr; und ein Wissen, welches diese Einseitigkeit zu seinem Wesen macht, ist eine der Gestalten des unvollendeten Bewusstseins, welche in den Verlauf des Weges selbst fällt und darin sich darbieten wird.

The fullstandingness of the forms of the not-real beknowingness gives itself through the needturningness of the forwardgoing and the togetherhanging itself. To make this graspable, it can in general [all-common] be bemarked, that the there-placing [representation] of the not true-graspable beknowingness in its not-truth, is not merely a *negative* bemoving. Such a onesided onlooking of it the natural beknowingness has taken overhead from [that there-placing]; and a knowing, which makes this onesidedness into its own being, is one of the shapes of the unended beknowingness, which falls itself in the running of the way and will offer itself therein.

Aber die Natur des Gegenstandes, den wir untersuchen, überhebt dieser Trennung oder dieses Scheins von Trennung und Voraussetzung. Das Be-

But the nature of the opposite standing thing [object] which we are underseeking rises above this splitting apart or this shine [appearance] of splitting apart

wusstsein gibt seinen Massstab an ihm selbst und die Untersuchung wird dadurch eine Vergleichung seiner mit sich selbst sein; denn die Unterscheidung, welche soeben gemacht worden ist, fällt in es.

and before-outsetting. The beknowingness gives its measuring-staff in itself, and the underseeking becomes therewith its likening of itself with itself; for the underdividing which has just been made falls into it.

The standard English rendition (which may appear no more intelligible to the lay reader) is as follows:

The completeness of the forms of unreal consciousness will be brought about precisely through the necessity of the advance and the necessity of their connection with one another. To make this comprehensible we may remark, by way of preliminary, that the exposition of untrue consciousness in its untruth is not a merely negative process. Such a one-sided view of it is what the natural consciousness generally adopts; and a knowledge, which makes this one-sidedness its essence, is one of those shapes assumed by incomplete consciousness which falls into the course of the inquiry itself and will come before us there.

But the nature of the object which we are examining surmounts this separation, or semblance of separation, and presupposition. Consciousness furnishes its own criterion in itself and the inquiry will thereby be a comparison of itself with its own self; for the distinction, just made, falls inside itself.

ENGLISH USE OF LOAN WORDS

English has not, however, made many of the bold compoundings out of native elements which might be suggested by these literal translations from Latin and German. Instead it has for historical reasons turned to outside sources for enrichment. This has been most conspicuous since the Norman Conquest, which temporarily divided England, in the eleventh century, into two communities, the rulers and the subjects, speaking two different languages. Later when Middle English emerged as the accepted national speech, it was a compromise of Anglo-Saxon structure together with an overwhelming numerical

majority of French loans. As was to be expected when the
feudal lords and representatives of government spoke French,
the underlings took over from them almost the entire vocabulary dealing with law, army, religion, the court, and official-
dom. The overlord could not be expected to learn the barbarous dialect (as it would appear to him) of the native English
peasants. Nor could he be expected to study and revere the
admirable literature that had been produced in the subject
speech. Countrymen who had dealings with him and his peers
were on the other hand expected to twist their tongues about
alien terms such as *duc, barun, cuntesse, sergaunt, justice,
benisun, malisun, marchaunt, chaumberlein, burgeis, homage,
fealté, truage, service,* and *rente* in dealing with the gentry, and
in the law courts they had to disentangle a maze of references
to *warrants, livreisuns* ("things delivered"), *hostages, prisun,
jugement, heritage, desheritage, jeopardy (jeu parti,* a "divided game" or "dangerous risk"), *puny (puis né,* "later born"),
cadet ("younger son"), *gibbet, banishment,* and other confusing or menacing matters. Naturally they adapted themselves to
the new vocabulary. Linguistic adaptation in the form of borrowing is usually left to underlings, and they have little choice
but to take over floods of words from ruling conquerors, even
if they cling to a skeletal structure of the native tongue.

The habit of borrowing persisted long after the linguistic
breach between two sections of the English population had
been closed. The great tide of early medieval loans seems to
have submerged almost completely the once living ability of
English to make fresh compounds out of its native roots and
endings. Henceforth the language was enriched rather by the
most hospitable inclusion of new words from all sorts of outside languages. Wherever the English people had direct contact with other cultures, whether by trade, conquest, cultural
interchange, or colonization, they plundered foreign vocabularies to enrich their own. This type of plundering, it may be
said, had one very great advantage over the harsher forms of

acquisition that often go with imperial expansion: it hurt nobody and left the givers no poorer than they were before.

A history of English loan words would reflect the colorful, sometimes sanguine history of English international relations. Since the Middle Ages a number of countries in succession have diversified the vocabulary. The fierce struggles with Spain in the sixteenth century over control of the New World are reflected in terms of political, commercial, and military significance, like *infanta, hidalgo, grande* (Anglicized "grandee"), *galleon,* "grenade" from *granada* ("pomegranate," so named from the fruity appearance), *armada, tornado, bastinado, peccadillo, puntillo* (Anglicized "punctillio"), *bravado, embargo*. Occasionally the article *el* was borrowed with the word: "alligator" comes from *el lagarto,* "the lizard." Many American Indian words reached English by way of the rival language. Thus came "canoe" (Spanish from Haitian), "hurricane" (Spanish *huracán,* Quiché *jurakan,* a Carib word), "potato" (*patata* from Haitian *batata*), "chocolate" (Mexican *chocolatl*), "tomato" (Mexican *tomatl*), *pampas* (pl., from Peruvian *bamba*), "tapioca" (by way of Portuguese and native Brazilian *tipioca*), and many other names of animals, plants, and other products emanating from New Spain.

How the name-procession of these strange new riches must have fired the imagination and the lust for conquest in the days of Henry's unflinching daughter, the Virgin Queen! Old Spain had already yielded a number of words ultimately sprung from Arabic: even in the Middle Ages they had begun to impart to the pages of English writers (geographers and the like) the exotic flavor and perfume of a strange civilization. "Cotton" from Arabic *qutun* was imported minus the definite article which Spanish has preserved in *algodón*. Words suggestive of rare food and drink, and of occult sciences, appeared—sometimes with and sometimes without the article *al*: *al anbīg,* meaning "the cup," gave "alembic," somehow suggesting something rarer than an ordinary vessel; *al qalīy* and *al iksir* yielded "alkali" and "elixir" respectively. "Alchemy," "algebra," "almagest," "almanac," "zenith," "zero," "cipher," "alcohol," "nadir," "caliber" bear witness to Arabic leadership in science. "Amber," "syrup" ("sherbet" too as alternate from the same Arabic word *sharāb*), "camphor," "henna," "lute," "tambour," "carat," "apricot," "hashish," "harem," "saraband" suggest English indebtedness to the luxuries and amenities disseminated by Spanish Arabs. The word "assassin," immediately derived from Italian *assassino,* is a corruption of *hashshāshīn,* "eaters of hashish"—a band of exalted desperados first encountered by Crusaders in the East, whose bravery was largely augmented by drugs.

Italian loans into English have been due on the whole to gentler cultural influences than the Spanish contacts. Trade with Italy and banking connections played an important part in English politics as early as the fourteenth century. Besides the practical allure of flourishing Italian city-states, there was the inexpressible glamour of the homeland of classic beauty, the intellectual ferment of late medieval and Renaissance thought housed there, the marbles and painting and palaces, and the hot sun, blue skies, and pointed cypress trees which have drawn chilled Anglo-Saxons southward with passionate longing, from the age of Chaucer down to the exodus thither of defeated or tubercular Victorians. Significantly enough, a number of the earliest loans have to do with the arts and civilized forms of living. Such pleasing terms as "carnival," "gondola," "madrigal," "fresco," "motto," "stanza," "viola da gamba" "canto," "inamorata," "cupola," "cornice," "cameo" are all recorded in English before 1600. The stream of words having to do with music has continued without break since the sixteenth century. To realize their importance, you need only try to imagine your concert program without them. In the nineteenth century German equivalents such as *kräftig, zärtlich, liebevoll* began to appear with the great upsurge of German music, but they did not succeed in displacing the *sforzato* and *amoroso* to which we had become accustomed. The more bellicose arts are not entirely unrepresented in the first Italian loans. *Battaglione,* reaching us by way of French, yielded our "battalion"; *squadrone, cittadella, duello, cavalcata, bandito* were but slightly modified when they were adapted.

English encounters with the rival naval power of Holland are reflected in Dutch loans of the seventeenth century, many of them nautical. So *aanslag* was Anglicized to "onslaught," *verlof* to "furlough," *jol* to "yawl," *kruisen* to "cruise," *gijben* to "jib," *sloep* to "sloop," *jacht* to "yacht," and *vrijbuiter* to "freebooter." (*Vrij* correponds to our "free"; *buiter* means "one who takes *booty.*") Trade and art supplemented the navy in enriching English from Dutch. One of the amusing terms connected with art is our "easel," derived from Dutch *ezel* "a donkey"—surely a graphic description of the patient three-legged stand used to support a painting.

Other European languages have furnished more limited lists of words. Russian gave a few political terms such as *ukaz, pogrom, tsar* (widened to apply to any powerful person, as in American journalistic expressions like "baseball tsar"), *duma, soviet,* and names of a few concrete objects like *samovar, droshki, knout.* Terms taken from the remoter European countries are pretty well limited to objects exclusively associated with those countries.

The enrichment from such sources continues to the present day. More and more distant parts of the world have been plundered. Even the minuscule additions add to the multicolored effect of our vocabulary. "Juggernaut" is a corruption of Hindi *jagannath,* "lord of the universe," applied to a figure of Vishnu; "punch" as a drink is a form of the Hindi *panch,* meaning "five," since the drink contained five ingredients. *Khākī,* Persian by way of Hindi, means "dusty" and has been very appropriately applied to uniforms of a protective dusty hue. "Shah," "dervish," "divan" are eloquent of Persian environment; "turban," "kaftan," "caviar" (*khāvyār*), "coffee" (*ka'hveh*), "kiosk," "fez," "kismet" (ultimately from Arabic *quismat*) evoke the Turkish. A woman who wears a hat shaped like a turban, who buys a newspaper at a kiosk and reads it in a café, is unconsciously acknowledging three Turkish debts. Even Dravidian, the non-Indo-European family of Southern India, has yielded a few words: "curry," "anaconda," "teak," "patchouli," "betel," "calico" (from the place-name Calicut). Hebrew loan words deal largely with more austere and elevated things such as "seraphim," "cherubim" (both in plural form with endings), "paschal," "manna," "shibboleth," "leviathan." Malay gives us a few eloquent terms such as "amok," "orangutan" (literally, "man of the woods"), "bantam," "sarong." The recent vogue of Polynesia as a setting for light fiction and escapist movies has added a whole series of pleasing vocables, mostly designating hedonistic objects or states of mind. A character in one of Mr. Earl Derr Biggers's mystery stories about Hawaii remarks (just to show how adept he is at linguistic assimilation), "I'm quite *pau*. Now I'm going *makai* to sit on the *lanai,* there to forget the *pilikia* of the day." The sense is: "I'm quite exhausted. Now I'm going towards the sea to sit on the terrace, there to forget the worries of the day."

Even remote Australia and inner Africa have contributed to some extent. From the former comes the very useful word "boomerang," so satisfying and so badly needed for metaphorical application in any language. From Bantu and other African languages come chiefly names for local flora and fauna, and a few for customs and social classes: "zebra," "tsetse," "gnu," "impi," "induna," "voodoo" are among these. Words so limited to the particular conditions of the country from which they came do not, however, gain wide circulation. In England they are kept alive chiefly, no doubt, by those retired colonials —civil servants and military men—who play so considerable a part in modern British fiction. From the displaced South African dialect of Dutch have come a few loans of somewhat wider currency: "trek," "veldt," "spoor."

NEW WORDS BY SHORTENING

Compounds and loan words have represented the two most important methods of enriching English; but there are a few other methods—though less productive than either—by which vocabulary is diversified. New words do arise from within by other curious procedures. Persons who are unrestrained by terror of a school master will modify and playfully distort the current vocabulary, thus creating new words. More cautious speakers are often shocked at first, but they frequently end by adopting these *neologisms* (that is, new word creations).

A *shortened* or clipped form of a word is sometimes created in defiance of its origin and component parts. Half-humorously, perhaps, we begin by saying: "The sculptor sculpts" or "The butler buttles," being quite aware at the time that the simple verb forms have not previously existed. In time, though, the humorous *back-formation,* as it is called, is often adopted and becomes an accepted word in all seriousness. The process of creation can be described as follows: The speaker says to himself (unconsciously, of course): "I can work back from *actor* to *act,* from *advisor* to *advise,* why not from *sculptor* to *sculpt?*" The common, accepted verb "edit" arose thus from "editor." This swift internal argument is known as reasoning by analogy. Others not yet admitted into standard speech are "to revolute" as a humorous verbal derivative from the noun "revolution"; "to enthuse" from "enthusiastic."

Some of these manglings are, indeed, more extreme than mere back formations. The division of a word into any kind of clipped form, regardless of etymology, actually gives rise at times to a new type of suffix and a new type of root. The *disjecta membra* are occasionally recombined in a very bizarre manner. We hear not only of "hamburgers" and "frankfurters," but "frankburgers" for sandwiches. Recently in the realm of cheap amusements in America there was an epidemic of endurance tests in dancing quaintly known as "dance Marathons." The second word of the compound was a very remote reference to the excellent runner who brought to Sparta the Athenians' appeal for help on the eve of the great battle of Marathon. By some obscure process the latter part of the word, "-athon," became associated with ability to survive any kind of severe physical test; and so sporadic currency was given to such amazing compounds as "dance-athon" and "walk-athon." One ingenious business firm apparently conceives of the termination "-lier," in the word "chandelier," as a usable suffix, and with its help has created the monstrous form "lightolier." The word "auditorium" has given rise to an occasional form "lubritorium," by the same process of treating the ending as a transferable suffix.

Clipped forms once considered daring or vulgar are now fully received: "mob" from Latin *mobile vulgus* ("excitable crowd"); "cab" from "cabriolet," "piano" from "pianoforte." Not generally accepted are "to vack" from "to vacuum" and "to perk" from "to percolate."

Student speech is filled with clipped forms such as "gym" for "gymnasium," "bio" for "biology," and "trig" for "trigonometry." The simple elements are not often used in compounding, yet this does occur at times. No student at Cornell would speak of the Domestic Economy building as anything but the "Domecon." Russian, highly inflected and breathtaking as it can be in its official terminology, has been driven to combine clipped forms in the same mechanical way, in order to avoid wasteful repetition of polysyllabic endings. The Government Printing House, which should strictly be called *Gosudarst'venoe Iz'datel'stvo,* has been clipped and compounded into the not very euphonious term *Gosizdat; fi'zicheskaia kul'tura* ("physical culture") has become *fizkul'tura.* German too has made some of these syllable-compoundings familiar throughout the world. *Gestapo* was a short-cut for *Geheime Staats-Polizei; Schupo* , an older combination derived from *Schutz-Polizei; Ka-de-we* was the popular and also the official term used for a department store, *Kaufhaus des Westens.* Sometimes the initial single sounds of a long phrase are made into a single anagram word, if the group of letters is pronounceable. Russian *Tsik,* presumably declined as a masculine noun, was the anagram of *tsen'tral'nyi ispol'nitel'nyi Komi't'et* (Central Executive Committee). In American there arose some attempts, mostly humorous, to create words out of familiar "New Deal" abbreviations such as S.E.C., E.R.B., and W.P.A. One has even heard "He's working for the woopa," and "The Ascap [American Society of Composers, Artists and Publishers] has settled its radio dispute." World War I brought us Anzac (Australian and New Zealand Army Corps) as a word. But in general English uses the anagram method little, since it is not obliged to dodge such wasteful (if sonorous) endings of many syllables as encumber the Russian.

PORTMANTEAU WORDS

A more intimate fusing of separate elements is accomplished sometimes with conscious humor in *portmanteau* words. "Brunch," out of "breakfast" and "lunch," is gaining currency as a description of that pleasing amphibious meal taken about noon on Sunday after a late rising. Columnists are good at creating such terms; some of them are both witty and trenchant. "Socialite" for "social light" is enjoying vogue at present. "Reno-vated" is a barbed description of a faded matron who has been legally divorced and spiritually refreshed in the mountains of Nevada. Lewis Carroll has made some portmanteau words like "chortle" and "galumphing" into classic creations for humorous discourse.

"POPULAR ETYMOLOGY"

A less conscious distortion of words occurs when speakers try to make an alien or unusual term sound like something comfortably familiar to them. Thus an entirely new word is sometimes created, as when a farmer, shying away from the learned "asparagus," turns it into "sparrow grass," although the vegetable has nothing to do with sparrows. Similarly our word "cockroach" was corrupted from the Spanish term *cucuracha* and given a quite fictitious connection with "cock"; "gargoyle," a name used as trade designation for a motor oil, is more plausibly distorted in illiterate speech into "gargle-oil." In one of Gissing's novels the name Penelope appears distorted, eloquently enough, as Pennyloaf. Pennies and loaves are far more familiar terms to the poor folk of the London slums than the name of the far-off patient spouse of Ulysses in ancient Ithaca. Among persons uninitiated in the mysteries of an American presidential election, the Electoral College (that almost mythical body) has been upon occasion converted into "Electrical College." (What, we may be given leave to wonder, are supposed to be the scintillant activities of its members?) In one of Dorothy Sayers's tales, *Clouds of Witness,* mention is made of an English inn whose over-literary name "The Bridge Embattled" was changed to the more familiar and also more beguiling "Bridge and Bottle."

This transformation of words is known as *popular etymology*. It can be observed in other languages. The French *Rue Vercingétorix* in Paris, intended to immortalize the memory of an early Gaulish hero, has been changed into *Rue Vingtcinq Liquoriste* by men who know not Caesar's Gallic War but do know their liquor. The Germans, having borrowed the French word *aventure,* "adventure," in the Middle Ages (together with the idea), converted it most appropriately into *Abenteuer,* under the not unnatural impression that an adventure characteristically befalls one in the *Abend* ("evening") and costs one *teuer* ("dear").

IMITATIVE WORDS

From time to time more or less onomatopoetic words may be created directly from an imitation of the sound designated. "Burp" is supposed to describe the slight, not too inelegant belching resultant upon potations of soda water or beer. Words already existent may be doubled or repeated with modified vowels to bring out the quality of sound, as in "flip-flap, clop-clop, hush-hush, slip-slap." This type of creation is not, however, extremely abundant in English today, in proportion to the sum total of our vocabulary. It may amuse you to observe what types of experience (physical, aesthetic, etc.) are designated by imitative neologisms.

CONSCIOUS CREATION OF LEARNED WORDS

Finally, there is one special sphere of modern life in which compounding of classical word-elements continues almost as vigorously as in ancient times. This is in the vocabulary of modern science, where terms like "thermo-dynamic," "psycho-therapy," "superheterodyne," "autointoxication," "appendectomy," "electro-magnetic," "schizo-phrenetic" flourish and proliferate. Here the prefixes, suffixes, and roots which are the heritage of Athens are still active, producing new formations. The results would surely mystify a son of the violet-crowned city of the old Aegean, if he could return to hear them—especially since they are sometimes combined with vocables derived from the speech of that other ancient city, the one of the seven hills. "Superheterodyne" was created by someone who felt no compunction about placing a Latin prefix cheek by jowl with a Greek one in the same word. These neo-classical compoundings engendered in the laboratory are favorable subjects for international circulation. The elements composing them are clear to anyone with the traditional classical education of European lycées, gymnasia, and "public" schools; they are sharply defined and unambiguous in the international realm of research, and in times when scientists enjoy the normal facilities of communication so precious to their fraternity, their verbal creations tend to pass freely from language to language as loan words.

COMPOUNDING IN NON-INDO-EUROPEAN LANGUAGES

The minting of words for the treasury of language goes forward without cease. In illustrating the processes involved, I have not permitted myself to wander far away from English and the best-known European languages. For the purposes of variety, however, it may be worth while to include a few examples from languages less close to home. None of the principles involved will seem startlingly new; in fact these additional examples will merely emphasize those already familiar in English itself.

Finnish, as has been pointed out, uses many suffixes and is capable of forming many compounds. The method is not dissimilar to that observed in our own compounds of Latin origin. For instance, if *pää* [pɛ] means "head" as part of the body, it is easy to see how *pää* plus *kaupunki*, "city," gives *pääkaupunki* or "capital." (Our own word uses the root for "head," Latin *caput*. The German word is *Hauptstadt*, also "head city.") *Pää* plus *lle-kirjoitus* (the latter element meaning "writing") gives "inscription" or "chief writing"; *pää* plus derivative *llys* plus *kenkä* "shoe" gives *päällyskenkä*, "overshoe"; *päätös* is "conclusion, exit." *Tuomio* is "judgment"; *tuomio-istuin* or "judgment sitting" means "court, tribunal"; *tuomitsee* is "condemn."

According to grammars of the Malay language, the simpler words are rather ambiguous as to function. It is not always possible to say definitely whether a word is a noun, verb, or adjective. Lack of elaborate inflexion facilitates the shifting about of function. But some prefixes and suffixes are used to derive more elaborate words from simple ones, such as *bĕrapi* "fiery" from *api*, "fire"; *bĕrkuda* "riding on horseback" from *kuda* "a horse"; *tĕrkechil, tĕrbesar,* "very small," "very big," from *kĕchil,* "small" and *bĕsar,* "big" respectively. Reduplication is also used: *langit* is "sky" and *langit-langit* is "ceiling cloth" or "roof of the mouth"; *kuda-kuda* is a "clothes horse" as distinct from *kuda,* the real horse; *api-api* is a "tree" (how related to "fire"?); *bĕsar-bĕsar* means "fairly great" (a limiting qualification; not "very great," as one might expect); *kĕchil-kĕchil* is "pretty small." Iteration reduces instead of magnifying in some of these cases. Compounds of completely separate words acquire a conventional meaning that would not belong to them taken separately. Some of these combinations are very picturesque. *Mata hari,* famous as the name of a spy glamorous in the annals of the movies, means "eye of the day" or "sun"; *mata-kaki,* "eye of the leg," is "ankle"; *orang utan,* "man of the woods," is "ape"; *orang bĕsar,* "man big," is "chief"; *orang rumah* "person of the house," is "wife."

A curious type of compounding has been noted in Chinese. Two adjectives meaning opposite qualities may be combined to make a sort of ambivalent abstract term. Thus *tô ʃaò* "much-little," is a noncommittal term for size; *k'îng-tʃung,* "light-heavy," for weight; *ʃi-fēi* "being-not-being," for a question whether or not . . . ; *ts'ün-wâng,* "survival-destruction" for existence. Thus one must be constantly reminded that life is made up of the paradoxical combinations of opposites! One of our few analogous compounds is the Italian *pianoforte,* literally "soft-loud," and perhaps also the learned Greek loan "oxymoron," literally "sharp-dull."

Some languages compound elements sufficient to make a whole sentence (according to our ideas) and treat the result as a single word. Von der Gabelentz cites the following construction in Greenlandish:

qasu - er - sar - fi - gssar - si - ngit   dluinar - nar - pog.
weary - un - make - where - wherewith - gain - not - entirely
[impersonal verb and indicative ending].

The meaning is: "One found no place at all to rest."

On the other hand, one of the simplest types of compounding, and one of the most universal (perhaps also one of the most primitive), arises when words are formed to designate new crafts and forms of labor. In English we tend to put the word for the activity first, and then the word for the agent, as in our recent formations like "confidence man" or "trainman" or "glamour girl." Other languages prefer to put the term for the agent first and then designate his or her occupation. Thus *tukang bĕsi* in Malay is "lord of the iron" or "blacksmith." In Chinese one of the few approaches to compounding can be found in similar formations which use *ʒîn,* "man" (written with the symbol ∧ suggesting a human biped) or *tsi,* "child," and other such terms, to express the agent. Thus *tsidng-ʒîn* is "work-man," *yük-ʒîn* is "jewel-man" or "jeweler," and *ʃì-ʒîn* is "arrow-man," or "arrow maker." Malay does this on occasion, too, when an occupation is indicated, as in *guru těnun* "weaving mistress."

Other languages prefer to put the term for the worker first as a matter of habit, and then give the name of the craft. In Cakchiquel (a Maya dialect), *aj* [ɑχ] has been standardized into a term meaning "man who" or "man of" to indicate performer of an act. Thus *aj chi* [ɑχ tʃi], "man of mouth" is an orator or talker; *aj bats* or "man of textile" is a weaver; *aj chak* is "man of work" or general term "worker." In Malay *tukang běsi* or "lord of the iron," or "blacksmith" is similarly compounded to show a trade.

COMPOUNDS AS METAPHORS

Many of the compounds reviewed here have been truly poetic creations. Malay *mata hari*, "eye of the day" for "sun" involves much more than a juxtaposition of two accurate, colorless terms for the sake of convenience. Like our own "daisy" from "day's eye," it is the result of a luminous perception of similarities, an elementary poetic act of comparison. Here again a linguistic whole—a compound—turns out to exceed the sum of its parts in scope. It could do so by virtue of the metaphor which created it.

But this means that compounds created by metaphor involve an important change in meaning. It is really impossible to discuss them without regard for the baffling problems of semantics (or the study of meaning). From the very beginning, this chapter has been introducing questions of semantic change surreptitiously and eluding their solution for the sake of convenience. Since the time when men first began putting together simple word elements into more complex ones, they have been widening the semantic scope of their creations, not arithmetically by simple addition, but by multiplication. It is high time to see how the territory of meaning shifts and expands while words are being made.

EXTENDING THE USE OF WORDS

Among the words first taught to children by their doting parents are the terms for the parts of the human body. Pressing down the diminutive button-like protuberance which shows signs of one day becoming a full-blown human nose, mama asks beguilingly: "What is this?" The child, shrewd and skilled already in the enormous task of humoring grown-ups, but nevertheless somewhat confused by the rain of new terminology about him, looks up co-operatively and suggests with hope but little conviction: "Baby's ear." "Oh, no!" the mellifluous voice proceeds, while the pressure is still maintained, "Baby's nose. *Nose!*" And so the baffling epithet is learned, presumably for a lifetime.

Now "nose" is a concrete term which will cause the child little trouble once he learns it, especially so long as he limits it to this bodily member of himself and his fellow human beings. He can even apply it to the corresponding members of familiar animals without being involved in confusion of meaning. This is also true of other members, such as eyes, ears, hands, elbows, knees, feet, and the rest. These elementary physiological identifications must give him a comfortable sense that things mean what they say. If we wish to amuse ourselves by speculating on the kinds of words which originated first in human speech, there is some reason for surmising that names for our bodily parts were among them.

But very soon in the life of a child comes the experience of metaphoric use. He is watching his mother peeling potatoes,

109

and begins to be aware of their shape and texture. Pointing to the buds visible on the surface of the brown tuber he asks: "Mama, what are these?" She replies: "The eyes of the potato." This designation is unhesitatingly accepted. In the first place, the elliptical depressions surrounding potato buds actually resemble human eye-sockets in shape. There is enough physical similarity to make the poetic image acceptable in place of a name. Besides, the child is in no position—as yet—to observe the difference in functioning between vegetables and animals which would cause him to challenge the existence of eyes in a potato: real eyes, that is, with a potential power of vision. He can hardly ask: "But has the potato a nervous system?!" He still lives in the mysterious, animistic world of fairy-tales, in which sticks and stones, knives and forks, tables and chairs possess souls. In such a world inanimate objects may confidently be expected to see and hear, to bless and curse, and in general to take definite attitudes of friendliness or hostility to little boys and girls. So it is not surprising if he pursues the subject of the potato-sprouts further and poses the (for him) quite logical question: "Then the Potato-man can *see* me?" This very plausible deduction is probably hailed by the mother with inner exultant glee. And aloud she may even go so far as to say: "Yes, if you're not good, the Potato-man will see you, *even in the dark* and at night he'll come for you, and *take you away*. . . ."

Thus metaphor is elevated into mythology. Fortunately for most children, these transparent lies are recognized at an early date. The slight change of tone that betrays them only complicates a bit more the day-long task of placating grown-ups. If the demonology of potatoes is taken too seriously, however, the results may be very serious. Those who have dealt with nervously maladjusted children are no doubt aware of the precise dangers involved. Considering the crude animism of the language surrounding children, it is a wonder that any of us escape undamaged.

METAPHORIC EXTENSION

When the bud of a potato is called an "eye," the designation is a metaphor. Physical similarity causes a transfer of an epithet originally clear, limited, and concrete in its application. A *semantic shift* has occurred, known as a simple transfer of meaning. It is useless to debate whether "eye" in the new context is a *new* word (in which case it should have been discussed under vocabulary and the creation of words) or not. In any event the application of the physical sound-symbol [ai] has widened. This is the extension of words to include new referents somehow resembling the original ones. Metaphor implies the perception of such resemblances. By means of this process meanings of words are constantly broadening and shifting. Here are some everyday examples:

Parts of the body are further used in references to many things which are themselves concrete and familiar. We speak of the "lip" and the "ears" of a cup, the "teeth" of a saw or a comb, the "legs" of tables and other immobile articles of furniture, the "elbows" of pipes and macaroni, the "hands" of a clock, the "tongue" of a balance or a bell, the "eye" of a needle, and the "head" of a hammer. When we travel we encounter the "foot" of a mountain, the "mouth" of a river, a "head"-land, the "shoulders"—even the "soft shoulders"—of a road, the "brow" of a hill, and the "neck" of the woods. The German speaks eloquently of a *Meeresbusen* ("bosom" of the sea or gulf). Slightly disguised from us today are the "core" (heart) of an apple—a Romance word; and "axle" (shoulder) of a wheel—cognate with German *Achsel*. In politics we hear of a "rump" session of parliament and a "head" of the state. Perhaps "ward-heeler" may be included here, though it is actually a compound.

Animal names and animal members appear in many of the least regarded units of our discourse. We have "wing" chairs and collars, clothes "horses," darning "eggs" and also "egg"-plants, the "fangs" of a machine, "goose-neck" lamps, "hare" lips, "rats" of hair. The last is, to be sure, dated; it was current only in the days when women wore pads of artificial hair to eke out what nature had given them. We refer ambiguously enough to the "cock" of a water-tap, the "beak" of a vessel, and the "crest" of a hill or wave. "Catspaw" is more than a descriptive designation of an object similar to something else, and so presumably is "monkey wrench." Value judgments are tied up with both of these.

Plants and their parts give us the "nut" of a screw, a shoe "tree," the "stem" of a glass, and the "root" of a tooth or a cancerous growth. When we talk of the "root of the matter" we are already moving on a higher level of abstraction.

Tools and simple inventions have long supplied names for similar objects elsewhere. Carpentry and engineering use "pin" for very solid joiners; "table"-land (Spanish *mesa*) refers to plateaus; valleys have "cups"; roads and trees have "forks"; the arid section of the United States is called the "Dust Bowl." The parts of the human body are often described by simple figures taken from engineering. Thus we have the "bridge" of the nose, the "arch" of the foot, the "roof" of the mouth, the "canal" of a tooth. In addition there are vocal "cords," eye "lids," and "club" feet. Simple metaphor even furnished the names of three small bones in the middle ear: "hammer," "anvil," and "stirrup," and the ear "drum" itself. Parts of musical instruments are described in terms of simpler tools: pianos have "hammers" and "keys," violins have "bridges" and "bows" in a sense unknown to primitive warriors.

All workers in special crafts can surely augment this list. What has happened is of course that an elementary similarity in external aspect has caused a shift of the word to a new function.

Other shifts occur when words having to do with time relations are applied to space, or the reverse. Sometimes it is hard to tell which came first. We say "The tree stands *before* my house" and also "I did this *before* the spring house cleaning."

Presumably one is a metaphoric application of the other. We transfer words describing impressions from one of the five senses, to make them apply to others. So it is quite usual to talk of a "sharp" tone, a "flat" taste, a "shrill" color, a "smooth" sensation of any sort. Finally, any of these physical terms can readily be applied to psychological states. "Bitter" grief is the kind that *bites* ("how sharper than a serpent's tooth . . ."); "anguish" is the kind that strangles, for the word is cognate with German *eng* and Latin *angustus* meaning "narrow, constricted." "Dreary" once meant "falling" or "dripping." Colors are taken to designate attributes of character: "He's *yellow*," or "That's mighty *white* of you" (regional U.S.A. dialect) in English. German has an expression *einem grün sein* meaning to be favorable or devoted to someone else; and Russian uses derivatives of the word *krasnyi* (red) for adjectives to express pleasure and approbation. (This, by the way, has nothing to do with politics. It is an old semantic shift no doubt connected with that preference for bright colors evinced in peasant embroideries and woodwork.)

When these rather elemental shifts occur it is easy to trace their course and to understand their cause. Some, however, are the result of more intricate psychological readjustments.

COMMUNICATION AND MISUNDERSTANDING

Two human beings who talk together are accomplishing an act of "communication," as we defined it in the first chapter. Since the effort succeeds so well in most cases, we are apt to forget that the act is and must always be an approximation. To each of his friends, even to his closest *alter ego,* a man talks out of a private world of his own: the sum total of his memories and experiences. Persons strongly attracted to each other by the emotions are prone to attempt a more intimate approaching of the two worlds, so that by some kind of magic extension of personality each one may reach back into the early days of the other and build the same structure of experience. But despite the torrents of eloquence with which the miracle is sometimes attempted, the isolation remains a dreary fact.

The reason is simple. It is impossible for any two persons ever to have learned the same word under precisely the same circumstances; occupying, as it were, the same space in time, and apprehending the new term with precisely the same background. Therefore each will take it into his consciousness ringed about with a special context of associations, differing from the associations of everyone else hearing it. This is what Hermann Paul means when he says that each linguistic creation—and re-creation—is and remains the work of an individual. Yet procedures repeat themselves and approximations of understanding do occur. Our speech is a compromise between the ultimate incommunicability of one person with another and the conventional communication values attached to certain symbols.

WORDS AND REFERENCES

Let us pause a moment to analyze what happens to us in normal conversation when we employ terms for things. Suppose the subject talked about is a spider. When the word is pronounced the sounds will call up in the mind of the listener a general background of experience, not always very vivid, and not always involving a sharp photographic image of remembered spiders. The background of experience in the listener's mind is called by some writers the *reference*, as distinguished from the *referent*, or the real spider existing in the world outside ourselves. It is important to keep the three elements in the situation quite distinct:

The *word*, which is merely a symbol made up of sounds, like ['spaidə(ɪ)];
The *referent*, or concrete object (a living animal);
The *reference*, or recalled experience of past spiders evoked in the mind of the listener.

Under certain circumstances, however, an extremely vivid image is recalled in connection with a given word. The reference is sharpened. This happens especially when the referent is associated with a strong emotion like love or fear. But the same stimulus, the spoken word [ˈspaidə(ɹ)], may produce nothing but a vague reference in one listener while it evokes a sharp one in another. Their experiences are by no means identical.

EMOTIONAL ASSOCIATIONS

For instance: when I first learned the word "spider," the circumstances were apparently tranquil. I had no cause for alarm, and my attention, so far as I recall, was chiefly captivated by the spinning activities of the creature. The word had no sinister connotations for me. A playmate of mine in those early days, however, must have learned the word under terrifying circumstances. She was never able to recall them or convey them to me in any way; but the mere pronunciation of the word (not to speak of the sight of an actual arachnidan creature) was enough to induce symptoms of panic amounting almost to a fit. If emotions may strongly color the reference of "spider," they may do so to some slight degree with less concrete terms such as "isosceles triangle." There is the illuminating story of a little girl who, having recently learned to read, was spelling out a political article in the newspaper. "Father," she asked, "what is Tammany Hall?" And father replied in the voice usually reserved for the taboos of social communication, "You'll understand that when you grow up, my dear." Acceding to this adult whim of evasion, she desisted from her inquiries; but something in Daddy's tone had convinced her that Tammany Hall must be connected with illicit *amour,* and for many years she could not hear this political institution mentioned without experiencing a secret non-political thrill. Another high school girl reports that the phrase "plane geometry" was first introduced to her in a context of deprecation, as applying to a science much less exciting and esoteric than something else (presumably "solid" geometry). So for a long time she understood "plane" in the sense of "plain"—a semantic confusion heightened by the homonyms of identical origin—appropriate for an unadorned Cinderella among the mathematical sisters; and it was only much later that she realized with a shock that the key word applied quite colorlessly to (imaginary) surfaces, having nothing to do with beauty or complexity.

With such varieties of individual experience in relation to words, there arise all sorts of *connotations,* as they are called, or nuances of association around the accepted factual definition. Some connotations (like the erotic aura around Tammany Hall for the little girl of our anecdote) remain strictly private and individual, the results of special accidents; others are coincidental for many persons and hence become currently attached to the word. If the sound-symbol is "spider," the situation can be thus represented:

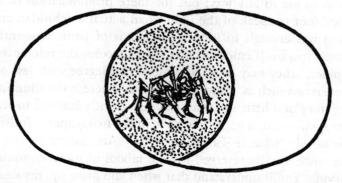

The unshaded sections in the ellipse of associations represent the special and private associations of the word due to the accidents of individual experience; the shaded portion represents a common store of connotations (tactile impressions approximately the same for anyone who has ever felt an arachnid crawl over his shin, generally current anecdotes or superstitions about spiders, etc.). In the heart of the overlapping associations is the word in its scientific sense: a designation of a biological type by (so far as possible) a colorless, unemotional scientific label. Even the label is a mere approximation of completely scientific denotation. The connotations cannot be kept away entirely, even from the abstract terms.

CHANGES IN MEANING

The shaded matter of our diagram differs in all experiences of speaking and listening. The shifts and instabilities may be great or little, but they exist. When repeated experiences tend to push the territory of common connotations generally in the same directions, a change in meaning will occur. The semantic development is often gradual, but it may end in a great transformation of meaning eventually. The general direction of the change will be determined by the prejudices, preoccupations, and interests prevailing over others in the community of speakers. Social tendencies appear more clearly in semantic than in phonetic change. This will be demonstrated more than once in the special types of change cited.

Pejorative change is one of the commonest and most readily observed. It means a degeneration in meaning from a comparatively noble and exalted significance to one of lower, if not downright contemptible or obscene, connotation. It has been suggested that there must be something groveling about human nature, since it has so often caused the besmirching of otherwise estimable terms. However, we must remember that here too the opposite of each tendency is perceptible concomitantly with it, and we must not despair too easily of any of the far-famed tendencies of human nature.

It is particularly words connected with sexual taboo and class snobbishness which tend to degenerate. Many words designating intimate articles of clothing have been shifted so often for this reason that it is difficult to keep abreast of them. So the homely "shirt" falls into disrepute and is replaced by "chemise." Speakers of the English language have often hidden behind an imported French word in order to spare their extremely delicate feelings. "Chemise" in its turn is either replaced by others still more vague, like "combination," or is eliminated entirely, together with the garment itself. The nether habiliments of gentlemen were at one time generally called "breeches"; later a sense of prudery caused this to be replaced by a loan word *pantaloons;* the new word was abbreviated to "pants," which quickly sank in the social scale and was superseded by "trousers." The corresponding diminutive garment of the ladies, formerly "pantalettes" or "panties" has shrunk to "step-ins," "scanties," and (adapting still another word from the masculine attire) "shorts."

In modern times many languages have witnessed a certain pejorative change in titles of class. "Sir," "lady," *monsieur, madame, Herr, Frau, señor, señora,* and the rest have lost their feudal connotations and are currently used for ordinary persons like you and me. "Bourgeois" too is by way of becoming a term of reproach after serving proudly the aspirations of a proud new class. In England, I am told, a wealthy club*woman* speaks of her "char*lady*." The reverse was formerly true. Malodorous and sinister subjects quickly cast a pejorative pall over their vocabulary. "Slaughter-house" is avoided for *abattoir;* "undertaker" was originally adopted as a euphemism, but has itself been replaced by "funeral director." An endless source of examples is to be found in the shamefaced phrases by which civilized human beings try to gloss over "natural needs" while alluding to them obliquely. "Toilet," which at one time referred to the entire process of gowning and beautifying oneself for appearance in public, fell into disrepute because of one aspect of that preparation; it is now disappearing before various evasive expressions like "rest-room" (but who "rests" in such a place?), "powder room," "lounge," "lavatory" (a British term), and others due to the jocular originality of individual tavern keepers. Further examples of this sort of thing will be found in a later chapter. The reader may amuse himself by extending the list. Names for underlings, for inhabitants of the country (as opposed to the sophisticated city), for foreigners, for death and certain types of sickness, are particularly prone to degenerate. At certain periods of history when the dominant culture happened to be in the hands of a cynical and dissipated group, many of the most innocent words have suffered degeneration. Allardyce Nicoll reports that the society comedies of the Restoration period in England tended to vilify any and all words applied to woman, even the most sacred and dignified. To us innocents it must appear an incredible situation to find the words "sister" and even "mother" degenerated to pornographic significance as they were in the seventeenth century. In our day such pejorative modifications are more strictly confined to the underworld; they do not appear so baldly in our accepted literature.

Ameliorative change is an elevation in meaning. Here too some of the clearest examples are connected with social levels and class distinctions. A "marshal" once meant a lad who looked after mares—that is, a stable boy; a "bishop" was one who had the job of looking (Greek *skopein*) things over (*epi*) —that is, a humble "overseer." An "angel" was merely a messenger, no more exalted than one of our gray-clad postmen before the theologians took the term and exalted it by using it to designate intermediaries between divine intelligence and man's intelligence. A *cathedra* (from the Greek) was once an ordinary chair; now it is associated only with exalted dignitaries. The bishop's seat was his cathedral town. The papal "see," from Latin *sedes,* has made the original word too sacrosanct for ordinary use.

With the development of a modern mercantile culture, some adjectives not originally laudatory have assumed meliorative connotation. A "shrewd" person was once "wicked, rascally"; now he's admired because he can beat his neighbors in the game of competition. A "smart" man, etymologically, is one to cause pain (think of German *Schmerz*); now we take our hats off to him. "Nimble" (from a verb *niman*) used to mean "good at taking things" as a pickpocket might be, but is now a synonym for general dexterity; "keen" meant "sharp," and both words have become terms of approval in the non-physical sphere; even "slick" contains overtones of admiration (albeit grudging), especially in America.

Narrowing or *restriction* of meaning occurs when a term that once applied to a general class of things is limited to special cases. This process often accompanies borrowing from one language to another. In Russian, *dog* doesn't mean the entire canine breed but only a great Dane; Russian *shtraf* (obviously taken from German) has narrowed from the sense of "punishment in general" to "money fine." Our word "corpse" is in origin identical with Latin *corpus,* meaning any sort of body, human or otherwise, alive or dead. Now it can only mean a cadaver or, as medical students would say, "a stiff." "Garage," a more recent loan word, comes from a French verbal noun originally meaning "place for storing anything," not exclusively automobiles. "Undertaker," already cited, shows narrowing as well as pejorative change. "See" as in "papal see" (quoted above) shows narrowing as well as ameliorative change.

Many words which were once abstract designations for a quality or a class have narrowed in the special direction of *concretization.* Latin *fructus* was once "the act of enjoying oneself"; now we limit "fruit" to the apples, pears, and oranges which help us to that desirable end in one definite form. Our word "city," designating a very tangible, visible, and in spots solid gathering of human beings meant "quality of citizenship" when it was first created as Latin *civitas.* "Faculty," which for academicians evokes a group of learned gentlemen —with a few ladies sprinkled in—robed in scholastic cap and gown, once had only the vaguer sense of "the possibility of doing (*facere*) something." We still use the word in this earlier sense when we speak of a man's "faculty" of concentration, or other talent. The word "faction," too, could have been applied to any sort of "act of doing" (*facere*). Now it is restricted to political groups within a larger body. This specialized and concretized use appears quite early. On the walls of Pompeii there are inscriptions using the verb form of *facere* in a narrow, political sense which has been interpreted as "unite, get together." Thus *Caupones, facite! Pomari, facite! Lignari, facite! Unguentari, facite!* would mean: "Tradesmen, unite! Dealers in apples, wood, and perfumes, get together!" It all sounds very familiar.

Expansion is of course the opposite of restriction. A term for an individual is adopted for a class. This is exemplified, for instance, whenever a proper name or a patented trade name is extended to cover a whole group. Soon after the phonograph was invented, one particular make, the "victrola," was popularly universalized for all. "Lynch" and "dunce," as your dictionary will tell you, come from the names of individual persons now forgotten in the larger idea. A "barn" formerly meant a "barley-place"; now it refers to a place of storage for all kinds of grain and for other things as well. "Box," once designating only receptacles made of *buxum* or boxwood, can now apply to all. "Manuscript" is often extended to cover material more accurately called "typescript." Bréal records a curious instance from the Sanskrit. Here *go-shtha* meant "cow-place" literally, but was universalized for any kind of stable, so that it was later possible to speak of an *açva-go-shtha* or "horse-cow-place." (*Açva*, nominative *açvas*, is cognate with Latin *equus*.)

Within the general field of metaphorical change which we have already briefly discussed, it is possible to distinguish a number of special types. The shift may occur in the direction of *hyperbole,* or deliberate exaggeration, causing expressions of great strength to diminish toward feebleness. Most of our intensive words go this way. "Awfully," "enormously," "tremendously" are adverbs used for quite trivial matters now. The tendency is still more marked with the more transitory expressions of disapproval which never achieve the dignity of accepted usage. "Stinking," "lousy," "vile," "putrid" are a few of those which have been recently current on both sides of the Atlantic. Naturally one's ears become jaded by these excessive stimulants, and they are quickly discounted as hyperbolic exaggerations. On the other hand *litotes,* or understatement, occurs when a weak or colorless word assumes strength from special uses. Some recent examples are: "protective custody" (which sounds reassuring on the face of it); to "co-ordinate" (*gleichschalten*), which under certain circumstances means quite ruthless elimination of opposition; to "strafe," from German *strafen,* a simple word for "to punish," now assuming connotations of bombed cities and civilian terror.

SHIFT TO OPPOSITE MEANINGS

When words are falling into disuse they sometimes take on new meanings because of association with the few stereotyped phrases in which they survive. "Desultory reading" means "disjointed, skipping" sort of reading. It might in fact be quite feverish in tempo. But since the phrase is now felt to be primarily an opposite of "continuous, orderly, *purposeful* reading," it has assumed connotations of "lazy, relaxed," which were once foreign to it. Apparently it is natural for us to think of qualities in pairs—each one together with its opposite. When I say "bright" I am unconsciously thinking "not dark." As Jost Trier, a German scholar, expresses it concisely in a recent study: "Every word spoken evokes its own opposite meaning." We exclude the opposite while at the same time we are aware of it as a kind of negative definition. But one word may have a whole series of opposites, due to the accidents of association. It is thus that "desultory" comes to mean "lazy"—by negation of an opposite not originally associated with it. So a person who had only encountered "otiose" in the single phrase of disapproval, "otiose epithet," might assume it meant "not decent, not polite," whereas it means only "not accurate; not needed; lazy, superfluous, functionless."

By such elimination "egregious" has become petrified in a few phrases which not only limit but essentially change its earlier sense. It is a vivid compound in its origin, from Latin *ē, ex,* "out of," and *grex, gregis,* "a flock." A sheep that stood out from the rest of the flock was, literally, an "outstanding" sheep, equally so, whether for good or ill. But words in English with the sense of "outstanding, conspicuous" readily assume the sense of "immodest, blatant, ungentlemanly." (A gentleman observes a well-bred conformity with the herd.) In this particular word the pejorative tendency is strengthened by the limitation of its use to a few obsolescent phrases like "an egregious error" and "an egregious ass." Who has ever heard denizens of a conservative club (where the word is most apt to be used) speak of one with "egregious talent" or "egregious virtues"? No; a gentleman's chief virtue is to have nothing in excess. Thus the accidents of association surrounding a word rarely used have modified it so that it is now felt to describe qualities with which it originally had no concern. Another instructive example is the semantic shift in the word "meat." The archaic use, found in the phrases "bread and meat" and "meat and drink," shows that the word once had a more general scope than now. But by new associations, especially new ideas about the foods it was meant to *exclude*, it became the equivalent of "non-vegetable" as well as "non-liquid" nourishment. This in turn caused a displacement of "flesh," which had been commonly used for food in expressions like "flesh meat," but is now used alone for the muscular part of any animal body apart from (*excluding*) connotations of edibility. In Spanish *carne* means both "meat" and "flesh."

Meaning and Grammatical Use

Some of the processes here cited are sure to have an effect on syntax, as we shall see. For the moment let it suffice to point out that the key words we use to express grammatical relations have often reached their present function by some of the semantic changes here indicated. A single word with a restricted application may have its scope widened so that it does the work for a whole class. Our verb "do" substitutes for many others in allusive sentences. ("Does she play?" "No, she *doesn't*.") The English "more," once a designation for an increased amount of some physical quantity, is now widely employed as a mere device to make other adjectives comparative:

"*more* beautiful," "*more* radiant," "*more* despicable." Its function has widened with its semantic widening. The same thing happened with the Romance languages, which took specific words like *magis* and *plus* and universalized them as signs of the comparative (Spanish *más*, French *plus*). Thus also do adverbs take on special functions as prepositions. In French, the grammatical form for negation has led to a curious transformation of positive terms into their opposites. There were expressions meaning "not a bit, not a step" *(ne . . . pas)*, "not a thing" *(ne . . . rien)* and "not a person" *(ne . . . personne)*. When part of a phrase or compound is suppressed and the remainder still has the meaning of the whole, we may call the process "shortening." But in abbreviated form, the very word meaning "not" *(ne)* might be suppressed, and the positive words for "thing" or "person" would still be felt to have negative significance. It is as if we changed "nobody" into ("body") and still felt it to be negative. That is why you say *personne* (literally "a person") in French if you wish to say "No one" in reply to a question like "Who is there?"

SEMANTIC ARCHAISMS

One special aspect of semantic change throws light on our earlier cultural history. When we invent new instruments we are apt to name them from something already known, thus continuing the elementary metaphors encountered by a child learning about "legs" of tables or "eyes" of potatoes. Or we name the new tool for materials long since superseded in the course of invention. This type of *substitution*, as it has been called, is a semantic change caused by changes in the outside world, not primarily by psychological factors. Yet it is impossible to separate the external and internal factors. Conservatism and inertia operate to keep our technological vocabulary archaic. We "sail" on boats which are innocent of sails. Little boys play with "marbles" which came from no quarries at all, since they are made of artificial compositions. Our "books" are so named from the "beech" tree, whose bark and branches

once served for the scratching of early runes. Our "manuscripts" are no longer written by hand (*manus*) but by machine, as our "*manu*factured" products are made. Our "paper"
is turned out from wood pulp, not from the papyrus reed for
which it was once named. Our "pens" are no longer feathers
(*pennae*). Our "pins" have little resemblance now to the primitive thorns (*spinae, spinulae;* cf. French *épingles*) once used
to hold together the earliest garments of man. Yet the development from thorn to pin is clear. Some of the brooches of
the early Irish, beautifully executed and elaborately designed

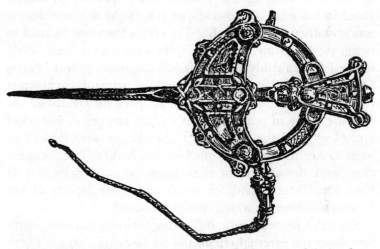

Tara Brooch Front. No. 13. National Museum of Ireland.

as they were, show unmistakably the imitation of the original
natural thorn.

Thus a little etymology helps us to go back quickly, by way
of palpable semantic change, to the very dawn of history, to the
cave dwellings of primitive man. You can try your own hand
at some of this semantic paleontology by looking up a few
key words in any good etymological dictionary. The German
word *Wand,* for "wall," will show you that woven or wattled
buildings persisted in Germanic territory into historical times.

Wand is related to our verb "to wind" (German *winden*) by a change in the root vowel. It is still used to apply to walls of stone, brick and mortar, with steel frames as skeletons—as far removed as possible from primitive wattles.

THE STUDY OF MEANINGS

Fascinating as the study of semantics is, it is one of the branches of language most recently explored. Long after the details of sound change and sound correspondence had been elaborately catalogued, scholars were still comparatively indifferent to the problems of meaning. The pioneer study was made by Michel Bréal in his *Essai de Sémantique* (1897). At this late date it was actually necessary for Bréal to *create* the word he used to designate his study. His principles were almost exclusively derived from a study of the classical languages (Greek, Latin, Sanskrit), and he appeared to regard the principles as abstract characteristics of "the mind" such as "need for clearness." At first the study of semantics was in fact limited to historical etymology, and the attempts at elucidation were limited to some rather unsatisfactory phrases like Bréal's. The "tendencies" were deduced from etymologies in an abstract way at first, with little regard for social and other aspects of the human situations in which change occurred.

Since this pioneer work, increasing curiosity has been manifest about the external circumstances favoring change. There must be something in the cultural history of a people which will help us understand why *fertig,* which in German once meant "ready for a journey," now means "ready for anything"; or why Anglo-Saxon *ceorl,* which once meant a freeborn husbandman, later degenerated to "churl." Hans Sperber has recently stressed the affective or emotional aura surrounding words as used by individual speakers: the coloring which, it will be remembered, was so very strong when one child heard or used "spider," and so slight when others did. If this aura of emotional connotation happened to coincide with the general preoccupations of a group in a certain age, it tended to spread. An example would be the connotations of nobility and admiration which gathered around the figure of a man on horseback in the Middle Ages. Men elevated the Vulgar Latin word for a "nag" or "old horse," *caballus,* into a progenitor of words like *chivalry, cavalier, caballero.* The emotional aura did correspond with a dominant prejudice—at least as felt by the feudal rulers themselves. It is easy to imagine the aura of affective associations which led to the sad decline in the word "quean" (cognate with "queen"). A still more glaring example is the enormous shift from the Spanish word *negro,* referring to the color "black," to the Southern American "Nigger," with its connotations of contempt (whether good- or bad-natured), intimidation, and even terror. Here the aura of associations due to the ruling group has gathered so thickly that it has darkened the literal blackness of the original meaning still more—clearly in coincidence with the attitudes of a very definite ruling group, in a ruling age.

Other recent work has stressed the need of including the field of associations and related meanings in dealing with the history and significance of words. By discussing the semantics of groups taken together we can more readily see how the overlappings, gaps, and duplications within the field cause some words to expand in application, others to contract, and still others to vanish. Jost Trier (to whose work we have already referred) has done this for words relating to the field of intelligence in Old and Middle High German texts. Another German scholar, W. Héraucourt, has recently made a semantic study of words for moral and ethical values in Chaucer. Such studies are more illuminating in many ways than an artificial isolation of individual words when their history is being discussed.

POPULAR STUDIES IN SEMANTICS

There has been, of late, a rather general flurry of popular interest in semantics, particularly in America. Many situations in the world about us have made people poignantly aware that they fail completely to understand each other even when they talk together volubly in the same language. The realization creates a sense of hurt loneliness, strongest in the least experienced persons. A moment's reflection shows that the counters of conversation most glibly employed, for instance in talk about politics, are the most ambiguous. The spheres of individual connotations (see the spider diagram) may overlap very slightly when terms like "dictatorship" are used. An optimist, struck by this fact, will quickly recover his good spirits and cry: "Very well, then; all we need is to get together and *define our terms*. Semantics—that's what we need!"

The solution, so expressed, sounds agreeably painless. The most obtuse observer will have guessed by now that there is something wrong with human affairs as we manage them, when they cause us to endure frequent major calamities like war, disease, and unemployment. How pleasant if it were only a matter of definitions!

For this reason, perhaps, one can understand the great popularity which has greeted a number of recent books on semantics written for the general public. By implication at least they promise general solutions for social ills, and so their current success is quite understandable. They have created a certain interest in language problems which linguists may find gratifying; but on the other hand they leave the ordinary reader with an inaccurate impression that semantics—only a single aspect of linguistics, after all—is the *Open Sesame* of otherwise impenetrable problems in both language and sociology.

Non-Linguists on the Need for Semantic Clarity

The current interest was stimulated to a large degree by *The Meaning of Meaning*, published by C. K. Ogden and I. A. Richards in 1923. This book served the very useful function of indicating clearly the complicated nature of the general problem. Others have been impelled as a consequence to approach it from different special points of view. Professor P. W. Bridgman, for instance, has explained for the layman in his *Logic of Modern Physics* just what semantic changes are involved when a specialist in his field uses ordinary words like "time," "space," "identity," and the like. For him these terms have a significance quite different from that which we attach to them in our daily speech. The problem in meanings leads Professor Bridgman to propose a new technique in definitions, which he calls "operationalism." He draws certain sociological deductions from his method of definition in a second book, *The Intelligent Individual and Society*. His thesis is: "The concept is synonymous with the operations by which you test for it," as you test for weight in the laboratory. When he applies the method to social concepts his results are discouraging. If you cannot test concepts like "democracy" or "duty" or "morality" by operations, he tells us, then they are "footless" (that is, meaningless) concepts, and should be abandoned. In the end nothing is left but the egocentric drives of the individuals constituting society.

The linguist and the sociologist alike may charge Bridgman with over-simplification. He has ignored the two-sided nature of a man's relation to the group, which is demonstrated afresh every time he learns and uses a new word. A speaker serves himself as well as the auditor both while he is listening and while he is speaking, The ability to talk withers and tends to die unless it is exercised in society. An equilibrium is desirable; the right degree of independence, the right degree of subordination, for linguistic fluency and presumably for health and social welfare also. It is true in particular of the creation of meanings by the collaboration of individual and group. When he talks about semantics, Bridgman overstresses the ego and understresses its necessary collaboration with others.

Thurman Arnold is another widely read non-linguist who deals with problems in semantics. Writing as a specialist in government and law, he discusses the problem of symbols, including words, and their power over us. In *The Folklore of Capitalism* he submits to sardonic and witty analysis the almost magic power of certain spell-binding references like "the

founders of this country," "The Constitution," and "government interference in business." His thesis is that we are ruled
by the manipulators of our symbols; and he leaves us with
the uneasy sense that very little can be done about the frequent
abuse of power by them, except tonic exercises in definition.

SEMANTIC STUDY NO PANACEA

One of the most influential of non-linguists to write on semantics is Alfred Korzybski, perhaps because he has made the most
extravagant promises in behalf of semantics as a panacea for
human ills. Stripped of elaborate verbalization and repetition,
his exhortations in *Science and Sanity* amount to a few salutary if not very original reminders: that the word—a symbol—
is *not* the thing (that is, the referent); that we must distinguish
sharply the levels of abstraction in the terms we use; that most
of our social problems center around ambiguous "multiordi-
nal" terms so interwoven with the emotions that our semantic
reactions become tragically confused. Personal, national, and
international maladjustments are reduced by Korzybski to
"neuro-semantic" reactions needing re-education. "In our
lives," he says, "most of our miseries do not originate in the
field where the terms 'true' and 'false' apply, but in the field
where they *do not apply;* namely, in the immense region
of propositional function and meaninglessness, where agreement must fail." Symbols (like money, for instance) are described by Korzybski as high-power abstractions that rule our
lives through the people who manipulate them. Like Arnold,
Korzybski suggests that our problem is to find the right manipulators, but he throws little light on the burning question:
How can we choose them, and how will they go to work on such
important symbols as money?

A number of more recent writers depend directly on Korzybski and acknowledge their indebtedness to him. Stuart
Chase, for instance, has undertaken to popularize the ideas
of *Science and Sanity* in his *Tyranny of Words.* His enthusiasm for semantic exercise as a panacea is even more vocal than

that of his predecessor. He repeatedly skirts the danger (when he does not fall headlong into it) of trying to exorcise critical practical issues by linguistic operations. His examples of the need for clarifying references and referents in law, economics, government, and sociology are most edifying, to be sure. But he also promises us too much in the way of automatic solutions to non-linguistic problems when once we have clarified the definitions and eliminated the meaningless terms.

Other disciples of Korzybski are more cautious in their promises. S. I. Hayakawa and Irving J. Lee both present useful popular texts explaining the principles of "neuro-semantics" for the layman. Their books give stimulating exercises to be worked out by the reader. The illustrations, taken from everyday life, are most instructive. The principles themselves, however, are less original than the authors appear to think. Exercises in denotative and connotative meaning have long been a part of college textbooks in rhetoric. Writers of Korzybski's school have made some contribution towards the techniques of definition by exploring some of the psychological aspects hitherto neglected. It is worth while to practice the techniques in their newer forms. Popular interest in them may be regarded as a gratifying sign of intellectual curiosity and alertness in the reading public. But readers at large may feel a corresponding disappointment, even despair, when they finally discover that semantic analysis will not solve their social problems for them after all.

VALUE OF SEMANTIC STUDIES

A student of language is apt to be more modest in his expectations and therefore less subject to disappointment than are the amateurs of popular semantics. There is no need to quit the subject on a note of complete skepticism. Even when we have discounted the exaggerated claims of the Korzybski school we may still concede the great importance and use of the study of meanings. Once the results of such study are before us, we naturally pose the question: What next? If irresponsible jour-

nalism, for instance, furnishes examples of deliberate confusion, deception by implication and connotation, and so on,
what shall we do about it? Obviously it is not enough to point
out the semantic malpractices.

The answer, says the linguist, lies outside my field. I do not
offer solutions in my capacity as linguist. But I am glad to help
my colleagues in journalism, economics, and sociology when
they deal with linguistic material. And I may even act with
them after the study has been made; but in that event
we shall all be acting together as citizens anxious to correct
an abuse. We shall have left our studies and laboratories to
participate in the affairs of the market place.

In the end, linguists will gain and give most in this field
when they unite the traditional scrupulous regard for scientific method with vivid and realistic awareness of social milieu
and its challenging problems. To do this they will have to receive help from, as well as give it to, other disciplines such as
sociology and psychology. Teachers of language can fructify
their material by availing themselves of pertinent discoveries
in the adjacent territories. No part of language study, indeed,
offers better occasion for scientific collaboration than the in-
vestigation of meanings against a social background. The practical effectiveness of this study will be increased rather than
diminished when the popular writers limit their claims to the
real advantages to be derived from it, without promising social
panaceas in addition.

6. Grammar, or the Building of Sentences

1. EUROPEAN LANGUAGES

MAKING INTELLIGIBLE SENTENCES

When we have begun to get an idea of what our fellow human beings mean by the words they use (all very approximate and relative, as the chapter on semantics has made clear), then there are further problems to baffle us. We must next decide how to put these words together in sentences so that we can say what we mean with them and also—again within limits!—can be understood as we wish to be understood. This means learning to adapt our words to the patterns used by the community about us. Otherwise we are condemned to one experience after another of quasi-intelligibility or downright unintelligibility.

Most persons have participated at one time or another in the efforts of a small child to put words together meaningfully. The units are at first disjointed. "Baby want go walk" can be made quite clear by the aid of gestures. But the words thus juxtaposed do violence to the language habits of an adult listener who speaks English. He is accustomed to small subordinate signs which will indicate with greater nuance how the four general ideas are related. So he obligingly undertakes to correct the struggling child, and says emphatically: "Baby *wants* . . ." Very quickly the child learns by imitation to suffix an -*s* to the first verb, to introduce the next one by an annunciatory particle like "to," and to affix -*ing* to the third when it is used to supplement "go." One day he is still isolating the words; the next day he suddenly makes use of the nuances.

There are many occasions when the child fails to make himself clear. A series of words like "Daddy naughty baby hurt cry" leaves the listener in some doubt as to who hurt whom, or whether a mere accident is being reported. No doubt eloquent gesture and vocal accompaniment would help to clarify the infant's exposition, but these are precisely the luxuries which more stoical adults feel themselves in honor bound to limit or forgo. To a certain extent, then, our grammatical inflections may be regarded as a substitute for elaborate gestures which might indicate the relationships of words more picturesquely, to be sure, but far less subtly.

"Parts of Speech"

In older school texts of English grammar (now all but forgotten) the elementary student was formerly initiated into a complicated lore known as "parts of speech." At an early age he was expected to babble freely of conjunctions and prepositions and other very abstract terms. He learned that nouns were names of things and that verbs designated actions, and then almost immediately ran head-on into a category of amphibious grammatical monsters, infinitives, participles, verbal nouns, and so on, which combined the functions of both nouns and verbs. The teacher explained that verbs could sometimes be nouns without ceasing to be verbs—a contradiction which might have caused serious disturbance for the docile student if he were not, fortunately, so healthily preoccupied with really important things at the moment, such as handball, dramatics, girls, and dogs. The metaphysics of grammar might otherwise have jeopardized his rational processes for life.

Of course the traditional terms, including the "parts of speech," have a use. They have been convenient in imparting to others some of the more persistent patterns in the relating of words to one another within complete expressions (sentences). Yet it should be recognized that the terms overlap and conflict. Above all, they do not signify the same things for all languages.

In English and the languages closest to us, the two most important items in the list of "parts of speech" are certainly *nouns* (names of things) and *verbs* (words denoting being or action).

NOMINAL ELEMENTS

We can extend the range of noun expressions, perhaps, by including under the same heading the substitute words which take the place of nouns, such as personal pronouns ("I," "you," "he," etc.) and demonstrative pronouns ("this," "that") and other economical substitutes for nouns ("some," "any"). These are all *nominal elements,* let us say. Even the words which qualify and describe nouns (adjectives, articles, demonstrative adjectives) may be regarded as nominal. They often appear strictly in a noun's capacity. You can say "Give me that," or "Hand me those" instead of "those eggs." A few adjectives in English can even be treated as nouns to the extent of having an -*s* added to make them plural. Such expressions are: "the fats and the leans," "the whites," "the blacks," "empties" (for "empty bottles"), "the slicks" (for magazines, as opposed to "the pulps"); "marked-downs" (overheard in a department store for "reduced dresses"). In German and the Romance languages the closeness of adjectives to nouns is much more apparent.

VERBAL ELEMENTS

If the nominal element includes all these time-honored parts of speech, then not a great deal more remains to be accounted for. The *verbal element* may be said to include all the words and expressions which report the doings or actions attributed to the other element (the *nominal*). As we have learned in school, verbs are modified and combined in various ways to show varying times of the action concerned. They also show conditions or aspects of the action. Thus "He *is hit*" is a special combination showing that the person designated by "he" (the subject) suffered the action. This is called *passive voice* (from *passus*, "having suffered"). If the subject performed it himself, as would be the case in "He hits," the voice would be *active*.

Other nuances are expressed by putting together two or more verbal forms: "He is hitting," "He does hit," "He will have been hit." Along with the verbal element one can consider words that make more specific the picture of the action in the verb, such as "He hits *accurately*." They are called adverbs, and their very name indicates their function. They are added to *(ad-)* the verbs. In English many adverbs end in *-ly*.

FUNCTIONAL WORDS

Finally we have a considerable number of words, mostly quite short, which are used to put together nominal and verbal elements. These are *functional* words, since they help to indicate the way the other chief elements are related or function together. *Prepositions* tell you of a variety of relations made possible by them between following nouns and other (preceding) elements: "the owner *of* the house," "speech *about* war," "to sail *from* the harbor." They are so called because they are placed in *position before (pre-)* the nouns. *Conjunctions* join other elements together with word-links such as "and," "but," "or," "than," "if," "when." The functional words have many origins, as we have seen in the chapter on vocabulary, but their chief significance for us today is that they make connections within the sentence. Most of them (though not quite all) remain unmodified under all conditions.

INFLECTIONS

Not so the verbal and nominal elements, however. Words falling in these categories are susceptible of some slight modifications which are known to grammarians as *inflections*. When we refer to more than one flame we say "flames." The adding of that final *-s* [z] is called an inflection of the noun.

In modern English we have few inflections left, though at one time the language had many. Professor Charles Carpenter Fries in a recent study speaks of "two major or live inflections."

These are the ones which have to do with number and tense respectively. Beyond these there are only a few minor ones left, such as declensions of a few pronouns, comparison of adjectives, and so on. That is why English presents a welcome relief to continental European students accustomed to memorizing long dull "paradigms" (meaning both declensions of nominal forms and conjugations of verbal ones) in other foreign languages. If only English had a rational system of spelling it would be easy in every way.

INFLECTION FOR NUMBER

Of the two living inflections, the forms for number appear most obviously in the noun. In the overwhelming majority of cases a simple device is used: -s (pronounced [s] or [z] according to the preceding sound) is suffixed to the simple word representing *one* object—the *singular*. In this way one or more objects are represented in what is known as the *plural*: thus "houses," "streets" stand for "more than one house" and "more than one street." A few nouns fail to conform to this pattern but use other methods. "Tooth" and "foot" are among those which show plurality by an internal vowel change. A very few show it by adding -en, like "oxen." As for the pronouns, they show plurality by the use of entirely different words. "We" is not a plural modification of "I," but a separate form. Here rules are of no help; the foreign student is forced to fall back on pure memory in learning "we" and "they."

In one inflection alone is the English verb concerned with number. If we are referring to a single thing or person the verb that goes with it will, for present action, take an -s ending: "He hits." This marks it off from verbs with plural subjects like "They hit." In the present tense of the English verb, therefore, the -s is a signal meaning exactly the opposite of an -s attached to a noun. It emphasizes singularity.[1] In all other tenses of the

---

[1] A group of words, "may," "can," "must," "might," "could," "would," "should," omit the -s for reasons which become clear if one studies the earlier history of English.

verb in English no difference is made between forms used with singular and those with plural subjects.[2] Forms like "drank" or "ate" or "landed" may be used indifferently with either "he" or "they" before them. When a verb *is* modified, however, in order to emphasize the singularity or plurality of its subject, grammarians are accustomed to say rather poetically that the verb "agrees," or shows "concord" or "congruence" with its subject. What they mean is that according to general usage you don't find singular subjects without the additional reminder -*s* to emphasize singularity in the present verb forms.

INFLECTION FOR TENSE

The one other "live" inflection in English is the change introduced in verbs to show change of time. "I *drink* your health" means that the speaker is performing the act now, in present time; "I *drank* your health" means that the speaker performed it in the past. As is well known, there are two ways of inflecting a verb in English for tense. The first is by changing the internal vowel according to a regular pattern ("drink, drank"; "sing, sang"), and is to be observed in some sixty-six verbs still in current use. These verbs are, for reasons best known to grammarians, called "strong." The other method is to add a suffix, a dental consonant [d] or [t], with or without a preceding pronounced vowel, as in "landed," "cleaned," and "leapt." These verbs are likewise mysteriously labeled "weak." They show no debility in numbers, as a matter of fact. Ever since Old English times the weak verbs have been increasing and the strong verbs diminishing. Formerly the past tense of "thrive" was "throve," according to one of the patterns of so-called strong verbs; now we tend to say "thrived," to rhyme with "dived," another verb of the same class.

When we wish to express other time relations than past as

2 Except, of course, for the verb "to be." This one alone shows a distinction of number in the past tense: "He was" as against "they were." This is a survival of a distinction once carried through the past tense of all strong verbs, universally and consistently.

opposed to present, we use a combination of verbal forms. Of these the first one in the series shows inflection most clearly: "He *has* not been hit," "They *are* being summoned," "He *had* intended to do otherwise." We also use combined forms to show that an action is continuous, or to emphasize it: "I *am* ringing the number for you," and "The party *doesn't* answer."

POSSESSIVE AND OTHER CASES

There is one minor inflection in English which deserves mention even in a sketchy survey like this. Nouns and pronouns are upon occasion subject to a modification to show their relationship to other nouns in order to indicate something like possession. "The boy's book" clearly shows possession of the book by the boy, and the relationship is signaled to eye and ear by the suffixed -*s*—that favorite inflectional form in English. (The apostrophe on the printed page is a visual symbol corresponding to nothing at all in speech values.) The plural possessive as in "*boys'* books" is indistinguishable in sound from the singular. Pronouns, too, show possession, as in "her," "his," "its," "their" and so on. So far as nouns are concerned the inflection is shrinking. It is being limited to words for human beings. We say "the boy's foot" but not usually "the hill's foot." For the latter expression, we substitute "the foot of the hill," a prepositional phrase.

Formerly the possessive was widely used, not only in relation to people but also to things. Such an inflection of a noun showing relation to another part of a sentence was called its *case*. We can still speak of "boy's" as being in the *possessive* "case" if we will. At an earlier time you could also tell by looking at a word like "boy" whether it was in the *nominative* case (for instance, used as subject of the sentence) as in "The boy ran" or the *objective* (also called *accusative*) case to designate the objective of some action as in "He hit the boy," or the so-called *dative* case of indirect object as in "I gave the boy a book." Now since we avoid even the possessive for a word like "hill," it may be said that the tendency in use of non-personal nouns is to ignore case altogether. Yet old-fashioned grammars still devote undue space to this moribund concept.

PARTS OF SENTENCES

The most important division in the English sentence is still, after all, the general one implied in the terms *subject* and *predicate*. The chief nominal form in the usual sentence, together with all its associated words (modifiers), is regarded as the subject or the thing talked about. The verbal form associated with it, together with all modifiers and complements, is the predicate. Since English has so very few inflectional forms to indicate by suffix what function a word performs in a sentence, we must depend on *word order* almost entirely to show relationships. It makes all the difference in the world whether you say "The man bites the dog" or "The dog bites the man." In German, where elaborate inflections survive to show the *case* or sentence use of a noun, the order can be reversed without changing sense. *Den Mann beisst der Hund* still reports the more usual event, in which the man is the victim and the dog is the aggressor, even though the victim appears first in the sentence. *Den,* the German article, corresponding to our "the," is so inflected as to show that its noun cannot possibly be the subject of the sentence but must be the object; *der,* on the other hand, shows by its ending that its noun, in the nominative case, must be the subject and cannot possibly be the object. Thus a German listener is in no doubt at all which creature bit which when he hears the inverted sentence.

PRESENTATIVE SENTENCES

Formal grammars teach us that every sentence must have a subject and a predicate. Still, in actual usage we often feel that phrasal locutions are complete and self-contained statements. Frequently, though not always, they are exclamations: "The old boy himself!" No particular verb is "understood," yet the phrase serves quite well to present the person concerned without any predicate. Hence it is called a *presentative sentence*.

Latin writers used verbless sentences like *Sus Minervam,* "The pig [undertakes to teach] Minerva," quite often. In most modern European languages, too, it is stylistically possible to write something like this in narrative prose: "He entered the room quietly. A moment of silence. 'Surprise,' he said." We also use presentative sentences often in informal but socially "correct" conversation. They cannot be classified according to rigid traditional doctrines about subjects and predicates.

"Psychological" Subjects and Predicates

It has been suggested, as a matter of fact, that there is often a kind of conflict between the formal subject of a sentence, which is given grammatical prominence, and the "psychological" subject, which is really the center of the speaker's attention. The latter may be placed in an unjustly obscure position. When we say "The result of the election constituted a vindication of his career," I suppose we may be concentrating upon the happy politico concealed behind the obscure pronoun "his" much more than on "result." Similarly the "psychological" verb, or action stressed by the speaker, may lurk in a noun. That action, then, constitutes the psychological predicate. In announcing that "The child has a toothache," the action (in this case, the suffering.) is not contained in the verb "has," which is a colorless connective, but in the noun. The psychological verb is implied in "toothache." What we really mean is something like "the child toothaches"—except that the habits of the English language will not permit such an expression. The discrepancy between a formal grammatical subject and the psychological subject of attention may result in "grammatical mistakes," as when we say "The sociological effect of these numerous wars were disastrous."

The problem of discovering the psychological subject in a sentence, and of giving it more emphasis, if possible, belongs under the general topic of style rather than grammar. It is instructive, however, to try one's hand at a practical discrimination between formal and stylistic structure in sentences.

When you have charted your way through certain newspaper editorials you frequently discover that the stress intended fails, whether by accident or design, to correspond with the stress of grammatical structure.

ILLOGICAL GRAMMAR

Grammarians have at times deluded themselves, one cannot help thinking, into an assumption that language is put together logically. Especially the grammarians who lay down rules for learners are apt to claim an inner logical harmony for the practices of sentence structure. When they declare "This is *right*," they often mean "This is the proper, unescapable, and logical way to say a thing." This is particularly true of those grammarians who have tried to establish a code of correctness; to dictate rules instead of reporting what is said.

Yet correct sentences are often put together in a way that, upon closer examination, turns out to be anything but logical. The intention is understood, rather than the exact or "literal" implication of the words. The "psychological" subject is detected by the listener no matter what the structure. When human beings—not only women, as the wags would have it—develop a modest or hypocritical or contradictory way of saying something the intent is grasped despite mood and tense. A reassuring statement too zealously uttered will make the listener think "Something is concealed here," and he will proceed to supply it. We all know how to interpret sentences beginning "Of course she's my best friend . . ." or "I feel that I must tell you for your own good" or "This hurts me more than it does you." Very often the thing literally said contradicts the thing intended in a most curious manner. Here are some examples:

We say "It's a beautiful day, isn't it?" Actually we mean affirmation instead of negation in the latter part of the sentence: something like "You agree, I hope?" Whatever the historical origin of the illogical "Isn't it?" or "Don't you?" the bare words are amazingly contradictory. When a gossipy woman says "She's very beautiful, *isn't* she?" there may be in truth a secret feline hope that the statement will be contradicted; but this situation is not the normal one. Similarly with the question "Isn't it a beautiful day?" which is obviously intended as a positive statement. In using present participial verb-forms we are guilty of strange inconsistencies. "A crying child" means one who cries, but an "eating" or a "cooking apple" is not one that eats or cooks, nor is a "hunting rifle" one that hunts. In a statement like "The streets were running with water" we are trying to say, really, that the *water* was running, but we twist it to something else. A machine "works," but the man who operates it is "working" it too.

In employing words like, "would," "could," "should," "might" and so forth, where power and desire are involved, we become involved in all sorts of polite evasions that end by reversing the sense of them. "Would you be so kind as to open the door?" really means "I know you *are* kind; therefore I do ask you to open the door." "I could have burst with pride" means "I had the false sensation of bursting, but I knew I couldn't." A most bizarre doubt is implied in the question "Might I come in?"

Agreement so often violates logical consistency, even in accepted usage, that we scarcely notice it. "Did someone call? Did *they* leave a message?" with its swift change of number, is so usual that the best writers use it in plays and novels. "The United States are a nation" may conform to strict grammatical congruence but it hurts the patriotic pride of an American. It implies that inner unity is lacking because a plural verb is, logically enough, put with a subject plural in form at least. The height of logical confusion is reached in a sentence like "She was given a book," which is sanctified by custom. We all know what it means; we know that "she" *wasn't* given, though the book was; and yet the words are mystifying if they are examined according to the rules and the expectations of English word order. What is one to understand by the subject of "*It* turned out differently every single time"?

LOGICAL SYNTAX

No wonder the logicians have looked at language and found it unsatisfactory for the purposes of strict statement and deduction. A student who wishes to be made aware of the ambiguities and illogicalities of ordinary speech can do no better than follow the initial exposition of Carnap's *The Logical Syntax of Language,* in which the principles of his special language are explained. Ordinary speech is so foggy and self-contradictory, Carnap remarks, that the task of disciplining and ordering it would defeat its own purpose. "In consequence of the unsystematic and logically imperfect structure of the natural word-languages (such as German or Latin), the statement of their formal rules of [logical] formation and transformation would be so complicated that it would hardly be feasible in practice." Language for a logician is a calculus or a system of conventions dealing with elements or symbols "about the nature of which nothing more is assumed than that they are distributed in various classes." Whereas in ordinary speech we say "The book is blue" or more generally "The object is blue," Carnap's special language employs a functional statement "Blue (a)" for "Blue is the object *a*." This is called a descriptive functor. The predicate is placed first. Similarly "Wr (a, b)" means "Warmer is a than b" and "Gr (7, 5)" means "7 is greater than 5" or "The object at position 7 is greater than the one at position 5." This is no place to pursue the elaboration of symbols by which Carnap designates in still more abstract terms the types of statements possible under his system. For a linguist one of the chief values of his work is that it provides, by implication, an imposing commentary on the inadequacies of everyday speech. But it does not deal with linguistics.

INFLUENCES OF LATIN GRAMMAR

Without doubt one of the reasons why logic and grammar have been confused is because both grammarians and logicians have so long been schooled in a classical training. The Latin language, which was formerly the core of a classical education, **is** a dead one. It has come down to us in written records which for the most part represent the most formal kind of speech, not the hasty, elliptical, inconsistent discourse of everyday. The Latin sentences of Cicero, for instance, make an elaborate and complex and almost inhumanly consistent pattern conforming to "rules" of grammar. A student who gets his ideas of grammatical relations first clarified by a study of Ciceronian Latin will tend to think of Latin relations as the model for all others. He will demand elaborate syntax and numerous inflections as ideal characteristics of a "literary" or "civilized" language. This is what has happened to many of the scholars who first undertook to write grammars of entirely different, non-Indo-European languages.

Let us examine for a moment the characteristics of this Latin grammar which has so widely influenced the formulation of other grammars. The briefest glance at a textbook will show you that Latin had fairly elaborate declensions: much more in the way of "cases" than anything surviving in English, or even than the more conservative German. Latin could indicate many relationships by a mere ending, often without the use of any functional particle like a preposition. In sentences like "They marched *for* six days" or "I gave the jewel *to* the girl" or "He lives *in* Rome" or "He is richer *than* his brother," the italicized words were not expressed. The suffixed ending indicated the relationship clearly enough. Classical grammarians used a series of fairly abstract terms to designate the cases thus formed:

Nominative for words used as subjects and predicatives of sentences.

Genitive, corresponding to our "possessive": also used in other ways, as in our expression "Forgetful *of* the event."

Dative used to indicate a recipient relationship as in "I spoke *to* the man" or "He gave the book *to me.*"

Accusative, corresponding to our direct object of a verb; also used after certain prepositions.

Ablative, a case implying separation. Used after many prepositions and many times without them, too.

Locative, to designate without preposition the place in which
a thing is placed; "I live in Athens." This case was limited to names
of cities and a few other nouns.

Vocative, or case of direct address, as in "*Charles,* come here."

Now the declensional endings which indicated these relationships were on the whole clear, regular, and unmistakable.
Whenever a student of Latin sees the ending *-orum* or *-arum*
he can say to himself: "This *must* be the genitive plural of
something: a noun, a pronoun, or a demonstrative adjective.
It can't be anything else." Not many case endings are so ambiguous as to cause grave confusion. So, despite the fairly high
number of case forms to be remembered, Latin may be called
an easy language because of its comparative orderliness.

The same is true of the verb. There are many suffixes to
show tense, number, person, mood, activity or passivity of the
action, but they are readily identified and interpreted. These
virtues may be found also in Sanskrit, Russian, Lithuanian,
and other conservative members of the Indo-European family.
The advantages somewhat counteract the wastefulness involved in attaching an identical or similar ending to a whole
series of words of the same number, gender, and case, as in the
expression meaning "of these beautiful Roman girls": *harum
formosarum puellarum Romanarum.* By the time one has
heard the fourth word in that series one feels like saying: "Yes,
I get the point. You are talking about something feminine in
the genitive case. It penetrates!"

The universal, almost superstitious regard for Latin grammar in Western European education has caused students to
accept it as a model of language structure. There has been an
unconscious tendency to regard it as a paragon of languages
which appeared full-fledged and perfect, highly inflected from
the start. And since the more archaic related languages resembled it in structure, parent Indo-European has been thought
of as essentially and immutably an "inflected" language. En-

thusiasts about so-called "Aryan superiority" have even claimed that an inflected language was necessary for subtle and elaborate thinking. You couldn't have one without the other, working both ways. All of which would leave small scope for the many languages (including English) employing other means of indicating relations.

ORIGIN OF INFLECTIONS

But Indo-European itself may have developed out of an earlier stage in which root-words and particles were loosely strung together as independent and semi-independent elements. Analytical study reveals traces of just such an early stage. There is clearly nothing sempiternal about inflections, not even the majestic and orderly ones we have learned in school grammars of Latin.

Let me suggest by example how the development may have occurred. In popular substandard English today, there is a demonstrative form "this-here," found in such sentences as "I recognize this-here guy." For some reason the combination "this-here" is frowned upon, perhaps because it is overemphatic. It is exactly analogous, however, to the perfectly respectable French *celui-ci, celui-là* ("this here, that there"). It is moreover not strikingly different from the acceptable "I see this man, here" or "Look at that man, over there." The small uninflected particles "here" and "there" can be loosely attached to preceding nouns to point out the positions of the objects mentioned. Such small words are called *deictic particles,* from the Greek *deiknumi* meaning "I show, I point." It is quite possible that, in the course of centuries, the habit develops of attaching a specific deictic particle to the subject of a sentence chiefly because the subject is the word receiving primary attention in the speaker's thought. Similarly, small uninflected words like "then" and "now" might become attached to preceding nouns in order to point out the relative positions of things in time, as "here" and "there" give their positions in space. Expressions like "that battle-there" or "this flood-now" or "the celebration-soon" show how closely allied are the words demonstrating place to the ones indicating time.

The process is the same whether small particles or recognizable independent words are attached to the ones preceding, as in the word "like," which is suffixed in the weakened form *-ly* to form English adverbs. The inflectional endings learned by students of Latin, Greek, or Russian are often made up of two or even more distinguishable elements called "determinatives." Hermann Hirt lists simple elements such as *om, ām, ā, ī, i, u, k, g, t, d, p, b, m, n, r, l, s, w* as the Indo-European determinatives which were used in combination or alone, to modify the meanings of root words. "At first," he says, "the meaning of the words was not essentially changed by the particles attached to them. Only conditioning relations of time and place were expressed. But gradually this sense was lost, and a new one was associated with the 'suffix.' Thus, for example, *-om* [Latin *-um*] became a sign of the neuter gender, *ā* the sign of the feminine, and so on."

If you have studied Latin grammar you have probably gained the impression that *-us, -a,* and *-um* (from earlier *-os, -ā,* and *-om*) are firmly tied up with questions of gender; and gender is, in our minds, firmly tied up with questions of sex (or its absence in non-living things). According to Hirt, then, this was not always so. What, you may wonder, was the significance of these endings if they had nothing to do with gender as we understand it? Here we can only guess. But it is quite possible that the *-s* of *-os* implied activity on the part of the person or thing thus designated. A *dominus* or "lord" (in what we now call the nominative case) was a man "acting like" a lord towards someone else. The *-m* of neuter *-om* may have meant passivity in a sense we now usually associate with verbs. It would have the same significance in the so-called "accusative" masculine form. Thus a *dominum* would be understood as a lord being acted upon by someone or something else. A *donum* ("gift") was an act of being given, whether as subject or object of the sentence. Possibly the feminine *-a* at one time expressed abstractness or collective numbers, as it still does in the so-called neuter plurals we have adopted into English: *memoranda, agenda, phenomena,* all ending in *-a.* Notice that our own usage is beginning to handle them as singulars once more, as when we say: "The agenda is ready."

It is at least clear that a division according to sex could not have been involved in all cases in the beginning. The terms masculine, feminine, and neuter suggest sex to our minds because a large number of nouns having a common suffix (Indo-European *-os,* Latin *-us*) referred to men and a large number in the group ending in *-a* referred to women. But it is clear that the primary intent of these suffixes must at one time have been something else; otherwise it would be difficult to explain words like *agricola* and *nauta,* meaning "farmer" and "sailor"—two conspicuously uneffeminate professions—which turn up in the so-called feminine declension.

What is true of nominal inflections is also true of verbal ones: there is no reason for supposing them to be everlasting. Certain verbal forms like infinitives, participles, and gerunds are nominal in function and can be regarded to an extent as suffixed nominal forms. Some are declined like nouns. Even the personal endings were at one time thought to be repetitions of the personal pronouns, later attached to the verbal theme. The evidence does not support this theory, and yet Indo-European verbal endings may have arisen from particles of some other sort. In any event some of the suffixes showing tense can be recognized as weakened forms of independent words later attached to the root. The process has been repeated in more recent times in the formation of certain tenses in Romance languages. The future, for instance, is a coalition of the infinitive and a weakened form of *habēre,* "to have." When a Frenchman says *j'aimerai* ("I will love") he is announcing (historically) "to-love-I-have," reduced to two words. What is now a simple inflected word quite clearly arose out of the combination of two independent parts. There is no obvious advantage in saying "to-love-have" rather than "shall love." Each is quite clear. In classical Latin, too, we have clues as to the origins of some personal endings of verbs. Thus *amamini,* "you are loved," has an ending identical in origin with a Greek adjectival suffix *-menoi* (plural) attached to verbs to indicate "having been acted upon." So *amāminī* was, literally, the equivalent of "you—the object of love" or "you—being loved." It was a verb lacking a strict verbal element (like "are"), but showing plurality just as a noun or adjective would.

2. NON-INDO-EUROPEAN LANGUAGES

"PARTS OF SPEECH" UNNECESSARY

A brief examination of Latin from the historical point of view shows, therefore, that its grammar was not always in the state in which Cicero found it and immortalized it. Its "cases" were not always "cases"; even its verbal inflections had multiple origins.

Let us try now to get away from the confines of languages familiar to us. Latin, Greek, Russian, Sanskrit, Old Irish—all of these, despite superficial differences, have similar grammars. It is from the study of them and of our mother tongue that we build up our ideas about nouns and verbs and other "parts of speech." It will be worth while to take a glance at remoter tongues which operate on quite different systems.

The Ewe language in Africa has been cited more than once because it is instructively different from our own in its manner of showing relations. Wilhelm Wundt writing on "folk-psychology" (as he called it) claimed over-zealously that this African tongue could give us an insight into the method of thinking of primitive man. He compared its methods to the methods of gesture language. He apparently regarded it as a case of arrested development in grammar, although he admitted that the sounds of the language have long since departed from the symbolic and imitative values he supposes they had at an earlier date. It would be more cautious, I think, to say that Ewe "grammar" is simply very different from ours.

It is innocent of many distinctions we think we have to make, and yet it gets along very successfully without them. To be sure, it is driven to the use of some awkward loose compounds; but German, an Indo-European language, is famous for some awkward tight ones, like *Vierwaldstätterseedampffahrtaktien-gesellschaft*. An Ewe visitor to Europe might well exclaim: "How unwieldy! At home we commit no such locutions as that!"

A European student of Ewe finds that words have a disconcerting habit of changing their "grammatical" function without changing or modifying their appearance. No suffix, no internal change may indicate to you that the word you heard (or saw) a few moments before used as a preposition is now being used as a verb, or the verb as a preposition. For instance: *de* (pronounced with a reverted [d], made by pointing the tongue backwards) means "to reach," but as a preposition it means "to." Thus *máyì dé avé me*,[3] "I shall go to the wood" literally means "I shall go-reach wood." The form *máyì*, future of *yi*, "to go," is itself a compound of *á* weakened from *vá*, "to come." Hence futurity is expressed by saying "come" before any verb. "I shall eat" is "I come eat."

The adverb "in the meantime" is expressed by a verb *gbɔ*, "come again," after the main verb. Thus *máyì gbɔ*, literally "I come-go come-again," is "I shall go in the meantime." The verb *yi*, "to go," after another verb of motion, means "towards." The verb *vá*, "to come," may also mean "here" or "hither." And strangely enough, *kpɔ*, "to see," if placed after another verb, serves as the adverb "ever." Thus: *ède afíma kpɔà*, "Were you ever there?" is literally: "You were there see there?"

Nouns and prepositions show the same chameleon quality, shifting functions as do verbs and prepositions. The single syllable ŋgɔ, we are told, has the meanings, "front," "place before," "surface of liquids," "future time," "before," "for-

---

[3] The accents indicate pitch: *é* is high, *á* middle, *è* or *e* low, *ê* falling and *ě* rising. This is Westermann's system. See note at end of this chapter.

wards," "in front." And *tá* has the bewildering versatility enabling it to function as "head," "skull," "intelligence," "point," "peak," "upper end," "edge," "part," "kind," and many other nouns, as well as the prepositions "over," "above," "on account of," "because." (The Irish word *ciann*, "head," also has prepositional uses, as we have seen.)

INFLECTIONS UNNECESSARY

The inflections proper in Ewe turn out, likewise, to be little more than words juxtaposed. The grammar by Westermann, written for Europeans, gives an impressive list of forms or conjugations for the verb, with learned appellations. At first glance you might suppose you were about to learn a subtly inflected temporal system like the Greek. Let us look at these formations for a moment, however, and see if they really deserve the names given them.

First there is the inflection called by Westermann "aorist" (from the Greek "indefinite past" tense), which, he admits, does not indicate any particular time. It can be past, present, or future according to context, but it is usually a vague past. Hence it has no similarity with "aorist" as applied to Greek verbs, where it meant a definite time. If Ewe *yi* is "to go," then "aorist" *meyi* means "I go, I went, I shall go." If *wɔ-dɔ* is "to do work," then *mewɔ dɔ* means "I work, worked, shall work." There is a delightful indefiniteness about such statements. Only when time relations are really important to the speaker or listener are they made clear—and then by the use of attached elements which are themselves independent words only slightly disguised. The "future" (to use our term) is formed by prefixing *vá*, assimilated to *á* after the pronoun, meaning "to come." *Máyì* is "I come-go" for "I shall go"; *máwɔ dɔ* is "I come-do work" for "I shall do work."

Other so-called conjugations or forms have been given impressive names by the grammarians of Ewe, and yet on their own account they show these to be combinations of words rather than tenses. The "habitual" form, to indicate action often repeated (like eating meals) adds a second verb, *na* or *nɔ*, "to be, to stay" after the main one. *Meyina,* "I usually go" is literally "I go-stay" or "stay going." The "progressive" means continuous action as in English, and as in English it uses a form of "to be" -*le*- with the main verb. The latter is reduplicated, and there is a suffix -*m* (used as a vowel). So we get *mele yiyim,* "I am going"; *mele wɔwɔm,* "I am doing." The "ingressive" or "intentional" creates a form like *mele yiyi gé,* "I am in the neighborhood of going"; the "cohortative" uses *ná* "to give" or *vá* "to come" as English would say "let me, let us . . ." do something.

The inflections of nouns should no more be regarded as declensions, probably, than the verbs should be thought of as having tense and conjugation in our sense. In Ewe, the plural is indicated by saying *wo,* "they," after the simple noun. The noun itself does not change, so it is probably unjust to speak of it as either singular or plural. It just exists. If for "houses" we said "house-they" we would have the same effect in English. *Ati* is "tree," and so *atúwo* is "trees"; *χɔ* is house and *χɔwó* is "houses." There is no case; the juxtaposition of words indicates relationship. Possession is expressed by a word *ʃe,* meaning something like "belong." *Fia ʃé χɔ* is "chief belong house" or "the chief's house."

Looking back over Ewe sentence structure, we can see how little scope it offers for the terminology of old-fashioned grammar as we have learned it from Latin. To give a true impression one should simply say of the verb forms, for instance: "Use *ná,* 'to give' or *vá* 'to come' if you want to suggest that something should be done." Of course this is roundabout; but it conveys the informal structure of Ewe better than an imposing term like "cohortative." It is difficult to clear our minds of the old Latin patterns, but it is quite necessary to do so if we are to feel our way in a language like Ewe.

To a greater or less degree this is true of many other languages. One more may be cited to provide further illustration. In Malay, we are assured by Winstedt, it is actually unscientific to try to classify words even as subject forms and predicate forms, after the fashion of earlier grammarians. Here too the function is imparted to a word entirely by its context. It is as much a chameleon as the Ewe word. These few examples will show how it takes on grammatical coloring from its surroundings:

tengah, having the general sense of "midst, mediate, middle" in—
  tengah hari, "mid-day"
  orang tengah, "umpire, man of mediation"
  potong tengah, "to cut in halves"
  tengah tidor, "whilst sleeping, in midst of sleep"

děkat, in general sense of "nearness"—
  rumah děkat, "neighboring house"
  děkat rumah, "near to a house"
  děkat habis, "nearly done, approaching completion"
  ia děkat, "he is near"

dalam, in general sense of "depth"—
  dalam rumah, "interior of a house"
  tělaga dalam, "deep well"
  dalam pěhan, "in the town"

In combinations like *rumah děkat,* as contrasted with *děkat rumah,* the word order is the only clue to grammatical function.[4]

WORD ORDER

We too depend on word order to a certain extent, as we have seen, in speaking English. To get an analogous example of position to show function, think of "jelly fish" as opposed to "fish jelly." The word that comes first is regarded as the modifier of the second; the opposite happens to be true in Malay. "Smoother surface" in English means one that has been com-

---

4 Malay does have some suffixes, however, which also indicate grammatical function. The ending *-nya* shows that a noun has been formed from an adjective: *běsar,* "big"; *běsar-nya,* "bigness, size"; *běsar nya rumah,* "size of the house."

pared with another in respect to smoothness; but "surface smoother" might mean an object used in planing surfaces.

Conventions of speaking within the several language communities are usually consistent enough to prevent any ambiguity. English is not always quite clear in these matters, however; perhaps Malay does better in avoiding such doubtful expressions as our phrase "the committee reports." This might be a statement consisting of a subject and a verb indicating that the committee is making a statement at the moment. But it might also be a noun phrase, the equivalent of "reports delivered by the committee"—especially if it occurs in a headline. Von der Gabelentz has given an example from Chinese of the way in which position alone (as often with us) shows the grammatical function of a word:

> wáng paò mín: king *protects* people;
> mîn paò: people *is protected*;
> mîn paò iǔ wáng: people *is protected* by king.

ALIEN INFLECTIONS

But some non-Indo-European languages *are* inflected, highly inflected. There is no intent to deny this. There is a certain danger, though, that we may read into alien inflections irrelevant concepts from our own language. This too is often done. Such a false approach puts up a barrier between ourselves and the people we are trying to understand. Besides, it often makes the job of learning far more difficult than it need be.

Take the verb, for instance. If I were to ask you what concept leaps to your mind most readily in connection with verbal forms, you would probably say, "Time." Principal parts of verbs exist so that we can discriminate time relations. The notions of temporality and verbality are inextricably connected in our heads. We who speak English assume that the question of paramount importance in verbal inflections is the determination of the time of an action in relation to other times of action, present, past, and so on.

VERBS WITHOUT TENSES

But this is not necessarily so. Intricate verbal inflections can exist which ignore or subordinate the notions of present, past, future, and perfect. The Ewe language may serve as an example, as we have seen. Person and number are also dispensable in a verbal system. In fact, there is little left of person or number in English. Other matters may be stressed instead. When a lad says in English "I am taking this girl out," his verbal form alone indicates that he is doing the action continuously and in the present; it also indicates—apart from the subject—that it is he, the *speaker,* who is doing it, since "am" could not go with "you" or "he." But his English *verb* neglected to indicate specifically that it was a masculine person speaking, or that a specifically feminine human object was about to be designated as the creature taken, instead of a book (let us say) being passively removed from the library. In other languages, however, the phrase equivalent to "am taking" might tell you of the speaker's masculinity, and of his preoccupation with a human object, and also of the repetitive nature of his assiduous "taking out,"—but it would leave you in some doubt about the time of the taking. The mode of the action and the nature of the recipient would be stressed, but not its temporal relations.

It is an instructive experience to try to set aside traditional English concepts about verbs and look at others with a fresh gaze. At this point only the briefest of excursions is possible, to be sure. Here are the examples: enough, at least, to convince anyone that grammar is a coy and elusive muse, too fickle even to have a name in mythology.

PRONOUNS WITH TENSE

In Mende (a Sudanese African language), a chief method of showing change of tense is by inflecting—not primarily the verb, but by "conjugating," if you will, the personal pronoun. A person speaking of himself in relation to present or future action says ηga_3; [5] negation of such action requires $nge{:}_{3\text{-}2}$; if he is talking about himself in relation to present action that is continuous, the "I" becomes $n\gamma a{:}_{3\text{-}2}$ for a positive statement and $\eta gi{:}_{3\text{-}2}$ for a negative. When the deed occurred in past time the "I" is ηgi_4 (positive) and $\eta gi{:}_{3\text{-}2}$ (negative). One can imagine that a naughty child or adult might find exculpation easier in Mende than it is in English. It is as if the Mende native were saying: "Yes, I *did* that some time ago; but I was a different 'me' at the time." There are also suffixes to indicate different tenses in the verb; but the pronoun has, so to speak, already announced them before the verb is spoken, thus:

ηga_4	wa_3	I come	ηgi_4	$wa_2 i_3 l\math905_2$	I came
ba_4	wa_3	you come	bi_4	$wa_2\ i_3\ l\math905_2$	you came
a_2	wa_3	he comes	i_2	$wa_2 i_3 l\math905_2$	he came
ma_4	wa_3	we come	mu_4	$wa_2\ i_3 l\math905_2$	we came
wa_4	wa_3	you come	wu_4	$wa_2\ i_3 l\math905_2$	you come
ta_4	wa_3	they come	ti_4	$wa_2\ i_3 l\math905_2$	they came

In Aneiteum, a dialect of Melanesian, the pronoun is also "conjugated" to show time. In Japanese, by the way, *adjectives* appear to show tense.

Verbs with Nominal Cases

In some languages a verb is really indistinguishable from a noun and is treated as one. When an individual wishes to express his relation to the action or being of a verb, he is really putting himself into a state of possession towards it. He says "My loving!" instead of "I love," or (more sadly) "My having loved!" instead of "I have loved." This sort of locution may appear fragmentary to us, but only because we are not accustomed to it. It need not sound the least bit tentative to those who are accustomed to hear such declarations. The Nenets language ("Samoyedic" of Siberia) makes use of such

[5] The subscript numbers from 1 to 4 represent musical pitch, covering approximately a fifth in music. Two numbers with a given syllable indicate a musical slur from one note to another.

a construction in making verbal statements where the action affects somebody or something as object. Compare the possessive endings attached to nouns with the identical endings attached to a transitive verb:

kula-ma:	"my crow"	*matuyua-ma:*	"I cut"
kula-ra:	"your crow"	*matuyua-ra:*	"you cut"
kula-du:	"his crow"	*matuyua-du:*	"he cuts"

Such usages in Nenets are of great help to students in reconstructing the probable verbal system of Primitive Uralic, since they represent archaic features lost in other Uralic languages. Maipure, an Indian dialect of Arawak (Orinoco), shows the same possessive treatment of the verb:

nu-ani:	"my son"	*nu-nawa:*	"I see; my see"
pi-ani:	"thy son"	*pi-nawa:*	"thou seest; thy see"
ani:	"(his) son"	*nawa:*	"(he) sees; (his) see"

In some languages there is but a trace of the point of view that your actions (verbal forms) are things "possessed" by you. In Quiché (Maya Indian language of Guatemala) possessive pronouns *may* be used with nominal verb forms in place of a conjugation as we understand it, and possessive forms appear occasionally in place of regular subject particles in the verbal inflection. Instead of being an innovation, such forms may perhaps point back to a time when names of actions were regarded as nouns and *had* to be so treated. When pronouns in one form or another are loosely attached to verbs which do not themselves change, it is quite logical to speak of "declining" the verb instead of conjugating it. Thus Lucien Adam speaks of verbal "declensions" in the Manchu language. Certainly the suffixed endings of verbs bear a marked resemblance to the pronoun subjects. In the form *bi ara-ha-bi,* "I have written," the personal ending *-bi* is identical with the subject "I" when used alone. We may recall the nominal form *amamini* in Latin, mentioned above. It too resembles an inflection not typical of verb forms.

ADJECTIVAL VERBS WITH GENDER

Another way of presenting a verb is to make it into an adjective that agrees with the subject. In other words, instead of saying "I love" or "My loving," you say: "I, the loving one" or "I, the having-loved one." Such a form is more understandable to us, with our linguistic prejudices, if we say to ourselves: "The verb 'am' is understood between 'I' and the adjectival 'loving.' It is a shortened way of saying, 'I am loving.' " Hebrew verbs in the present tense really do something like this. Hence they are inflected for gender. "He-learning" (with the "is" unexpressed) is *hū lōmēd;* "she-learning" is *hī lōmēdah.* With our own linguistic prejudices we may find it hard to understand why a different verbal form is needed when a "she" is learning, as distinct from the form for a "he." It is the attitude towards the verb which is involved, not any discrimination, necessarily, between the respective powers of girls and boys in learning.

THE LIVING AND THE NON-LIVING IN VERB FORMS

If English-speaking persons think it strange to express gender in relation to verbs, there are other still stranger categories which are to be found in the verbal systems of other languages. In Nahuatl (Modern Aztec), for instance, it is felt to be necessary to express in advance, in certain verbal forms, whether the object of the action affects a person or an inanimate object. To us speakers of English, it is verbally indifferent whether we say "I *look at* the pretty child" or "I *look at* the pretty dress." We make no distinction. The more circumspect Aztec warns you beforehand what sort of object is fixing his attention. If it's human, he prefixes *te-* to certain verb forms; if non-human, *tla-.* If, for example, the verb is "to eat," with the root *cua,* the Aztec hastens to prefix *tla-* in order to assure you he is not a cannibal! A mistake in this delicate matter might give a most unfortunate impression. The distinction is clearest in verbal nouns like *te-tlazohtlani,* "one who loves [people],'' as contrasted with *tla-tlazohtlani,* "one who loves [things]"; *tla-machtilli,* "pupil," is one who is concerned with the act of learning in relation to things, while *te-machtihqui,* "teacher," is one who is concerned with learning in relation to people.

Transitive and Intransitive Forms

Another distinction expressed in advance by the Nahuatl verb is the one between actions which involve an object and those which do not. In English we say "I sleep" and "I cut meat" with no outward sign that there is any grammatical difference between the intransitive and the transitive verbs. Nahuatl makes a difference in the personal prefixes of the two types of verbs. The signal is the presence or absence of a *k*-sound at the end of the verbal prefixes which indicate person:

1. *nehua ni-cochi* "I sleep"   *nehua nic-tequi* "I cut [an object]"
2. *tehua ti-cochi* "you sleep"   *tehua tic-tequi* "you cut [an object]"
3. *yehua   cochi* "he sleeps"   *yehua qui-tequi* "he cuts [an object]"

and so on. A distinction between transitive and intransitive is also made in the verbs of the Dravidian languages of Southern India. In these latter tongues several devices are listed by the grammarians as methods by which an intransitive verb may be made transitive: the final consonant of the root is made voiceless, or a particle is added, or the initial consonant of the tense suffix is made voiceless. No doubt an outsider learning to speak Tamil, for instance (one of the Dravidian languages), could make himself clear even if he violated these fine distinctions, but he would be regarded as an awkward barbarian in his mistreatment of conventional patterns.

It will be seen from these few examples that verbs, or what we call verbs, may be required to express many ideas in addition to time, mood, and voice familiar to us. This does not mean that time relations are quite neglected in most of the language families remote from Indo-European, or that all aborigines of lands distant from Europe show a noteworthy indifference to present, past, and future. The Sudanese Chi chewa is very specific about the range of time represented in some of his tense forms. For instance:

1. Non-committal present tense: *nikú dja,* "I am eating."
2. Recent past with present influence. This applies to action occurring any time between the night before and the moment of speaking. It appears to be included in any statement of present situation which arose recently. Thus *na·dja* means "I have eaten recently; the effects of the eating still hold; hence I am not hungry now"—all implied in one verbal form.
3. Recent past without present influence. The effect of the action has worn off. Hence, *ṇná·dja* means "I have eaten, but that doesn't do me any good now—I'm hungry!"
4. Remote past with present influence. This refers to action occurring before the preceding night. "I have eaten (some time ago) and therefore I'm not hungry now."
5. Remote past without present influence: "I have eaten some time ago but now it's all over—I'm hungry."
6. Past descriptive and habitual: "I was eating, I used to eat."

This is much more elaborately explicit than anything we are accustomed to. When a verb tells you sharply just when the effect of a preceding action (like eating) has ceased, you must supply in your own mind, it appears, the action or state that replaces it. To employ a concept like "eating," you must be ready to supply the complementary one of "being hungry." Chichewa requires this perpetual contrasting of actions and states.

Aspects of Verbs

As for our own Indo-European verbal tenses, although we now regard them as aspects of time, they may at an earlier date have expressed something else. The oldest type of tense change in Indo-European is represented by verbs like "drink—drank," with an internal vowel-change. The "present" tense was associated with a high front vowel, and the "past" with a low back one. A similar association has been remarked in the Semitic languages. Perhaps the vowel changes involve a sound symbolism which contrasted things near in place as well as time, with things far away in place as well as time. (Perhaps, indeed, place was the relationship to be designated before time was involved in the matter.) "It is an empiric fact," says Prokosch, "that high oral resonance is apt to be accompanied by high tension of the vocal cords, low resonance by their relaxation, so that resonance and vocal pitch generally, though not necessarily, coincide. . . . Now, muscle tension implies interest, and in speech this holds true especially for the tension of the vocal cords. It would seem, then, that the IE [Indo-European] 'present tense' is fundamentally the expression of interest in an action going on and is expressed by articulation with tense vocal cords favoring the selection of a front vowel. Inversely, forms of rather abstract, remote meaning, such as verbal nouns, tend towards relaxation of the vocal cords and, indirectly, towards back vowels."

NEARNESS AND DISTANCE

Wundt suggested some years ago that vowel position and vowel pitch had grammatical meaning in early languages because they could thus symbolize contrasted states. Not only nearness and present time would normally be implied by high position, but also activity and other qualities like it; low position would imply distance, past time, passivity, and related concepts. Von der Gabelentz pointed out that sounds from a distance have a deeper, lower quality than those heard near at hand. From this he explained the vowel change in expressions like "bing, bang"; "ding, dong"; "rim, ram, ruff"; "tick, tock," and so on. These in turn are related as are the tense forms of a verb like "drink, drank, drunk." In nursery language the same type of sound symbolism is sometimes employed spontaneously, in coined names and expressions. Therefore it is not difficult to surmise an original connection between the ideas "here—close to me—now" contrasted with "there—far away—then." Temporal and deictic (i.e., "pointing-out") categories are associated in gesture: a motion with the right thumb backwards over the right shoulder may mean "before now" as well as "back there."

MASCULINE AND FEMININE

Some of our other abstract grammatical distinctions may go back to more elemental ones like "near" as opposed to "far." The classical languages and some of the modern ones most familiar to us make use of a category known as gender with which we inevitably associate ideas of sex. This can scarcely be otherwise, since as school children we are taught to classify nouns as masculine, feminine, and neuter. But we have already seen, in reviewing the characteristics of Latin grammar, that the distinctions according to sex are not always carried out. They are present, to be sure, in a pair of words like *dominus— domina,* where the distinction is precisely the same as in the corresponding English words "master—mistress." We have noticed, however, that very masculine words like "farmer" and "sailor" are assigned to the so-called feminine Latin declension and so we were led to surmise that the distinction was once of a general demonstrative character having nothing to do with sex. Let us see how other languages handle gender and kindred distinctions.

In the first place, some languages are quite innocent of any *formal* division of words according to sex. Yet the biological distinction may be important for practical reasons in talking (for instance) about domestic animals, fowl, and so forth. In such cases, the speaker of a genderless language attaches another word to the common noun in order to make his meaning clear. The same effect is obtained in the Biblical English expression "he-goats and she-goats." Another method would have been to say "goats-male and goats-female." In Nahuatl, the useful distinction is made by prefixing the words for "man" and "woman" respectively. Thus, if *tototl* is "bird" in the general sense, *oquich-tototl* means "male bird" and *cihua-tototl* means "female bird."

In Manchu there is a very limited place for gender as a grammatical distinction. Most nouns do not show it, but the beginnings of grammatical gender according to sex do appear in certain words. Here, curiously enough, the distinction is expressed by change of vowel *within* the word (vowel gradation), not by a suffix. For instance:

haha, "man"	*hehe,* "woman"
amba, "older brother"	*ambu,* "older sister"
amila, "male bird"	*emile,* "female bird"

Since, however, the same sort of internal vowel change distinguishes verbs with opposite meanings (*wasime,* "descend" and *wesime,* "mount"), it is doubtful whether sexual contrast is the basic, original one intended.

Living and Non-living, Rational and Irrational in Nouns

In place of gender according to sex we often find other distinctions elaborated. Animate objects (regardless of sex) are sometimes sharply set off from inanimate; shape is sometimes designated carefully while more urgent matters (to our way of thinking) are ignored. In Potawatomi (an Algonquian Indian dialect), the generic distinction of nouns as animate or inanimate objects is also carried into the verb, which must observe the distinction of the subject. In Dravidian dialects the chief division of nouns is into two classes, according as the subjects possess reason or do not. The former, including celestial and infernal deities and human beings, show, in the singular, attributes of sex gender which are of comparatively recent date. The second class, on the other hand, includes creatures and objects destitute of reason, whether animate or inanimate. It is worth noting that native Telugu grammarians designate the "rational" category as majors and the "non-rational" as minors; while Tamil grammarians use the terms (borrowed from class distinctions) of "high-caste" and "casteless." An interesting study could be made of the assignment of creatures and things to "higher" and "lower" categories in those languages which use types of evaluations like "high" and "low" in place of gender.

SIZE AND NUMBER

Distinctions of size sometimes overlap other generic distinctions. In Latin it was possible to indicate small size as well as gender by the modified endings *-illus* (masculine) and *-illa* (feminine). Modern Italian is unusually rich among European languages in suffixes that indicate bigness and littleness: *libro,* "book"; *libretto,* "little book"; *librone,* "big book." (All these words have gender as well. They are masculine.) In some languages reduplication is used to intensify the concept of size or number, whether to aggrandize or diminish. Compare the infantile form "teeny-weeny." In the Solomon Isles, where a Melanesian language is spoken, reduplication is used to designate a wild fruit as opposed to the same species cultivated. In the Polynesian languages reduplication is used for so many different purposes, as a matter of fact, that it cannot be compared with any single category in our grammar. In Hawaiian, *poo* is "head," but *poopoo* is a ball of oval shape; *lima* is either "five" or "hand" (the semantic connection is clear), but *lima-lima* is "handle." In Mangarevan (another dialect of Polynesian) *rakau* is "tree," but *rakarakau* is "branch."

Number is one of the many categories which can be expressed by reduplication. To repeat a word is one very obvious way of indicating plurality. In nursery talk there may be partial reduplication as well as a plural ending: "piggy-wiggies." We are accustomed to think of two grammatical numbers only: singular and plural; one "house" as opposed to a "muchness of houses." At an older period English, like other Indo-European languages, had a dual as well as a singular and plural number. There was a special way of saying "we two" or "you two" in one word. Sanskrit had dual forms for all nouns and adjectives and verbal conjugations. Micronesian has even more: singular, dual, trial, and quatrial forms! There is nothing obligatory or universal about the limitation of number to the two forms we know.

INCLUSIVE AND EXCLUSIVE

A special aspect of number is interesting from the point of view of human psychology. Some languages make a sharp distinction in the plural pronouns (first and second persons) between "inclusive" and "exclusive" forms. It is one thing to say "we" including the person addressed: that is, "you and I" or "you and these others." But it is another thing to exclude him: "I and these others—*not* you." The latter seems a bit snobbish to us who are not accustomed to it. Spanish uses only the exclusive pronouns in the two plurals: *nosotros, vosotros,* literally "we others," "you others." Manchu has a special inclusive first plural pronoun: *muse,* "we including you." In one of the Munda languages, Santal, spoken in southeastern India, the forms are:

	Inclusive	Exclusive
1st pl.	*bo, bon:* "we and you"	*le, lo,* etc.: "we without you."
2nd pl.	[lacking]	*pe:* "you without us"
1st dual	*lang:* "I with thee"	*pen, ping:* "we two without you (thee)"

The so-called case-endings of nouns are also capable of varied treatment. We have observed repeatedly how particles of demonstrative and adverbial significance can be loosely appended to words. Often they appear to us as prepositions misplaced. In such languages it is as if one said "morning-from, evening-to" instead of "from morning to evening." Probably students find it easier to learn the suffixes as loose postpositions than to memorize a case name for every possible suffix. Finnish grammars for English readers might well present the matter in this fashion, avoiding if possible the awe-inspiring names (modeled on Latin grammar) for the fifteen "cases"—inessive, elative, illative, adessive, ablative, allative, and so on. The mere learning of these names of cases requires a considerable effort, better devoted to the words themselves.

AGREEMENT IN GRAMMAR

When the student of an inflected language has learned his conjugations and inflections, there is still one very important problem left. He must discover what words "agree" or correspond to others in the sentence, by expressing the same grammatical category. To go back to the child who still lisps in isolated words, "Baby want go walk," we feel that something is wrong with them because the verb doesn't remind us that (as we already know) the subject is singular. This rare instance of openly expressed agreement is tenacious in English speech. Other verb forms have lost the endings which formerly expressed agreement with the subject.

There is no particular reason why a verb should agree with its subject if another means, such as word order, can show that it is the baby and not someone else who does the wanting. Other languages demand agreements unknown to ours which naturally appear superfluous to us. The French participial forms in perfect tenses agree with preceding pronoun objects. If a man is talking of some girls and says "I have seen them," he knows the feminine gender (here identified with sex) of "them," and makes "seen" agree with it: *Je les ai vues*. If the object had been men or boys he would have said: *Je les ai vus*. It must be added, however, that spelling alone makes the distinction. It was once indicated in the spoken sounds as well; but today there is no difference in pronunciation.

The oldest Indo-European languages demanded complex agreements throughout a sentence. All forms—demonstratives, adjectives, nouns—referring to the same object in identical relationship were obliged to show this by their endings. But even this obligation was much less burdensome than similar requirements in some non-Indo-European languages.

COMPLEX AGREEMENTS OUTSIDE OF INDO-EUROPEAN

In Bantu, for instance, the concord class to which a subject noun belongs is expressed not only in the noun itself, but in adjectives, verbs, verbal objectives, and other qualificatives. When you have launched on a Bantu sentence you are kept firmly moored to the basic nominal concept with which you began. Here is an example from the Chichewa dialect:

a-sirikali	βá·káli	βát-ámiŋg git·tsa	βa-ná	βábú·li
policemen	angry	they are chasing	children	innocent

βá·-ká·li   (from βáβá-ká·li)
they them   are catching.

The prefix *a-* (alternate form for *βa-*) at the beginning of the first word shows that we have to do with the plural of a noun of class 1, which happens to contain a number of names for persons. (The word "Bantu" itself is one of them.) It will be clear at a glance that this prefix in its fuller form is echoed throughout the sentence. There is little chance to forget what sort of noun began the exciting narrative. Perhaps the Bantu people have a sharper sense of syntax, or sentence organization, than we have; but of course it is an acquired sense, learned in the act of mastering the native tongue. The elaborate co-ordinations come to them without reflection. But to outsiders like ourselves, who have to learn such forms and rules if we wish to use the language, the elaboration must appear little short of terrifying.

COMPARATIVE GRAMMAR AND HUMAN VALUES

There has been a double value, I hope, in the presentation of sample usages in grammar, culled from various parts of the world, which differ widely from our own. For one thing, the bewildered reader may return home to English with an increased sense of gratitude for its comparative simplicity. For another, he may have been able to free himself of some of the natural prejudices with which anyone starts out when he begins to study alien tongues. Because of his own speech habits, every learner is prone to begin with such ideas as: "Every verb *must* agree with its subject," or "All nouns have gender," or "All verbs have tenses." The sooner he divorces himself from these prejudices the better, especially if he is going to work on some of the remoter languages. In addition he may be greatly helped if he attempts to put himself into a sympathetic frame of mind towards the new language. Instead of saying: "Aren't these foreigners funny? They conjugate pronouns!" he will do well to say: "So they conjugate pronouns. Why not? The person speaking *was* different last year, and he will be different again a year from now." This more sympathetic attitude will be of practical assistance in so far as it will aid in the mere mechanical effort to master paradigms. And more than that: it will make the learner at the same time a more humane person; more deeply aware of underlying kinships within the human race despite all linguistic barriers; better able to understand the fraternity of all of us who are speaking animals. The ability to apprehend a very different type of grammar does something to your imagination. Sympathetically pursued, linguistics can be a truly humane study.

7. Kaleidoscope of Sound

GUESSING WORDS FROM SOUNDS

Over and over you must have had an experience like this. You have, let us say, been devoting a certain amount of your already crowded time to the acquisition of some Spanish, in order to equip yourself for the more savory enjoyment of a coming holiday in Cuba. Being a normal American you are terribly "rushed"; you must economize time in every way, and make every minute devoted to your hedonistic pursuit of Spanish repay you to the full. So you impress into service all similarities and relationships which will save you time and effort in memorizing new forms. When your teacher tells you that the "perfect passive participle of verbs ending in *-ar* is formed with *-ado*," you think of our English loan word "incommunicado" which indicates a most unhappy degree of passivity; the suffix "clicks" with something you already know, and you are ready to leap ahead to the next fact. Your teacher adds: "Feminine forms of this participle end in *-ada*." Again you summon up an English word, "Armada," with its memories of the Spanish threat to Queen Elizabeth's expanding empire, and you nod intelligently, even impatiently, so obvious is the fact to you. Later in the lesson you encounter the word *oscuridad*. Falling back on your vague reminiscences of high-school Latin, you realize that this abstract noun, like many others in Spanish with the ending *-dad*, must come from the inflected Latin case suffix *-tate*, as in *obscuritate*, English "obscurity." Likewise the participial endings *-ado*, *-ada* must have come from Latin forms with [t] between the vowels.

So you begin to guess, whenever you see or hear an intervocalic (between-vowel) [d] in Spanish, that *perhaps* it represents a [t] between vowels in a word already familiar to you in English or Latin. (The better for you if you know both.)

Then you find yourself in Havana at last, with many opportunities presented to your eye and ear to test out your ability in perceiving Spanish and English sound relations. One day you are standing on a street corner, and your eyes turn to the label on an approaching bus. You are skeptical about the legend marking its destination, but as it approaches you along the Malecón you realize that it does indeed read as you had thought: Vedado. And your mind, by now trained to analysis of such forms, provides the following commentary: "If those *d*'s have the usual history, the word comes from an earlier *vetato,* corresponding to Latin *vetatum,* 'that which is forbidden.' It is the verb familiar to us in the phrase '*veto a law.*' As a place-name one would expect it to mean Paradise."

If you inquire of a Cuban friend, he will assure you that there *is* a reason for the name. In colonial times, a certain part of the city was marked off and forbidden *(vedado)* to slaves. It was like the "Pale" in medieval Dublin, forbidden to the native Irish. Hence the puzzling and alluring name. Your amateur etymology was quite accurate. It was only insufficient knowledge of the historical background which left you puzzled.

Adults who learn new languages are constantly looking for such guides to help them guess the meanings of new words. Older children do so to a certain extent too, and they are surprisingly grateful for hints enabling them to discover such relations. High school teachers are often amazed at the responsiveness of pupils to any explanation that "makes sense" out of dull rules and paradigms.

CHANGES IN SOUNDS

The behavior of Latin *t*'s in Spanish words illustrates, then, a principle of linguistic change that has very practical value for the student. It can be paralleled in many other languages. There are about a dozen such principles, very easy to learn, which serve repeatedly as short cuts in understanding, and therefore in memorizing, new forms. When you understand why and how *vedado* is related to "veto," the word used by Roman tribunes and presidents of the United States to prevent passage of a law, then you are much less apt to forget it. The reason why *t*'s become *d*'s will be explained in its place. The curious thing about these general tendencies is that they exist in pairs, each one usually being accompanied by its opposite. Of course it is most unlikely that a given tendency (such as voicing of consonants in certain positions) should be accompanied by its opposite (unvoicing of consonants in other positions) to the same degree at the same time within any given language. In general one or the other tendency predominates and the opposite one is distinctly subsidiary.

Assimilation and Dissimilation

Assimilation is one of the tendencies most easily recognized, and it is one of those most often encountered. It simply means that unlike sounds are apt to be made more similar, especially if they form a group in juxtaposition which is hard to pronounce. Even the Russian tongue, which ordinarily surmounts the most bristling clusters of consonants easily, is balked at a combination like *'solntse,* "sun," and habitually simplifies it to *'sontse* in ordinary speech.

Colloquial English is full of assimilations. We hear "gimme," "wanna," "lemme," "govemment" for "give me," "want to," "let me," "government." What happens is that the speaker's eager thought, leaping ahead to the sounds about to come, causes him to put his speech organs in position for them before the due moment. As a result he anticipates.[1] He may make a slight abortive motion in the direction of the final consonants in "give," "let," but the sound doesn't come forth,

---

[1] For a simpler account of this change in non-technical language see the Preface, p. viii.

though he may imagine he actually made it. The same psychological tendency to leap ahead causes us to misspell words in typing by anticipating a coming letter too soon.

Other languages give even more abundant examples than English. Italian is full of them: *Absoluto has become assoluto; *Hectore has become Ettore; *nocte, notte; *exacto, esatto; *Septembre, Settembre. In many European languages a spelling with a so-called double consonant indicates that assimilation was once at work. Spanish has simplified these doubled letters; it writes comisionar where we have "to commission." In Italian, on the other hand, the spelling is not only preserved but the doubled consonant is actually prolonged in speech. Our English words with such spellings which come from Latin are a historical record of assimilations which took place long ago, before the heyday of classical literature. Thus "assimilation" itself must go back to an old form *adsimilatio; "possible" to an older *potsibile (with a root like the one in "potent"), and so on.

Sometimes the assimilation is only partial. Two dissimilar sounds are made more like, but they do not become identical. If a form like *in-possible existed in early Latin, it was modified to the familiar im-possible by the approximation of unlike sounds. For the same reason we say "Stamford" instead of "Stanford," and "Pemberton" for "Penberton." We say "Dambury" though the official spelling is "Danbury." The dental nasals [n] have been made into labial nasals [m] in anticipation of the coming labials [f] and [b]. We know that assimilation has been at work here because other words preserve the consonants of the prefixed syllables in unmodified form. "Stam-" is a form of "stone" and "Pem-" is a form of "Penn," the Welsh word for "head."

The usual tendency of assimilation is regressive: that is, the sound causing the change works backward on an earlier one. This may happen, by the way, to sounds not juxtaposed, but separated by intervening syllables. You can easily slip up on "Massachusetts" and make it "Mashachusetts" (partial assimilation), or change "blatant brigandage" into "bratant bringandage." Latin *quinque* thus came from an older form **penque*. But sometimes it is the later consonant that is modified. In English we affix an ending -*d* or -*t* to our weak verbs, depending on the sound at the end of the root word: "dreamed" and "seemed" beside "leapt," "slept." The voiced sound is the older one; when you find [t] it is because of a *progressive* influence exerted by a voiceless consonant like [p] on the sound following. In this way Latin *collis,* "a hill," whence French *colline,* was derived from older **colnis.*

Vowels can be assimilated also. Just as your tongue anticipates the position of a coming consonant, it will anticipate the level of a coming vowel. It will fail to go as high or low as it should, because of the foreknowledge you have of the position of the next vowel. So in pronouncing the expletive "Gemini!"—the twin gods by whom the Romans swore—we say "Jiminy!" We don't drop our tongues from [i] to [e] in pronouncing the second syllable of "irresistible"; here the effect would be the same whether the influence were progressive or regressive. In any event we say [ɪɹɪ'zɪstəbl̩]. In Primitive Germanic the plural form for "man," namely **maniz,* was eventually changed to **meniz* (whence our plural "men") by partial assimilation of the [ɑ] towards the [i]. This type of vowel change is called *umlaut* by specialists. It is simply a form of vowel assimilation. The same tendency caused Latin *similis* ("like") to develop out of older **semilis,* and a prehistoric Germanic **esti* to become German *ist,* "is." The plurals of German nouns which show *umlaut* or vowel change can be explained by this anticipatory movement of the tongue in forming vowel sounds. Originally the vowels of the endings caused the changes. Vowel harmony, which we have observed in Magyar and Finno-Ugric, is a form of progressive vowel assimilation.

Dissimilation, obviously the opposite tendency, results from a wish to avoid too many similar sounds. Speed and a desire for facility or simplification will take us just so far towards a leveling of our sounds, but the tendency does not go unchecked. We want variety too. It is as difficult to enunciate a series of too-similar sounds accurately as it is to produce a cluster of very dissimilar ones. If you doubt this, try saying one of the well-known tongue-twisters like "Peter picked a peck of pickled peppers." Even at a moderate tempo you will feel the tendency to dissimilate against your will.

A series of liquids [l, r] and (or) nasals [m, n, ŋ] is most apt to cause trouble. One way of diversifying them is to introduce ordinary stop-consonants within the monotonous series. That is why we say "tender" from Latin *tener*, "timber" from an older form "timmer" (still used without [b] in Dutch), and "remainder" where you would expect a noun "remainer" from the verb. Popular pronunciations like "fam*b*ly" and "chim*b*ley" illustrate the same tendency. French has introduced extra consonants in words like *plaindre, nombre, peindre,* which lacked them originally.

Another way of avoiding monotony in sounds is to omit one of the offending liquids or nasals, as in the English "feeble" derived from Latin *flebilis* ("something to weep about") or the Spanish name Federico from an older Frederico. Or else the full number of sounds may be retained, except that one is shifted to become less like the others. Thus, "turtle" was dissimilated from Latin *turtur*. Finally, several forms of dissimilation may occur in the same word. English "marble," originating ultimately in Latin *marmor,* has changed the second [r] to [l], eliminated the second [m], and introduced a [b] to diversify the consonant group. The whole word now looks very different from the original simple reduplication. Spanish, too, has changed *homine* ("man") to *hombre* by dissimilating the second nasal to a liquid [r] and inserting [b] between them.

You will hear dissimilation, like other sound changes, exemplified in the momentary lapses of tired or preoccupied persons. They will say "Flederick" or "irreplessible" or "illogicary" or "merancholy" (a form often used in old French), or "testimory" despite themselves.

VOICING AND UNVOICING

Consonants are subject to another pair of influences working in opposite directions: voicing and unvoicing. As the words indicate, they refer to the changes in the use of vibration by the vocal cords.

Voicing occurs when the unvibrated sounds like [p], [t], [k] become [b], [d], [g]. There are two very common causes of this. One is assimilation, which we have already discussed; the other is a relaxation in the speech organs due to lack of stress. It takes more energy to pronounce a sharp voiceless sound. Hence consonants in unaccented syllables are particularly apt to slump into voicing. In colloquial English, "city" becomes ['sɪdɪ], "butter" becomes ['bʌdə], "committee" becomes [kə'mɪdɪ], even [gə'mɪdɪ]. Lack of stress in word or sentence caused the Spanish forms like *vedado* and *estado,* already mentioned, to develop out of **vetato* and **stato*. The ending became universal in time for all verbs. The same lack of stress also explains why Danish *tage* (pronounced with a voiced pallatal continuant [ĵ] in the second syllable) corresponds with English "take." Both come from an older Scandinavian form *taka*. English has kept the voiceless [k] in standard pronunciation, but one often hears "Take it away!" rendered as [teig ɪd e'weɪ]. The tendency for consonants to assume voicing when a strong stress accent does *not* fall on the preceding syllable is called "Verner's law" by specialists in Germanic philology. But it is by no means limited to Germanic languages. Old Irish, for instance, showed abundant examples of it.

Unvoicing is of course the opposite, and is frequently associated with strong stress on the consonant concerned. We do not have many examples of actual unvoicing in English,[2] but

[2] There are cases which at first glance might appear to be loss of voicing because of stress: for instance, the emphatic adverbial form "off" as compared to the unstressed form "of." However, it is the preposition which has changed in becoming voiced; the older form of *both* is preserved in the unvoiced [f] of the adverb.

in German and Russian the tendency is exemplified at the ends of words which are spelled with a voiced consonant. The spelling indicates the older pronunciation. In speaking, the sound is now given as the corresponding voiceless consonant. German *Hand* is pronounced [hɑnt], Russian *gorod* ("city") as ['gɔrɔt]. The tendency to do this is called in German by the imposing name of *Auslautsgesetz,* meaning "the law of final sounds." It explains the proneness of German Americans to speak in sentences like "I haff to liff" and "Giff me your hant" —a characteristic recognized and used freely by writers of dialect comedy.

VOCALIZATION AND CONSONANTIZATION

Just as consonants can change their nature with respect to the presence or absence of voicing, so they can become vowels, and vowels become consonants. In fact there is no sharp line of division between the two. Certain sounds like [m], [n], [l], [r] can, as we have seen, serve either as the one or the other.

Vocalization is the change by which a consonant becomes a vowel. In American speech the final *l*-sound is often pronounced as a [ʊ]. We say [weʊ] for "well" and [peiʊ] for "pale." Notice that in these cases the result is a diphthong, or even a triphthong, as the new vowel is pronounced in the same syllable as the original one. In the same way, an original [l] was vocalized in Old French words if another consonant followed. Our English words "altar" and "fault" correspond to French *autel* and *faute,* in which the spelling still indicates an earlier dipththong resulting from vocalized [l]. We have restored the *l*-sounds in English as a result of pedantic desire to go back to the Latin forms, *altaris* and **fallita;* this occurred in the Renaissance, when a mistaken zeal for Latinity distorted some of the words we had already adopted in their French forms. In our versions of "palm," "psalm" and others, we write the *l* but don't pronounce it. The French equivalents are *paume* and *psaume.*

Some languages vocalize [l] in a different fashion. In Italian, it becomes [i], or rather [j], between a consonant and a *following* vowel. Thus Latin *clamare* turns up as *chiamare* ("to call out"; compare English "clamorous"); *flamma* as *fiamma* ("flame"); *flore* as *fiore* ("flower"); and *plano* as *piano* (meaning "even, gentle, soft" or "plane").

Other sounds which vocalize readily are [r], and also the guttural [g] in various positions after it has been made a continuant [γ] or [j]. We have examples of [r] in modern English, where "there" is pronounced [ðɛ:ə]. It may be said that the [ə] is a vocalized survival of the [r]. As for the variations of [g] after a vowel, their history may be traced in English words derived from French. The Latin *legalis,* for instance, became French *leial,* later *loial.* We have both the older form and the vocalized one in our words "legal" and "loyal" respectively. In the same way *regalis* yields "regal" and "royal." The same transformation has produced the diphthong in our word "way" [wei] from an older *weg.* The sound [γ], voiced guttural continuant corresponding to [g], is apt to become [w], especially near a back vowel like [ɑ] or [ɔ]. Our "dawn" is derived from an older *dagan,* which meant "coming of day"; [3] our "bough" developed the diphthong still indicated by our spelling because of the *g* [γ] which has since been lost. Spanish *agua* is very close to [awa] in Mexico. The sounds [b] and [v] tend towards [u] in some languages. Spanish has *ausencia* for our "absence."

Consonantization, or the change from vowels to consonants, is comparatively rare. It can be detected in cases where two vowels come together in hiatus: that is, in separate syllables although no consonant stands between them. In the three-syllable word "poetic," there is a tendency to say "pwetic" ['pwetik]; "coöperate" also inclines to ['kwɑpəɹeit], and "Victoria" to [vik̑tɔ:ɹjɑ]. In the days of Vulgar Latin, words ending in *-ia* went the way of the last-named word. The last two syllables of

[3] The noun "day" itself is from an older *dæg.* Here the final consonant vocalized into [i] because the preceding vowel had been "fronted," or raised from [a] to [æ].

words like *gloria, historia,* and *memoria* apparently became
-*ja*. Even between two words one can hear consonantization:
"My eye" sounds like [maɪ jaɪ] because the off-glide of the "my"
assumes consonantal coloring before the initial vowel of the
noun. If it were to develop still farther it might become [dʒ]
or [ʒ], as the Latin word *maior* did in developing through
French into English "major" ['meɪdʒə]. The Russians have
chosen to consonantize the second element of diphthongs like
[aʊ] and [eu] appearing in foreign words. They say *avtor* for
"author" and *Evgenii* for our "Eugene." It is a transformation
which to us at least appears to be a change from the easier to
the harder pronunciation.

SHORTENING, LENGTHENING, AND
DIPHTHONGIZATION OF VOWELS

Certain changes affecting vowels alone have to do with their
length and their shifts back and forth between simple sounds
and diphthongs.

Shortening occurs when a vowel originally long is abbreviated. If you say "breakfast" as a noun you pronounce the first
vowel as a short sound; yet as a separate work "break" has a
long vowel, as in the verbal expression "to break one's fast."
For some time there has been a marked tendency in English
to pronounce vowels short in front of heavy consonant combinations. The first element in the word "husband" was once
identical with the word "house" (then pronounced [hu:s]);
the first in "wisdom" was identical with "wise" (then pronounced [wi:s]). So in modern German there is a noticeable
drift towards the shortening of [e] in the past tense *lebte,* "he
lived," although the present infinitive is *leben* with a long
accented vowel. Our own past tense form "crept" is related to
"creep" in precisely the same way.

Another very general cause of shortening is loss of stress.
So long as a syllable preserves an accent upon it, there is little
likelihood that its quantity will change, especially in a language like English. (That is, unless a consonant cluster of the

type just described exercises a shortening influence.) But if the same syllable loses its accent it is likely to be slurred and hence shortened. Pairs of related words in English illustrate this:

able	[ˈeɪbl̩]	beside	[əˈbɪlɪtɪ]
reform	[ɹɪˈfɔːm]	”	[ɹefɔˈmeɪʃn̩]
repute	[ɹɪˈpjuːt]	”	[ɹepjuˈteɪʃn̩]
dispute	[dɪsˈpjuːt]	”	[dɪspjuˈteɪʃn̩]
fate	[feɪt]	”	[fəˈtælɪtɪ]

Moreover, English possesses two forms of certain words pronounced long or short according as they are stressed or unstressed in the sentence. "The" and "a," for instance, were at one time pronounced with long vowels exclusively: [ði:] and [ɑː], later [ei]. More recently these were reduced to short syllables [ðə] and [ə] for all purposes except emphatic use. We say "the man" [ðə ˈmæn], but "Spell *the*" [spel ði:].

Lengthening, conversely, may be brought about by a shift of accent to a syllable formerly unstressed. The list just given illustrates lengthening as well as shortening. In some languages particular vowels are lengthened in an open accented syllable (i.e., a syllable in which the vowel is final, not "closed" by a consonant). The accented syllables in "shaken" and "undertaken" were originally short [ɑ], but because of their position they were lengthened. And just as certain awkward consonant clusters like -sd or -sb caused shortening, so other more pronounceable ones have caused lengthening. The vowels of English "wild," "blind," "climb" were originally short (as they still are in cognate words in modern German: *wild, blind, klimmen*), but combinations of liquids [l, r] or nasals [m, n, ŋ] plus voiced stops made with the same tongue position have caused lengthening in English.

A very common cause of lengthening is the loss of a consonant in the neighborhood of a vowel. This is known as compensatory lengthening. In a word like "far," when it is pronounced [fɑː], the loss of [r] has prolonged the [ɑ] sound.

In "light," once pronounced with the guttural as in German, the [i] was then short, but when the following consonant was eliminated it became [iː] and was later diphthongized to [aɪ].

Diphthongization occurred in the examples just cited after the vowels had lengthened. After the intermediate stage [wiːld, bliːnd, cliːmb] came Modern English [waɪld, blaɪnd, klaɪm]. The development of a diphthong out of a simple long pure sound is due apparently to a combination of physical and psychological causes. It is difficult to maintain our impatient speech organs in the same position for a markedly lengthened sound while our thoughts are hurrying ahead to the next one. It is also difficult to sing a long pure tone on the same musical note. The more the length is augmented the more apt we are to introduce qualitative variety. When someone says "Listen to me—e!" with a prolonged final vowel (let us say in comic distress), he diversifies it to [miːj] or [miːə]. Such minor shadings within a lengthened vowel are the first step towards diphthongization.

There are two common sources of diphthongs, therefore: an inner change in a vowel, and the development of a new vowel out of a neighboring consonant (vocalization). A third method is the development of a new glide sound between the vowel and a neighboring consonant even when the latter is retained. For instance, in local dialects "milk" becomes something like [miulk]. In Old English of the time of King Alfred, many consonants appeared with such glide-vowels before or after them, thus causing diphthongs (both short and long ones) to appear in place of original single vowels. There are many examples: *heort* for earlier *hert* ("hart"), *sceolde* for earlier *sculde* ("should"), ȝeat for earlier ȝæt ("gate"), ȝiest for earlier ȝest ("guest"). In special works this particular form of diphthongization is called *breaking*.

Monophthongization is naturally the opposite of diphthongization. It is the process by which a diphthong is simplified into a single sound. It is also a very common tendency. When Vulgar Latin was developing into the Romance languages it simplified old diphthongs while it was developing new ones. Names like Augustus, Caesar, Cloelia were often misspelled Ogustus, Cesar, Clelia, thus reflecting the general drift. Ordinary words like *audire, caedere, coepere* ("to hear," "to slay," "to begin") appeared as *odire* or even *oire* (cf. Spanish *oir*, Old French *oyer*), *cedere*, and *cepere*. English has repeatedly simplified older diphthongs, just as it has repeatedly diphthongized simple vowels. Among the simple vowels most recently developed in English are [lɔ:] in "law" from older [lɑʊ]; and the vowels in "would," "could," and "walk" which at one time had diphthongs.

About the time of King Alfred diphthongs were a conspicuous feature of English words, but these were generally simplified in the Middle English period. Then new diphthongs arose, chiefly from vocalized or partly vocalized consonants, so that not all words contained simple vowels even after the elimination of Old English diphthongs. When these new diphthongs were in turn being eliminated, the long simple vowels began to diphthongize once more. It will be seen, in fact, that English has passed through several cycles in which the dominant tendency has alternated between diphthongization and monophthongization. Both have always been present, but one or the other has always been in the lead. At present English leans heavily towards diphthongs.

ADDITIONS AND LOSSES

Additions and *losses* of sounds occur occasionally by processes slightly different from any thus far described. Sometimes, for instance, a difficult consonant group is evaded, not by assimilation, but by the introduction of what is known as a "parasitic vowel." (This type of addition may be compared with the form of dissimilation discussed in words like "number." In a broad sense it may be regarded as another form of dissimilation.) Children tend to say "fillum," "arum," "atheletic" to facilitate pronunciation. When *st-* comes at the beginning of a word a vowel is prefixed for the same purpose in certain dia-

lects. If you are out of breath you may catch yourself saying
[ə'stænd] for "stand." The prefixed vowel must have been
fairly widespread in Vulgar Latin, which produced a form
like *estato from the classical status. Hence Spanish estado,
and the Old French estat (later état) giving English "estate."
A Spaniard speaking English is prone to say "e-street" for
"street." The same desire to avoid the initial st- combination
caused the prefixing of y in Welsh words like ystad (also a loan
from the Latin).

Vowels and consonants may be affixed to words because of
a mistaken idea that they are related to other words through
grammatical function or meaning. People add a -t to the word
"once" because it suggests "first" in form and meaning. Originally "wicked" lacked a final -d, but received it because, no
doubt, the word was felt to be like past participles ("damnéd,
perverted, corrupted") with similar meanings. Unaccented
final vowels receive an unhistorical [ɹ] before words beginning with another vowel in the Maine dialect of the United
States because many words with a genuine historical [ɹ] occur
in this position. When you have been using phrases like "the
painter is . . ." or "the actor is . . ." [də 'peɪntə-ɹ-ɪz, ði 'æktə-ɹ-ɪz]
it is easy to say "the idear is" [ði aɪ'diː:ə-ɹ-ɪz]. The pattern of
sounds is being extended beyond its original scope: that is all.
In other words, there is always some kind of "reason" for the
addition of such final consonants. Similar locutions often give
the key to it.

Even more commonplace is loss of consonants in such position. Anyone who studies French must be aware of this. Originally the "unpronounced" final consonants which one must
learn to write in correct French orthography were given their
full value in speech. They have been dropped gradually in
the course of centuries. Certain consonants in intervocalic
(between-vowel) position are also apt to disappear. One of the
weakest is [d]. You can easily drop it out in the English word
"meadow." The Dutch word weder ("weather") has become
wêer, and Latin audire, as we have seen, produced Spanish oir,

Old French *oyer*. On the other hand, consonants at the beginning of a word are apt to be faithfully preserved. Attention and energy are strongest when we begin to speak; they flag towards the end of a group of sounds.

PALATALIZATION

A special form of assimilative change known as *palatalization* is important enough to receive special treatment.

Any consonant followed by the palatal semi-vowel [j] is likely to be modified—that is, shifted from its original position. This is true whether the [j] is original (possibly consonantized from [i]), or is itself a glide-sound developed between a back consonant and a front vowel. Such a glide appears when the word "car" is pronounced [cjɑ:]. The shift will naturally be directed towards front palatal position for the consonant, which is thus partly assimilated towards the [j]. If you wish to convince yourself that such readjustments occur, try to pronounce our word "sugar" with the [s] separate and distinct from the following [j]. You will find it difficult. Almost inevitably you must change the [s] to a more palatal position, namely [ʃ]. What was once [ˈsʲugaɹ] has become [ˈʃjʊgə]. The shift from [s] to [ʃ] before a palatal glide like [j] is one of the commonest cases of palatalization. The same sort of shift in Old English caused all sorts of words with original *sk-* ("sc-") at the beginning to shift to [ʃ], which we spell "sh." Thus "shield" comes from older **skild;* "should" from older **skulde.*[4]

Certain simple and complex sounds in various languages are to be explained as the result of palatalization. It is not difficult to reconstruct the unpalatalized consonant when you have had a little practice. The sounds in question are, in addition to

4 Words in Modern English beginning with [sk-] are loan words, mostly from Scandinavian languages. They were imported into English in large numbers at the time of the Danish invasions, from the eighth to the eleventh centuries. Examples are "sky," "skull," "skill," "skirt." Modern Danish has preserved the [sk]-sound; Swedish has palatalized it to [ʃ].

[ʃ]: [tʃ], [dʒ], [ts], [j]. The palatalized group is common in Russian. Modern Castilian Spanish shows [χ] and [θ] resulting from palatalization. Some languages, like American Spanish and Modern French develop a palatalized [kʲ] all the way to an [s], as in the words *cielo, ciel* from Vulgar Latin **cjelo,* "heaven."

Some examples will make the development clearer. When [t] is followed by [j] it readily becomes [tʃj]. "Tube" [tjub] slides easily into [tʃjub] if you are not careful; or it may become a simple [s]. The development into [θ] is more likely for Spanish tongues. Examples of the various possibilities are afforded by an unaccented syllable [-tja] in a Vulgar Latin word **platja* (from older *platea*) meaning an open square or public place. It became Italian *piazza* ['pjɑt:sɑ:], German *Platz*, French *place*, Spanish *plaza*. Another possibility is the development of [tj] into the similar combination [tʃ]. The Russian word for "tea," derived from Chinese *te*, is *chai* [tʃai].

When [k] is followed by [j] or even [i] or [e] it is first raised to [c] and then shifts frequently to other palatal sounds such as [tʃ], later possibly to [ʃ] or, as we have just seen, even to [s]. Romance forms of Caesar's name show these possibilities with Spanish employing [θ] here also. German kept an unpalatalized form in *Kaiser*. In English we occasionally find both palatal and unpalatal forms of the same initial consonant: for instance, *chart* and *card* (older *carte*); *cattle* and *chattel*. The variety is due to the fact that English borrowed from more than one dialect of French in the Middle Ages. The Parisian dialect had palatalized [k] to [tʃ] even before an [a]. Old English also transformed initial [k]-sounds if a front (or fronted) vowel followed them. First the glide [j] was introduced; then the consonant itself was changed. Even Latin words showed this transformation if they were borrowed early enough. Roman camps had been called by the name *castra* in Latin; this term was adopted early by the Anglo-Saxons and developed from [kɑstrɑ] to [kæstr̩] to [cjæster] to [tʃjæster], written *ceaster*. Hence our suffix "chester" in place names like Westchester.

So "cheese" has come from a Vulgar Latin *caseo, and "chamber" from camara (with dissimilation). Germanic *kerl became Anglo-Saxon ceorl [tʃjɔrl], modern English "churl."

The palatalized form of [d] can be heard frequently in contemporary pronunciation of "due," which is at times almost identical with "Jew" [dʒju:]. An example is modern Italian raggio [ŕadʒ:jo], from Latin radius, *radio. The sound has been obscured in French to a mere [j], as in Old French rai from the same Latin form. Other palatalized consonants, like [bj], and even original [j] alone, can give rise to the sound [dʒ]. This sound [dʒ] was fairly common in Old French. When we borrowed it in French words at an early date we have kept it, as in words like "judge" from juge [dʒydʒə]. But in recent times the French have simplified [dʒ] to [ʒ], so that more recent loans from that language appear with the softer sound; for instance, rouge (which comes from rubeus, *rubjo with palatalized [b]).

Other consonants which are often affected by a neighboring palatal are [l], [n], [g]. For instance, [lj] has been reduced to a simple [j] in French words like merveille (from mirabilia). Spanish changed the combinations [pl, kl] at the beginning of a word into [lj], which in Latin America is pronounced simply as [j]. Words like plorare, clamare, meaning "to weep," "to call out" simplified first to llorar, llamar, and are now spoken as [ljɔ'rar, lja'mar] in Castile, but [jɔ'rar, ja'mar] in South and Central America. An original [lj] in Latin, however, such as is contained in mulier ("woman") gave the sound [χ]: mujer. Palatalized [n], or [ɲ], does not undergo very spectacular transformations. It is similar to the initial sound of our word "new" [nju:], and is familiar in "canyon" or cañon, a Spanish word. As for [gj], exemplified in Vulgar Latin *legione, its development into [dʒ, ʒ] appears in such words as French légion, English "legion," Italian leggione. Old Spanish often eliminated [g] before a palatal vowel: hermano, "brother," comes from *gʲermano.

ASPIRATION, OR STRONG BREATH EXPLOSION

There is, finally, another situation within a word which is apt to make consonants change. Strong aspiration of stop consonants like [p, t, k], when expelled as if [h] came after them, will tend to shift them into the rank of continuants. When our Germanic ancestors began to explode these sounds as [pʰ, tʰ, kʰ], they initiated a development which eventually produced [f, θ, χ]. A form like *piskis (from which Latin piscis was derived) turns up in Germanic (Gothic) as fisks, English "fish." If you aspirate the initial sound of "true" you may find yourself saying "through"; likewise an aspirated "please" may sound like "fleas." The statement of a whole series of sound-changes like this, which occurred in Primitive Germanic, is known as Grimm's Law.⁵ For an example of two forms of [p], both aspirated and not, observe the word "peept" [pʰiːpt], preterite of "peep." The initial consonant keeps its aspiration because a vowel follows; the second [p] loses it because a following consonant blocks it off. It is the first, or aspirated [p] in this word which may become [f] if you explode it too strongly.

RECONSTRUCTING SOUNDS

It is partly by a knowledge of general tendencies such as these that we are able to surmise the nature of an older language, even one that perished without being written down. Reasoning backwards from the sounds preserved in living languages

⁵ The full statement is this: the voiceless stops [p, t, k], whether originally aspirated or not, became the voiceless continuants [f, θ, χ]; the voiced stops [b, d, g] became the voiceless stops [p, t, k]; the somewhat problematical sounds represented as [bʰ, dʰ, gʰ] became [b, d, g]. Curiously enough, a similar shift occurred in Armenian. Just as Germanic shifted original [d] to [t], as exemplified in "two" beside Latin duo, so Armenian also substitutes [t] for the same sound. Here the word meaning "I give" is tam, cognate with Latin dāre and Russian dam, "I shall give." The word cognate with Latin genus is [cin], showing the same sort of shift we have in English "kin." For reference to comparable consonant changes in Hebrew, see chapter 3, note 3.

today, and knowing in general the reasons for shifts, scholars are able to make a very good guess about the phonological aspect of the parent Indo-European speech. They are aided in their surmises, of course, by loan words into non-Indo-European tongues at an early date, and by the earliest records of the most archaic descended languages. These give concrete evidence for a period soon after the scattering of sections of the linguistic family.

CONSONANTS AND VOWELS OF INDO-EUROPEAN

The consonants are not difficult to reconstruct, since they have been comparatively stable. It is thought that the parent language contained [p, t, k] (both aspirated and unaspirated), [b, d, g], and a series of sounds, possibly spirants or continuants, which are represented in textbooks as [bʰ, dʰ, gʰ]. Their exact nature is not clear; but they correspond to a series of consonants in Old Indian in which an aspiration really was heard after the voiced stops. There were in addition the series of nasals [m, n, ɲ, ŋ], and the liquids [l, r] which could serve either as vowels or consonants. (In exactly the same way [l] is a vowel in our word "table" but a consonant in "tabulation.") The sound [s] also existed; and [z] developed from it in certain positions. The semi-vowels [j, w] must have been close to [i, u] in pronunciation.

The most important vowels were apparently [a, e, o], both long and short. The other two, [i, u], were most conspicuously used to form second, less stressed, elements in falling diphthongs such as [ei, eu, oi, oʊ].

EXAMPLES OF INDO-EUROPEAN SOUNDS

Here are some examples of words in related languages which have preserved consonants from Indo-European:

[p] in Latin *patēr*, Greek *patér;* cf. English "paternal."
[t] in Latin *trēs*, Greek *treîs;* cf. English "tri-une."
[k] in Latin *clepō*, Greek *kleptō* ("I steal"); cf. English "kleptomaniac."

[b] in Latin *baculum,* Greek *baktron;* cf. English "bacillus," meaning "little staff."

[d] in Latin *dens, dentis,* Greek *o-dōn, o-dontos;* cf. English "dental."

[g] in Latin *genus,* Greek *genos;* cf. English "generic." [6]

Shifting of Vowel Sounds in Indo-European

Although vowels are notoriously less stable than consonants, we have a fairly clear picture of their behavior in parent Indo-European.

For one thing, we know that they were subject to change according to the movements of the accent in various related forms of the same word or root. The same changes can be observed in Modern English. Take, for instance, the striking differences in vowel sound which result from shift of accent in these two words:

define	[dɪ'faɪn];	definition	[defɪ'nɪʃn̩]
address (verb)	[ə'dɹes];	address (noun)	['ædɹes]

Sometimes a polysyllabic word may have its accent shifted over as many as three syllables in various forms:

history	['hɪstɹɪ];	historic	[hɪs'tɔɹɪk];	historicity [hɪstəɹ'ɪsɪtɪ]
memory	['mem(ə)ɹɪ];	memorial	[mə'mɔɹɪəl];	memorability [meməɹə'bɪlɪtɪ]

In all of these variations we observe, once more, that stressed vowels are clearly preserved, and unstressed ones are reduced or disappear entirely. Throughout the declensions and conjugations of the parent Indo-European language, vowels behaved in the same way. They were clear if the accent fell on them, but became diminished or even eliminated entirely if the accent was moved away. They could be lengthened, too, if

---

[6] The English words are of course not native, but borrowed from the classical languages. When cognate words appear in the Germanic heritage of English they have been shifted. For instance the *native* English words corresponding to *patēr* and *trēs* are "father" and "three." See note 4.

a following syllable completely disappeared from lack of stress. These shifts are known as *gradations*. The names for the various stages are: lengthened, normal, reduced, and vanishing gradation. In the word "history," for instance, it may be said that we use vanishing gradation of the middle vowel. Except in extremely elaborate discourse the *o* which we spell so carefully has vanished from speech. The related word "historical" shows normal gradation of the same syllable, since here accent insures its clarity; and in "historicity" we have the same sound in reduced gradation. The entire range of possibilities is termed *quantitative gradation*.[7] The various shifts have affected quantity or length.

The principles of gradation have really been discussed above, under the general heading of lengthening and shortening. They were not different in Indo-European from the same general principles operating in Modern English. But Indo-European appears to have made thorough and systematic use of them. Diphthongs were subject to the same processes of lengthening and eliminating as normal single vowels. The only difference was that "vanishing gradation" of a diphthong meant elimination *only* of the first element, so that the unaccented form of [ei] or [oi] was [i], and of [eu] or [ou] was [u].

EXAMPLES OF VOWEL CHANGE OR GRADATION

Certain words in English have come down to us in forms which show traces of gradation dating back to Indo-European. For example: there was a root **pet-* which meant "to fly." The normal form of it was used to make a word **petnā,* "feather," which

---

7 The term used by German writers for gradation is *Ablaut*. In addition to quantitative gradation, Indo-European also employed qualitative gradation in words of the same root. It is clear that Latin *tegere,* "to cover," is related to *toga,* "a covering robe"; Greek *legere* "to speak" with *logos* "a word." In *both* cases there is normal gradation, but the quality is different. Such alternation (the French call it *alternance vocalique*) was used, among other things, to show change of tense. In Greek it is still clear: the diphthong [ei] alternates with [oi] and a vanishing form [ı] in verbal forms. In English we still have qualitative gradation in our strong verbs, "sing, sang, sung" (from **sengh, songh, sṇgh*).

in Latin became *penna*.[8] However, when a word was constructed from the same root to mean "winged," the accent was placed on the ending, and as a result the root syllable lost its vowel. The word appeared as Greek *pterós,* which is used by us in learned Greek compounds like "pterodactyl," meaning "wing-fingered." Here loss of accent has put the root into the vanishing gradation, leaving nothing but the difficult combination [pt]. In the same way **gen,* meaning "to know," appears in vanishing gradation in the word "gnosis" (a heretical belief). Latin *s-umus* "we are" represents vanishing gradation of a root **es-,* meaning "to be."

Various forms of a root **pelə* or **plē* have produced words like "com*plete,*" "plenty," Greek *polu* ("many," as in our prefix "poly-syllabic"), and by Grimm's Law "full" (since the original [p] became [f]). When loss of a vowel left a liquid or nasal in the same syllable, it could assume the function of a vowel like the [l] in our word "table." Later it might develop a new vowel, somewhat as we do when we say "fillum" for "film." English has developed a short [u] before such liquids and nasals in syllables representing vanishing gradation. Hence the vowel in our word "full," from Indo-European **plnós,* appears as [ʊ]. Our prefix "un-," meaning "not," comes from an older **n̩* alone, vanishing gradation of some syllable like **en.* In Latin the same vanishing gradation produced *in-.* The Germanic form exists in our word "unlikely"; the Latin form in "incontrovertible." Both alike go back to an unaccented form which had lost its vowel completely but later developed a secondary or "parasitic" vowel sound. If you see a short [ʊ] before [l, r, m, n] in a Germanic word, like "sung" or "drunk," you can assume that it goes back to a form with no vowel at all: that is, vanishing gradation, with the liquid or nasal doing the work of a vowel.

All of this is the same in principle as the gradation in living English words like "history" and "historicity."

---

8 Our English "feather" contains the same root, with the consonants, [p] and [t], transformed by Grimm's law to [f] and [θ] respectively.

PRACTICAL USES OF PHONOLOGY

These are the chief principles involved in the phonological changes of a language. When you have mastered them you will be able to make many canny guesses about words you encounter in foreign languages. To take an obvious case: you will see that the word "Nazi" ['nɑːtsi], an abbreviation of National-Socialist when pronounced German fashion, contains a form of palatalization of the sound combination [tʲ]. When you learn in Russian that the first person singular of *isʹkatʲ* ("to search for") is *ishchu* [iʃtʃʲu], you will remark: "Quite understandable and easy to remember: the first person singular has merely palatalized the *-sk-* of the infinitive." You can share the pleasures of learned specialists, who must devote much time to reconstructing lost forms, and at the same time hasten your acquisition of living languages. What makes language study so painfully slow for most people is the seeming absence of logical arrangement in the patterns of sound. It is true that at best one must rely very largely on mere memory. Nevertheless, knowledge of sound changes often tells you what to expect in various forms of a word to be studied. It helps you to guess relations intelligently, and by putting order in the place of arbitrariness it makes your task of learning more pleasurable. The reward is surely worth the effort required to grasp the sound changes as a whole.

8. Life-History of the English Language

IMPORTANCE OF STUDYING ENGLISH HISTORICALLY

Very often throughout this book it has been necessary to explain puzzling modern words or expressions by reference to earlier forms. Our English language is in fact such a curious mixture from many sources that a brief sketch of its biography is really essential to an understanding of its structure today. Moreover there is an interesting parallel to be drawn between the development of the language and the vicissitudes of the people speaking it. If we trace the history of English, we shall observe historical relationships which also obtain in the histories of other languages.

THE ROMAN PERIOD

Under the later Roman emperors, as everyone knows, Britain was a Roman province with a flourishing colonial culture. The population was predominantly Celtic, to be sure, and spoke a language akin to modern Welsh. (See chapter 3, p. 56.) The native dialect no doubt persisted in the countryside, but the cities grew up about former Roman camps and included many Roman families, patrician and plebeian, who used Latin habitually. They did so even when they intermarried with the British or employed them as workers and slaves. All the amenities of Latin culture were enjoyed in the cities of this distant province: baths, forums or market places, comfortable villas with plumbing and tessellated floors, schools of rhetoric, theaters, and libraries. The Roman army was famous for making itself at home and mingling with native populations everywhere, with or without official formalities. It deserves indeed much of the credit for spreading Vulgar Latin as an international language among the common people of the ancient world. Cultured Britons were Roman citizens and used the recognized dominant language of the empire with slight modifications. In due time they were adopting the new religion, Christianity, which was rapidly becoming the chief Roman faith in the fourth century.

THE ANGLO-SAXONS

The ancestor of the English language appeared first in Albion when some tribes from Northern Germany, the Angles, Saxons, and Jutes, began to harry the shores and invade the island. This happened in the middle of the fifth century A.D. The raids were part of a larger diffuse movement known to historians as the *Völkerwanderung* or folk migrations. From the shores of the Black Sea to the coasts of Britain, the northern boundaries of the *Imperium Romanum* were harassed by restless Germanic peoples: Ostrogoths, Visigoths, Vandals, Franks, Langobards, Burgundians, and the so-called Anglo-Saxons, who sought foothold within the provinces. Roman resistance was weakened for many reasons, and the Germanic peoples were able to establish themselves in the heart of some of the most fertile sections. The struggle was at its height when the Angles and Saxons began the invasion of Britain. The mother cities, Rome and Constantinople, could give no help. More than that: Rome was obliged to call on the British provincial army to give aid on the continent. So Britain was doubly exposed. By the year 500 the Germanic invaders were established. There was an end of the sophisticated urban culture of the Romans, with their debates and theaters, their laws, government, army, and incipient Christian Church.

The newcomers were pagans, worshipers of Woden and other Teutonic gods. Their organization was tribal rather than urban. They were described by contemporaries as tall, blond, and blue-eyed. In the early days of the "Germanic peril" it had been the fashion for Roman matrons to dye their hair or wear wigs in imitation of barbaric blondness. By this time, however, the threat had become grim earnest; no mere subject for coiffeurs' modes.

The languages spoken by all the Germanic tribes about 450 A.D. were closely alike. They might more properly be called dialects of a General Germanic tongue shared by all, as English now is divided into dialects throughout the English-speaking world. The Germanic dialects had in turn, as we have seen, sprung from a fairly unified (lost) ancestor which we call Primitive Germanic.

EARLY OLD ENGLISH

We have no written documents in the Anglo-Saxon or Old English of the first few hundred years. Later, when Christianity was re-established in Britain in the early seventh century, schools, books, and the art of writing followed it. From two sources the newly converted Anglo-Saxons received instruction in these amenities. The missionaries from Rome acted as pedagogues chiefly in the south, in the kingdoms of Kent, Sussex, Wessex, and Mercia. In Northumbria some excellent work was done by Irish Christian missionaries, whose influence was felt in places like Lindisfarne, Yarrow, and Whitby. The alphabet taught here shows clearly its kinship with the Old Irish characters still used in Modern Gaelic. The first blooming of Old English literature occurred

Reproduced from the *Lindisfarne Gospels*. Cotton Nero D. iv, folio 139.

in this north country in the latter seventh and the eighth centuries. To the northern English schools of writing belonged Cynewulf, Caedmon, the Venerable Bede (who, like Alcuin, wrote in Latin), and the unknown author of *Beowulf*. Epic poems were written on the native heroic pagan traditions, and

Christian themes were also treated in lyrical and heroic style —all in the Northern dialect. Unfortunately this glorious promise was cut short by the violence of the Danish invasions, beginning at the end of the eighth century. Monastic schools were reduced to smoking ruins, the learned writers scattered or killed, and precious manuscripts were destroyed.

WEST SAXON

A revival of letters occurred later, despite the persistent fierce onslaughts of the Danes, in the kingdom of Wessex under King Alfred. The king was acutely aware of the need for education among his followers. According to his own account, even the clergy had sunk into a distressing condition of illiteracy. It was his wish "that all the freeborn youth of England who have sufficient means to devote themselves thereto, be set to learning so long as they are not strong enough for any other occupation, until such time as they can well read English writing. Let those be taught Latin whom it is proposed to educate further, and promote to higher office."

The language spoken by Alfred and his court was the Wessex or West Saxon dialect of Old English. It may be compared to Modern German in respect to declensions, for in both there are nouns with four cases in the singular and plural. There were approximately half a dozen different schemes of declension. In Modern German it is necessary to know what declension a noun "belongs to" in order to give it the proper forms in a sentence (according to use or "construction"); this too was true of Old English. The similarity of pattern is clear if one compares the inflection of two cognate or related words meaning "stone," a masculine noun:

	SINGULAR		PLURAL	
	Old Eng.	*Germ.*	*Old Eng.*	*Germ.*
Nom.	*stān*	*Stein*	*stānas*	*Steine*
Gen.	*stānes*	*Steines*	*stāna*	*Steine*
Dat.	*stāne*	*Steine*	*stānum*	*Steinen*
Acc.	*stān*	*Stein*	*stānas*	*Steine*

There are reasons for the differences to be noted in the plurals. However, the kinship is clear enough. Modern German is a conservative first cousin of Old English.

A Roman missionary trying to learn Anglo-Saxon for purposes of persuasion had to remember which of about six patterns to follow with every new noun acquired. It would have been felt to be a bad blunder if, for instance, he had used the "-e" ending of the plural of a feminine noun to make a plural for *stān*. In precisely the same way Americans who learn German are constantly in danger of falling into barbarous error if they choose the wrong pattern in inflecting a newly acquired noun. Since articles and adjectives presented forms for every case, gender, and number, and each form had to be carefully chosen so as to agree with the coming noun, the difficulty was greatly increased.

A Latin-speaking missionary might find all this entirely natural and understandable, since his native speech was also highly inflected, but he would have been puzzled by the existence of two separate and distinct declensions for all adjectives, the "strong" and the "weak." The former was used when the adjective alone preceded a noun, as in "good man"; the latter when an article or demonstrative came before the adjective, as in "the good man." Latin had no such distinction, but German had and still has:

STRONG SINGULAR DATIVE		WEAK SINGULAR DATIVE
O.E.	*gōdum manne*	*þǣm gōdan manne*
	"[to] good man"	"[to] the good men"
Germ.	*gutem Manne*	*dem guten Manne*

OLD ENGLISH VERBS

In the system of verbs one can see many resemblances between Old English and German. Both languages show a large number of verbs, called "strong," which indicate changes in tense by internal vowel change. The pattern is a very ancient one based on the vowel gradations of the old parent language

(Indo-European). Some words still show the basic similarity of pattern:

	INFINITIVE	PAST		PAST PARTICIPLE
O.E.	*rīdan*	*rād,*	*ridon*	*riden*
Germ.	*reiten*		*ritt*	*geritten*
Eng.	ride	rode		ridden
O.E.	*bindan*	*band,*	*bundon*	*bunden*
Germ.	*binden*	*band*		*gebunden*
Eng.	bind		bound	bound
O.E.	*etan*	*æt,*	*ǣton*	*eten*
Germ.	*essen*	*ass*		*gegessen*
Eng.	eat	("et")	ate	eaten

In both German and Old English too, there existed a second, larger group of verbs which used a different method for forming tenses. These "weak" verbs used a suffix instead: an added syllable containing a dental consonant. In modern German the suffix is always *-te,* but in Old English it varied. The possible forms were *-de, -ode, -te.* The past tense of Old English *dēman,* "to deem, to judge," was *dēmde,* "deemed"; of *lōcian,* "to look," it was *lōcode;* of *sēcan,* "to seek," it was *sōhte,* "sought."

Old English Sounds Compared to Modern German

The close relation between Old English and German is further indicated by constant relations in the sound patterns. When you encounter a strange word in the former you can often guess quite accurately what its cognate is in Modern German. Certain consonants have shifted away from the common Germanic position of an earlier day, but the kinship is still clear.

    O.E. *drincan* resembles German *trinken* (drink) d: t
    "   *þencan* [θεɲkʲan] resembles German *denken* (think) þ: d
    "   *twelf* resembles German *zwölf* (twelve) t: z [ts]
    "   *dēop* resembles German *tief* (deep) þ: f

By applying a few simple correspondences like these you can use German to help you learn Old English, or Old English to help you learn German. Moreover, even the vowels show fairly consistent parallelism. The Old English *ā* [ɑ:] parallels Modern German *ei,* pronounced [ai], in a multitude of words: *stān, Stein* (stone); *bān, Bein* (bone); *ān, ein* (one), etc. So with the Old English diphthong *ēa* [ɛ:a] and Modern German *au* [aʊ]: *hēap, Haufen* (heap); *lēapan, laufen* (run, leap); *ēac, auch* (also, eke). It is useful to compile your own list as you proceed.

To be sure, minor changes in both languages have by now obscured some of the neat correspondences. Old English was particularly prone to assimilations of various sorts: palatalizations which changed [k] into [tʃ]—as you will note in the pair of words "church," *Kirche*—and subtle changes in vowels, also of an assimilatory character. The causes of these changes become apparent, usually, when the Old English forms are compared with others in the related Germanic dialects. For practical purposes Modern Dutch is even more useful than Modern German in showing family similarities.

A few lines of Old English, from a Biblical translation, will illustrate some of the characteristics of the language: [1]

Ond Pharāōnes dohter cwæđ tō hire: "Underfōh þis cild ond fēd hit mē, ond ic sylle þē þīne mēde." þæt wīf underfēng þone cnapan, ond hine fēdde ond sealde Pharāōnes dehter.

Ond hēo hine lufode ond hæfde for sunu hyre, ond nemde his naman Moises, ond cwaeđ: "Forþāmþe ic hine of wætere genam."

Exodus 2:9-10

And Pharaoh's daughter quoth to her: "Receive this child and feed it (for) me, and I (shall) give thee thy meed." The woman took the boy and fed him and gave (him) to Pharaoh's daughter.

And she loved him and had (him) as her son, and named his name Moses, and quoth: "Because I took him (out) of water." (Literal translation)

CONNECTIONS WITH INDO-EUROPEAN

Even in this short passage there are a few words which show the more remote kinship of Old English with languages outside

1 Note that þ, đ stand for [θ] and [đ] indiscriminately. The letter *h* stood for a rougher sound than ours today, something like [χ].

the closely knit Germanic family. No specialized knowledge is required in order to see these similarities:

O.E. *sunu* (son) corresponds to Russian *syn*, Sanskrit *sūnú*.
" *nama* (name) corresponds to Latin *nōmen*, Greek *onoma*.
" *dohtor* (daughter) corresponds to Greek *thugátēr*, Sanskrit *duhitá*.
" *mē* (me) corresponds to Latin *mē*, Russian *me'n'a*.

It is by resemblances such as these that the wider relationships are established among the various families called Indo-European.

INFLUENCE OF LATIN ON OLD ENGLISH

Once the language of the Anglo-Saxons began to be written and to be studied along with Latin, it was brought into contact with the wide currents of world culture still pulsing strongly from the great center of Rome. The influence was felt in several ways. First of all, the study of classical Roman writers, which was more enthusiastic and intense than many readers may suppose, made Old English authors conscious of style and sentence structure in their own language. They began to cultivate certain effects they had admired in writers like Virgil, Ovid, and the prose historians. That is why the great prose translations and even the original works fostered in Old English by King Alfred have the air of being done by cultured, sophisticated writers, who knew very well what effect they were striving for. At times their admiration of Roman prose style led to unfelicitous imitation. When the translator of *Apollonius of Tyre* writes "all these things thus being done" (*ðisum eallum ðus gedōnum*) in the dative case, he is trying slavishly to follow a famous Latin construction in the ablative case: something like *hīs omnibus ita factīs*. It just doesn't fit. The effect remains foreign and awkward. But other writers combined planned intricacy and simplicity with more success. There are passages in the Alfredian translations of Bede, St. Gregory, Boethius, and Orosius which represent a happy marriage of Roman rhetoric with native English usage in sentence structure. In describing the death of Cædmon, the Old English version of Bede's history shifts from elaborate description to the direct recording of Cædmon's simple request: *"Beraþ mē hūsl tō"* (Bring me last sacrament). Nothing could be more English, including the ancient and entirely legitimate ending of a sentence with a preposition or adverb-particle. Thus while vigor of native idiom was retained, the very architecture of English was somewhat modified, at least among the cultured few at the courts and churches and schools, by association with the Roman literary heritage.

In the second place, the Old English vocabulary was enriched by a number of direct loans from Latin. The implanting of Christianity brought a number of direct transfers from one language to the other. Most have survived to this day. The list includes:

abbot	hymn	organ	shrive
altar	martyr	pope	synod
angel	mass	priest	relic
candle	noon	psalm	temple
deacon	nun	shrine	

Flourishing trade with Roman merchants continued the borrowings which had begun long ago on the continent when Germanic tribes first encountered salesmen from the Mediterranean. To the list above belong words like *cycene* (kitchen) from *coquīna; disc* (dish) from *discus; cīese* (cheese) from *cāseus; pund* (pound) from *pondus; mynet* ("mint" of money), from *moneta; copor* (copper) from *cuprum; tigele* (tile) from *tegula; strǣt* (street) from *strāta via;* and *ynce* (inch) from *unica.*

The debt to Roman word material was increased in another less obvious manner. For abstract learned concepts the Anglo-Saxon writers frequently coined words out of simple forms already existent in their own language. But they did this by translating literally the elements of the Latin words. We have already discussed the general procedure in chapter 4. Thus the Old English vocabulary was increased under Roman inspiration without sacrifice of native ingredients. German has often followed the same method of constructing new learned words out of native elements, with an eye to the Latin model. The similar method of compounding appears in these typical examples:

O.E.	GERMAN	ENGLISH
efen-sārgian	*mit-leiden*	com-miserate
fore-sprǣc	*Vor-wort*	pre-face
mid-wyrhta	*Mit-arbeiter*	col-laborator
ofer-ferian	*über-führen*	trans-fer
wið-standan	*wider-stehen*	op-pose
ūt-drǣfan	*aus-treiben*	ex-pel

Old English writers were thus exploring the possibilities of elaborate compounding in order to express new ideas. They never went very far in this direction—not so far, say, as some modern German writers—but it is possible that the tendency might have led to unwieldy polysyllables if Old English had developed into Modern with no disturbances from without.

INFLUENCE OF DANISH

There was one other foreign language besides Latin which exercised a measurable influence on Old English. The long-continued attacks by Danes and other Scandinavians on the English coasts were attended by some measure of success. At one time a Danish king, Knut or Canute, actually ruled the country. Large settlements were established, especially in the northern districts. They eventually remained on a peaceful footing, and the settlers merged with the English population. Before losing their identity entirely, however, they contributed a list of loan words to the English vocabulary. Most of them are so homely and practical that we may be sure that the immigrants rapidly attained neighborly status with the people they had but recently been harrying. Words borrowed at this period include "husband," "fellow," "law," "take," "store," "gate," "skill," "sky," "ransack," "call," "thrive," "skull." A personal pronoun was taken over bodily. We owe our plural forms, "they, their, them" to the Scandinavian *þeir, þeira, þeim* which gradually displaced Old English *hīe, hīera, hem* (confusingly like the singular masculine pronoun). The loans show the intimacy finally achieved by northern settlers who must have been at first bitterly resented.

LATE OLD ENGLISH

By the end of the Old English period, then, England had what might be called a recognized literary language, already used for several hundreds of years for important creative and translated writings. By the year 1000, however, certain changes were beginning to affect the literary language. The multiplicity of endings was gradually being reduced. Cases originally kept distinct were beginning to fall together with identical terminations. You could no longer be sure, without relying more and more on context, whether a given form meant a dative singular or a dative plural. If the confusion was appearing in formal documents written by men at least semi-learned, it was no doubt far more widespread among the unlearned. And very soon the process of confusion or leveling was speeded up by an important political event.

THE NORMAN CONQUEST

In 1066, as every school child knows, England was invaded and conquered by William, Duke of Normandy, commonly called "the Bastard." He used as pretext a doubtful claim to the English crown after the death of Edward the Confessor, "last of the Saxon Kings." The army attendant upon William was chiefly composed of Normans, men speaking a provincial dialect of French but related by blood to the Danes. Their forefathers, most of them, had migrated from Scandinavia and conquered the land of Normandy even as they themselves were now proposing to conquer England. Their success meant more than a mere change in dynastic rule for the inhabitants of Britain. The old local kingdoms and tribal organizations were swept away—such as had survived the period of unified Danish rule. In their stead the whole of England, excluding Scotland and Wales, was placed under a single complex feudal system of administration.

FEUDALISM IN ENGLAND

Feudalism of course was a highly stratified organization of society. In France there were already many ranks or orders of men, from the lowly unfree serf, up through free traders and workers, landless knights, land-owning knights, little barons, big barons, and recognized kings. Military service and other obligations were the basis of land ownership. Rights and prerogatives were at times vague or conflicting, and hence gave rise to fierce combats. Feudal France was divided into great duchies, each with a hereditary overlord at its head. Roughly speaking the dialects of medieval French corresponded to these feudal divisions. Within the confines of each duchy there was not a great deal of difference between the language of the lower and the higher orders, except insofar as differences of interest and preoccupation tended to mark off the stores of words used. The husbandman talked about agricultural matters, using more or less simple sentences studded with the technical terms of his job; the knight employed a more aristocratic vocabulary referring to tournaments, etiquette, literature, and art (within limits!), terms of inheritance, and the techniques of warfare; but in general they spoke the same dialect within the same region. The regional dialect divisions were probably much more noticeable than class divisions, apart from limited items of specialized vocabulary.

BILINGUAL ENGLAND

When William of Normandy transferred this feudal organization to England, the linguistic situation became more complex. At once the lowest orders were doubly marked, not only by inferior economic position but also by the use of a separate, despised tongue. Since the Church, which conducted most of the schooling of the time, was also taken over by Norman-French bishops, abbots, and other prelates, instruction in English practically ceased. Most of the native speakers became necessarily illiterate and remained so for several generations. The recording of English was very much reduced almost everywhere. While English thus remained neglected in writing and uncorrected by formal teaching, it tended to change more rapidly than it had been doing before 1066. The leveling of forms, now accelerated, produced a greatly simplified grammar. Many of the distinctions of Old English were lost in the process. Earlier writers like Sir Walter Scott have probably exaggerated the cleavage between Norman French and English, and the length of time it endured. But it was sufficiently marked at least to intensify the drive towards simplicity, already noticeable in Old English.

EARLY MIDDLE ENGLISH

English re-emerged as a literary language in the hands of churchly writers in the latter twelfth century. These men, schooled primarily in Latin and Norman French, merely adapted the classroom spelling of these upper-class languages to the native idiom. Some few may have known a little about the Old English written before 1066, especially in places where efforts had been made to keep the old *Anglo-Saxon Chronicle* up to date under the Normans. In all cases they tried to write what they actually heard, phonetically. Where inconsistencies arose they were due to regional dialects in English itself, or to a conflict between French and traditional English orthography. In Old English, for instance, the word *hūs* for "house" was pronounced with a single long vowel [hu:s], and was so written. In the so-called Middle English period, from 1100 to 1400, it was still being pronounced as before, but under French influence the spelling became *hous* for [hu:s]. We can be fairly certain of the pronunciation because of the general consistency. Some writers, moreover, were interested enough in the problem to indicate the reasons for their spelling, and what it was supposed to represent.

CHANGES IN GRAMMAR

With the reduction of Old English declensions the English sentence fell increasingly into the word order habitual with us today: subject, predicate, complement. Otherwise it would have been impossible, eventually, to distinguish one part from the other. (Old English sentences had used the inverted order and delayed clausal verbs to be found in Modern German.) Almost all the nouns were attracted into the declension represented by *stān*, with a plural in *-as* later weakened into *-es*. Only a few survived in the other declensions. The vowels of unaccented endings were reduced to the obscure sound [ə], written *-e-*. The verbs retained endings not unlike those current in the time of King Alfred:

Ī singe	*we singen* [2]
þū singest	*yē singen*
hē singeth	*þei singen*

The adjectives retained vestiges of inflection, even slightly differentiating strong forms from weak; but the elaborate declensions of Old English adjectives were forgotten. The reduction of endings to short, unstressed syllables gave the language a trochaic and dactylic effect.

CHANGES IN SOUNDS

Although the consonants survived with little change, there was some shifting in the quality of the vowels. Old diphthongs were simplified and new ones arose. Old long vowels were shortened

---

[2] This is the Midland form of the plural. In the South it was *singeth*, in the North *singes*. The distinction is typical of many others which demarked the dialects from one another.

and short ones were lengthened under special conditions and for special reasons which need not be rehearsed here. In general the resulting new vowels were pronounced as in Modern Italian, Spanish, or German: in short, with the so-called "continental" values. Thus:

ā was [ɑ:] as in "father";
ē was [e:] or [ɛ:] as in "they" or "there," respectively;
ī was [i:] as in "machine";
ō was [o:] (not [oʊ]) as in "lone";
ū was [u:], sometimes written "ou", as in "rouge";
ȳ was identical with ī in pronunciation.

All vowels were intended to be spoken, except when two coming together in a sentence were elided (*thē intente* became *th' intente,* with three syllables to the second word). Diphthongs were pronounced by giving the above values to the separate parts: thus *"au"* represented [ɑ] plus [u] in one syllable. When you have grasped these few principles you can read Middle English aloud and enjoy the music of it along with the sense.

PERSISTENCE OF OLD ENGLISH WORDS

The earliest Middle English texts were still composed with an almost pure English vocabulary. The spelling, too, was conservative for a time, especially in the South, so that a casual glance at some of the early texts (ca. 1200) leaves the impression that Old English was still being written. A closer examination, however, shows that the simplification of forms was already far advanced at this time. Here is a short passage from a poem written in the South about 1170. It deals in a quaint medieval manner with the transitoriness of earthly happiness, yet there is a perennial appeal about its grave simplicity:

Ich æm elder þen ich wes a wintre and a lore;
Ic wælde more þanne ic dude; mi wit ah to ben more.
Wel lange ic habbe child i-beon a weorde and ech a dede;

þeh ic beo a wintre eald, to ying I eom a rede. . . .
Ylde me is bestolen on ær ic hit awyste;
Ne mihte ic iseon before me for smeche ne for miste.

(I am older than I was in winters and in lore; I have more strength
than I did; my wit ought to be more. For a long time I have been a
child in word and eke in deed; though I be in winters old, too
young I am in rede. Old age has stolen on me before I ever wist it; I
could not see before me for the smoke and for the mist.)

Some of the lyrics retain pure English vocabulary at an even
later date, because they deal with warm intimate things which
we still prefer to express with the "Anglo-Saxon" part of our
language.

Wynter wakeneth al my care,
Nou thise leves waxeth bare;
Oft I sike and mourne sore   [sigh and mourn sorely]
   When hit cometh in my thoht
   Of this worldes joie, hou hit geth al to noht.

Nou hit is, an nou hit nys,
Al so hit ner were, ywys;
That moni mon seith, soth hit ys:
   Al goth bote Godes wille;
   Alle we shule deye, thoh us like ylle.   [though it displeases us]

French Loan Words

Meanwhile, however, French was still the language of court,
school, diplomacy, and Parliament. Even as late as the fourteenth century some outstanding English men of letters wrote
exclusively in French. The English vocabulary could not long
remain unaffected by this environment. What had at first been
a mere infiltration of French words into English increased until by 1300 it was flood-tide. The new terms came from many
occupations: from law, philosophy, theology, and military science; cookery, weaving, architecture, book-making; and the
trade in wool, wine, and other commodities. Many of the more

learned importations were long words which must have seemed by their vagueness imposing and slightly awesome to English ears. French words like *contritioún, transubstantioún, reverénce, penaúnce, obligacioún, dominacioún* must have arrived with double impressiveness: first because they referred to lofty matters of religion and government which the common man uneasily shies away from; and second because they simply sounded different from the native vocabulary. During the years when it was chiefly the language of illiterates, English had naturally veered away from the tendency to form lengthy compound abstractions out of native elements. Only a few like *rihtwysnesse* ("righteousness") and *agenbit* ("remorse") had survived. On the whole the native vocabulary had conserved best the basic non-abstract terms and hence turned now to an alien treasury for the needed terminology of learning.

The loans were conspicuous for another reason besides their length. They still preserved the French accentuation on the last syllable, in direct opposition to the English tendency to throw accents forward. Even when this English tendency began to affect the French importations, a strong secondary stress was retained on the last syllable: *con-trí-ci-oùn, ré-ve-rèn-ce, dó-mi-ná-ci-oùn*. The struggle between French and English tendencies in accentuation produced a wave-like rise and fall of stress which added even more dignity, it may well be, to the physical impressiveness of the words. The alternation of strongly stressed root syllables in native English, followed by the shrinking unstressed endings, was already contributing to the same effect. Out of these divergent sources came the iambic-trochaic movements of English which Chaucer used so brilliantly in his narrative verse.

THE COMBINED VOCABULARY IN CHAUCER

And Chaucer illustrates, too, the aesthetic uses to be made of the new polyglot vocabulary. No one knew better than he how to juxtapose, contrast, or temporarily isolate the dual elements of fourteenth-century English. In this respect he may be com-

pared to his own advantage with many modern poets. At one
time Chaucer permits the full grandeur of the French polysyllables to roll out:

> For of *fortúnes* sharpe *adversité*
> The worste kynde of *infortúne* is this:
> A man to han been in *prospérité,*
> And it remembren when it passed is.
>> (*Troilus and Cressida,* III, l. 1625 ff.)

This poignant comment on human felicity, paraphrased from
Dante, gains in dignity from the use of the italicized Romance
words. At the same time, the last line has a simplicity of everyday speech, the more effective by contrast; and the delayed
verb in the archaic Old English style gives it a falling cadence
which heightens the wistfulness. The same artful contrast of
polysyllabic dignity and native simplicity is found in many
other Chaucerian passages. In the ballade called "Fortune"
he begins:

> This wrecched worldes *trānsmutácioùn*
> As wele or wo, now povre and now *honoúr*
> Withouten ordre or wys *discrécioùn*
> *Govérned* is by Fórtunès *erroúr.*

He laments the passing of a happier day when people told the
truth and their word was as good as their bond:

> Sometyme this world was so stedfast and stable
> That mannes word was *obligácioùn.* . . .
>> ("Lak of Stedfastnesse")

You will notice that the melody of Chaucer's lines depends
on a correct rendering of the unaccented syllables. Unless the
vowels are pronounced in these, the verse is harsh and un-
metrical. Give due value to the unstressed vowels (including
final *-e*'s), however, and retain strong secondary stress at the
end of French loan words, and you will have verse as musical
and diversified as any in English.

In less exalted moods Chaucer often undertook to describe

the lives and persons and small adventures of common folk. Here his brilliant realism was re-enforced by an appropriate vocabulary and a sentence structure echoing the cadences of ordinary speech. In drawing the picture of an elderly carpenter's young wife, with her gay amorous ways, her "likerous eye" and her "middle gent and smal" as any weasel's, he concludes gustily:

Hir mouth was sweete as bragot or the meeth,   [ale or mead]
Or hoord of apples leyd in hey or heeth.   [hay or heath]
Wynsynge she was, as is a joly colt,
Long as a mast, and upright as a bolt. . . .
Hir shoes were laced on hir legges hye.
She was a prymerole, a piggesnye   [primrose or "pig's-
For any lord to leggen in his bedde,   eye" (a flower)]
Or yet for any good yeman to wedde.

The homely details and comparisons expressed in everyday language—"sweet as apples laid in heath or hay"—are enough to make the reader's mouth water, as indeed they were intended to do. And the simple vocabulary of ordinary life is beautifully used when the same fair Alison rebuffs (but not permanently!) an amorous overture by her boarder, a handsome young student:

> [She] seyde, "I wol nat kisse thee, by my fey!
> Why, lat be," quod she, "lat be, Nicholas,
> Or I wol crie 'out, harrow' and 'allas'!
> *Do wey youre handes,* for youre curteisye!"
> ("Miller's Tale," *CT*, A3261 ff.)

With the English vernacular being handled in so masterful a manner, it had surely reached legal majority and could no longer be regarded as a subject dialect. Conversely, it was because English had already won recognition that Chaucer devoted his genius to it rather than French or Latin. Significantly enough, Parliament was first opened in English in 1362, and the chronicler Trevisa tells us the native language was used in the schools in 1385. Both events fell in Chaucer's lifetime.

THE FIFTEENTH CENTURY

Soon after Chaucer's death, in the fifteenth century, there was a renewed drift towards simplification in English. Final un-accented vowels, by 1400 already reduced to a very slight mur-mur, were entirely lost. Still more nouns were shifted to the majority declension (with plurals in -*s*) out of the small group left in the minority declensions. More and more verbs were shifted to the weak conjugation from those still retaining the internal vowel change. For a time, of course, there was a choice of forms: Malory could decide between either "he clave" or "he clefte" in telling how one knight smote another asunder, as they were so frequently engaged in doing in the *Morte d'Arthur*. Similar fluctuations arose between "he clomb" and "he climbed"; "he halp" and "he helped." Some of the quaint surviving constructions out of Old English, such as impersonal verbs with the dative, the inflected genitive case for nouns de-noting things, and the double negative, began to fall into dis-use. They persist in the fifteenth century, indeed even into the sixteenth, but they are felt increasingly to be archaic survivals.

Where Chaucer said:	Later English has:
He *nevere* yet *no* vileynye *ne* sayde	He never said *any*thing villain-ous about *any*body
In al his lif unto *no* manner wight.	In all his life to *any* person.
Me [to me] were levere a thou-sand fold to dye.	*I'd* liefer [rather] die a thousand times over.
Me thynketh *it* acordaunt to resoun.	*It* seems reasonable *to me*.
Our present *worldes lyves* space. . . .	The space *of* our present life *of* [in] this world.
In hope to stonden in his *lady* [gen. sing. fem.] grace. . . .	In hope to stand in his *lady's* grace.

Another important usage became increasingly prevalent in the fifteenth and early sixteenth century: the bolstering of verbs with a number of auxiliaries derived from "do" and "be." In Middle English a question was asked with the simple form of the verb in inverted position: "What say you? What think you?" For a couple of centuries after 1400 this was still done habitually, but more and more people fell into the habit of saying "What do you say? What do you think?" The "do" was colorless and merely brought about a deferment of the main verb. In effect it makes our English usage somewhat like Russian, which says "What you say? What you think?" without any inversion of the verb before the subject. In simple statements the "do" forms were used for situations where we no longer feel the need for them. An Elizabethan would say "I do greatly fear it" (an unrestricted statement). We should use the less emphatic "I fear it greatly." Compare Shakespeare's

> I *do prophesy* the election lights
> On Fortinbras; he has my dying voice—

and many other instances.

During the same period there began the gradual spread of the so-called progressive conjugation, with forms of "to be": "I *am coming;* he *is sitting* down." These two special forms of English conjugation have developed an intricate etiquette, with many modifications of usage, which cause great trouble to the foreign student. One of the last distinctions he masters is the one between "I eat breakfast every morning" and "I am eating breakfast now"; between "I believe that" and "I do indeed believe that."

One of the most fateful innovations in English culture, the use of the printing press, had its effects on the language in many ways. The dialect of London, which had for over a century been gaining in currency and prestige, took an enormous spurt when it was more or less codified as the language of the press. As Caxton and his successors normalized it, roughly speaking, it became the language of officialdom, of polite letters, of the spreading commerce centered at the capital. The local dialects competed with it even less successfully than formerly. The art of reading, though still a privilege of the favored few, was extended lower into the ranks of the middle classes. With the secularizing of education later on, the mastery of the printed page was extended to still humbler folk. Boys who, like William Shakespeare, were sons of small-town merchants and craftsmen, could learn to read their Virgil and Ovid and Holy Writ even if they had no intention of entering the Church. Times had distinctly changed since the thirteenth century. It may be added that changes in society—the gradual emergence of a mercantile civilization out of feudalism—gave scope to printing which it would never have had in the earlier Middle Ages. The invention was timely in more than one sense.

All this may have been anticipated by the early printers. Their technological innovations may have been expected to facilitate the spread of culture. But they could not have foreseen that the spelling which they standardized, more or less, as the record of contemporary pronunciation, would have been perpetuated for centuries afterwards. Today, when our pronunciation has become quite different, we are still teaching our unhappy children to spell as Caxton did. Respect for the printed page has become something like fetish-worship. A few idiosyncrasies have been carefully preserved although the reason for them is no longer understood. When Caxton first set up the new business in London he brought with him Flemish workers from the Low Countries, where he himself had learned it. Now the Flemish used the spelling "gh" to represent their own voiced guttural continuant, a long-rolled-out sound $[\gamma]$ unlike our English$[g]$. English had no such sound at the time, but the employees in Caxton's shop were accustomed to combining the two letters, and continued to do so in setting up certain English words. In words like "ghost" and "ghastly" it has persisted, one of the many mute witnesses to orthographical conservatism.

HUMANISM AND CLASSICAL INFLUENCES

English vocabulary continued to be diversified as printing and increased communication with the continent diversified its cultural needs and interests. The Renaissance (a term we shall not attempt to define here) brought with it widened interest in pagan classical learning. It was not so much an innovation as an extension of the already lively medieval interest in the same heritage. But linguistically the debt was expressed in a new manner. Whereas Roman words had formerly been taken over in French form, with all the modifications due to centuries of use, now the Latin vocabulary was plundered direct, at least to a much greater extent than before. Writers who knew some classical philology did not hesitate to adopt into English a number of forms unmodified except for a slightly Anglicized ending. Words like "armipotent," "obtestate," "maturity," "splendidous," "matutine," and "adjuvate" had not been in French popular use for centuries before reaching English; they were lifted directly out of classical texts with little change. Browne's *Religio Medici* furnishes many examples. Some writers went to such lengths that their language was crusted over with Latinisms.

The tendency had begun in the fifteenth century and went to absurd lengths in the sixteenth. Ben Jonson satirized it in his *Poetaster,* a play in which a character guilty of pretentious verbal concoctions is made to vomit them forth in a basin, in sight of all. The victim, named Crispinus, is supposed to stand for the playwright Marston who actually committed verbal atrocities of the sort. When the pill is administered Crispinus cries out:

Crispinus.	Oh, I am sick—
Horace.	A basin, a basin quickly, our physic works. Faint not, man.
Crispinus.	Oh—*retrograde—reciprocal—incubus.*
Caesar.	What's that, Horace?
Horace.	*Retrograde,* and *reciprocal, incubus* are come up.
Gallus.	Thanks be to Jupiter.
Crispinus.	Oh—*glibbery—lubrical—defunct;* oh! . . .
Tibullus.	What's that?

Horace.	Nothing, yet.
Crispinus.	*Magnificate.*
Maecenas.	*Magnificate?* That came up somewhat hard.

Among other words thus "brought up" are "inflate," "turgidous," "oblatrant," "furibund," "fatuate," "prorumped," and "obstupefact." The ungentle satire concludes with admonitions by Virgil to the exhausted Crispinus: among other things

> You must not hunt for wild, outlandish terms,
> To stuff out a peculiar dialect;
> But let your *matter* run before your *words;*
> And if, at any time, you chance to meet
> Some Gallo-Belgic phrase, you shall not straight
> Rack your poor verse to give it entertainment,
> But let it pass. . . .

The critical attitude represented by Jonson was exaggerated in some cases into a fanatical purism. There were some who leaned over backwards in their attempts to avoid English neologisms out of Latin or Greek. If they went too far it was because the "ink-horn" terms of "aureate" or gilded English had become a kind of stylistic rash on the literary language. Still, many of the conscious creations of this period filled a real need, and were permanently adopted into standard speech.

Another consequence of the renewed, if not at all new, devotion to Latin was the freshened awareness of the component parts of Latin words in English. In the hands of gifted poets this resulted in a semantic rejuvenation of words which will be further discussed in the next chapter. Even spelling was affected by this awareness. Words pronounced still in a French manner were given a Latinized orthography which did not correspond to usage: thus "victuals" for ['vit̩lz] from French *vitaille.*

LATIN SYNTAX IN ENGLISH

Not only the English vocabulary was affected by the intensified devotion to Latin. Many attempts were made to have syntax and sentence structure conform too. There were attempts to implant long absolute constructions as an imitation of the Latin ablative absolute, and to make the sentence a tissue of intricately related clauses. The results were at times monstrous. This is one sentence committed by Sir Philip Sidney in the *Arcadia*:

But then, Demagoras assuring himself, that now Parthenia was her own, she would never be his, and receiving as much by her own determinate answere, not more desiring his own happiness, envying Argalus, whom he saw with narrow eyes, even ready to enjoy the perfection of his desires; strengthening his conceite with all the mischievous counsels which disdained love, and envious pride could give unto him; the wicked wretch (taking a time that Argalus was gone to his country, to fetch some of his principal friends to honor the marriage, which Parthenia had most joyfully consented unto), the wicked Demagoras (I say) desiring to speak with her, with unmerciful force (her weak arms in vain resisting), rubbed all over her face a most horrible poison: the effect whereof was such that never leper looked more ugly than she did: which done, having his men and horses ready, departed away in spite of her servants, as ready to revenge as they could be, in such an unexpected mischief.

You can amuse yourself by counting up the numbers of times you are delayed in this sentence by participial constructions in *-ing* ("assuring," "desiring," "strengthening") just when you are waiting breathlessly for the main verb. The end of the sentence (after the last colon) starts with "which done," something as close as we can get to a passive absolute construction on Latin lines; and it omits a necessary pronoun subject to "departed," since Latin verbs do not normally need to express "he" or "she" or "it" as subjects. Moreover, a number of words are used by Sidney in their original Latin sense rather than the familiar English one: "perfection" means "accomplishment, completion" as *perficere, perfectus* had meant "to complete."

LATIN STYLE IN ENGLISH

Even those authors who tried to eschew an excessive Latin vocabulary sometimes followed Latin sentence structure and idiom very closely. Reginald Pecock begins one of his sentences thus:

Even as grammar and divinity are 2 diverse faculties and cunnings, and therefore are unmeddled [distinct from each other], and each of them hath his proper to him bounds and marks, how far and no farther he shall stretch himself upon matters, truths, and conclusions. . . .

Every reader will notice how foreign-sounding is the expression "his proper-to-him bounds." Today we should consider it impossible to thrust a modifying phrase between "his" and the word it limits. But the phrase was so handled by Pecock, no doubt, because he was thinking of the Latin *fines sibi proprias*. The "how far" clause modifying "marks" has a Latin flavor also, recalling *quousque* clauses.

Notice too how Pecock creates new English idioms by translating literally certain Latin compounds. By "stretch himself upon," used in the non-physical sense, our author means "extend," from Latin *ex-tendere* "stretch out." In all self-conscious writers of the time there was a strong inclination to build elaborately balanced sentences, with clause counterweighing clause, in the manner of Roman rhetoricians. Pecock did this too. In formal exposition there was great use of constructions to contrast ideas "on the one hand"—"and on the other hand. . . ." In belles-lettres these elaborate balancings, both great and small, were often underscored by alliteration, making an intricate pattern of sound to correspond to the pattern of sense:

It happened this young imp to arrive at Naples, a *p*lace of more *p*leasure than *p*rofit, and yet of more *p*rofit than *p*iety, the very *w*alls and *w*indows whereof showed it rather to be the *t*abernacle of *V*enus than the *t*emple of *V*esta.

Thus John Lyly starts his hero Euphues on the artfully worded chronicle of his adventures. The italicized letters show how alliteration calls attention to the ideas put in antithesis. And once again we find illustration of Latin sentence structure used contrary to English idiom. It is not natural for us to say "It happened this young imp to arrive"—with "imp" presumably in an oblique (inflected) case as subject of the infinitive; nor was it probably a natural way of talking in Lyly's day. It is, however, a literal rendering of the Latin accusative with infinitive—*contigit iuvenem pervenīre.*

One more instance of non-English structure has persisted in limited scope into our day. It is the placement of adjectives after nouns on the model of both French and Latin—more particularly the former. Phrases like "lords appellants," "blood royal," "siege apostolic" are paralleled in contemporary use by surviving legal inversions: "notary public," "estates general," "body politic." Only the stereotyped inversions live on in ordinary speech, but poets avail themselves of the ability to create new ones when they are trying for an exalted effect. Thus Hart Crane, writing "wings imperious" and "junctions elegiac" is carrying on a minor Latin-Romance heritage of word order. In a phrase like "court martial" the unaccustomed inversion adds to the sense of ominous strangeness. Poets use this atmosphere to heighten desired effects deliberately.

UNSTANDARDIZED ELIZABETHAN GRAMMAR

Attempts to stretch English on the Procrustes bed of Latin grammar delayed the achievement of a generally accepted style of vigor and simplicity. (Francis Bacon represented simplicity of a sort, but it was highly mannered.) Besides, English grammar was in a fairly unstable condition. There were conflicts of usage due to the heritage of archaisms from the Middle English period, and the competition of dialect forms from the regions outside of London, which persisted into the Elizabethan era.

The third singular present of the verb is a good example of this fluctuation. If Shakespeare, writing in London, had followed the London tradition in this he would have used the *-eth* ending always, and consistently set down "singeth, loveth, creepeth." But another ending, *-(e)s,* had been gaining popularity at the expense of *-eth*. Originally *-es* developed in the North country, but it spread southwards until in the sixteenth century it was becoming as acceptable as the native southern form. Shakespeare was able to use the two indifferently: "the bird of dawning *singeth* all night long" but "Tomorrow and tomorrow and tomorrow *Creeps* in this petty pace from day to day."

Other matters of grammar were less rigidly established in Shakespeare's day than ours. There were still strong traces of grammatical gender in the use of "he" and "she" for inanimate objects where we should say "it." Pecock, it will be noticed, spoke of each faculty having "his" proper bounds, instead of "its." Shakespeare wrote, "The corn hath rotted ere *his* youth attained a beard," and spoke of the soul as "she," as when Hamlet says to Horatio:

> Since my dear soul was mistress of *her* choice
> And could of men distinguish, *her* election
> Hath seal'd thee for *herself*. . . .
>
> (*Hamlet,* III, ii)

The leveling of forms having proceeded with uneven tempo, there was considerable latitude of usage in inflected forms. Nominative and oblique cases of pronouns became somewhat confused; the newer usages have in many cases been approved by custom. The plays give us such forms as "My father hath no child *but I*," "When *him* we serve's away," "And damned be *him* that first cries 'Hold, enough!' " and "*Who* does he accuse?" There are also examples of compound subjects and even straight plural subjects with singular verbs, singular verbs with plural subjects, plural pronouns like "they" referring to singular indefinites like "everyone," double comparatives like "more braver"—in short, most of the hair-raising mistakes which cost students bad marks today. In formal prose there was more rigid usage than this, but the drama, closer to current speech, reflects a wider tolerance. In addition there were commonly accepted formulas which we now feel to be quaint rather than wrong. We are accustomed to think of abstract qualities such as "honor," "truth," and "courtesy" as single indivisible units: an Elizabethan, however, often made plural forms to indicate distributive use. His "Commend me to their loves," a very fair way of expressing things, simply appears odd to us, like the numerous words and phrases that have fallen into disuse: "I fain would know it," and so on.

THE AGE OF CLASSICISM AND FORMAL RULES

In the seventeenth and eighteenth centuries there was a strong reaction away from Elizabethan laxity and in favor of formal regularity of grammatical usage. Once more Latin exerted an influence, this time for the legislation of "rules": the intricate "do's" and "don'ts" to be observed if, as simple people often express it, one is to "talk grammar." The drive toward regularity and conformity in speech may be considered part and parcel of the general cultural manifestation known as "classicism," another term which we shall not attempt to define here. At least there is a certain appropriateness in the fact that grammatical relations were treated with a free and easy tolerance during an age of exploration, conquest, and colonization when plain piracy and robbery of land were being idealized; and that decorum and strict congruence were demanded as matters of taste (not only in grammar) when conquest had been organized into accepted, consolidated, and hence respectable empire. The parallelism may be worked out by students of culture in the large.

What we do know is that grammarians of the classical period set down fixed rules for the behavior of pronouns and verbs with a definiteness new in the history of English. A "good" writer could no longer put down "Between who?" even for the stage, if he intended it to be spoken by a prince like Hamlet. Such a locution was limited to low-class characters on the rare occasions when they were permitted to appear (for relief) in polite literature. When in doubt, the legislators of grammar appealed to Latin for authority. Was there some doubt about expressions such as "It is I," "It is me" or even "It am I"? The Latin rule about nominative cases as predicates after a finite form of "to be" decided the matter, and "It is I" was decreed despite a strong native tendency to say "It's me." In this period too, the fluctuating uses of "shall" and "will" were subjected to rules with complicated minor ramifications. Significantly enough, it was not a native Englishman but a French grammarian (George Mason) writing in 1622 for foreigners, who first tried to lay down the rules. In France as well as in England the dominant cultural tendencies favored regularity, probably for the same reasons. A Frenchman learning English would have been shocked at anything so chaotic as the "shall-will" conjugation, and it was natural for him, at that particular period, to try to give it a formal (if intricate) pattern.

Such an attitude affected the conservation of grammatical distinctions, too. While it regularized it also arrested leveling. For instance, the subjunctive in forms like "If I *were* you" or "If it *be* possible" had been giving way to the indicative, but a clear distinction was now reaffirmed in the precepts of eighteenth-century grammar. That codification has remained in force until our own times. Teaching has as usual had a conservative effect. If it were not for the careful preservation of these dying forms in school books, I should have begun this sentence with the words "If it was not. . . ." As it is, we tend to limit the few surviving subjunctives to formal discourse, printed or spoken.

In France an Academy had been established in order to give final, authoritative judgment on disputed questions of grammar and usage. Some writers in England advocated the establishment of a similar British Academy to legislate for the English language. It was felt in some quarters that refinement and formality should be made official. However, the project was never realized. Historians of English explain the resistance to it by citing the rugged independence of English character. This is no doubt true as far as it goes, but it is not a basic explanation. The rugged independence paradoxically manifested even in an age of conformity must itself be explained: perhaps by reference to the political interlude of the English Commonwealth, which effectively and permanently checked absolutism in government in the seventeenth century. It could not be successfully tried for any length of time after 1649. Any tendency towards absolutism in language was to some extent, therefore, checked by the changed political atmosphere resulting from the Commonwealth. Voltaire found this atmosphere to be very libertarian as compared with the French. Despite great similarities between French and English taste, there were great differences. France, lacking such a check as the experience of a republican government in the seventeenth century, showed the exaggerated effects of absolutism in both linguistic and cultural matters, down to 1789. The readjustment was the more drastic because it was so long delayed. The French Revolution, too, had its effect on the style and vocabulary of accepted speech—not only in France, but in England to a certain extent. The vogue of "simple" speech and rural dialects (one of the aspects of "romanticism") is connected with shifts in taste which heralded and accompanied the French Revolution.

IMPERIAL EXPANSION

Meanwhile the English language had been spread far and wide over the globe, following the course of imperial expansion. India, at first settled and claimed by the French as rival colonists, fell under exclusively English sway in the eighteenth century. In North America also French claims were forced to yield throughout the entire territory represented by Canada and the Thirteen Colonies. French survived as a language only in the Quebec region of Canada. English discoveries and settlements led to the claim over Australia and New Zealand. In the nineteenth century the greater part of the continent of Africa fell under English sway, both direct and indirect. The Dutch Colony of South Africa was taken over after the Boer War; large territories like the English Sudan became British dependencies in the form of colonies of "backward" peoples;

and some countries like Egypt were in practice directed by British commercial and administrative interests while maintaining formal independent statehood. Not everywhere in this far-flung territory has English been adopted as the prevalent speech. The dominions use it, of course; but in some of the colonies there has been little attempt to disseminate it beyond the circle of resident administrators, and in certain quarters (in India, for instance) it has met with conscious opposition.

The linguistic results of imperial expansion were manifold. We have already noticed the influx of foreign loan words into English from all quarters of the globe (chapter 4). In addition, each colonial dialect separated from the mother country has developed its own special idiosyncrasies, so that English-speaking visitors to England can be labeled, by their pronunciation, as emanating from Canada, Australia, South Africa, or "the States."

The settlement of Englishmen in India was particularly momentous for the history of linguistic science. When the dust of battle died down somewhat and peaceful contacts became possible, administrators with the gift of intellectual curiosity began to be impressed with the character of the various Indian languages belonging to the Indo-European family. When some of the bolder spirits extended their inquiry so far as to undertake the study of ancient Sanskrit, the classical literary language, they were further impressed by its affinities with the known classical languages of Europe. Sir William Jones was able to draw the proper conclusion as early as 1786: he wrote that Sanskrit, when compared to Greek and Latin,

bears a stronger affinity, both in the roots of verbs and in the forms of grammar, than could possibly have been produced by accident; so strong, indeed, that no philologer could examine them all three without believing them to have sprung from some common source, which, perhaps, no longer exists: there is a similar reason, though not quite so forcible, for supposing that both the Gothick and the Celtick, though blended with a very different idiom, had the same origin with the Sanskrit.

Sir William was quite right. His studies may be said to have opened the door on comparative philology, encouraged the work of Rask, Bopp, Grimm, Leskien, and the other pioneers who established family relations among languages in the nineteenth century.

CONTEMPORARY ENGLISH

In the recent past our language has shown no new tendencies of major importance. A great vowel shift has occurred since 1500, producing the modern sounds we associate with the printed symbols. The host of borrowed words is increasing daily, from all parts of the world. A supplementary list is being created from Latin and Greek roots to serve the purposes of scientific research. There is a revolt—within limits—against the rigid rules of classical grammarians. "Good" writers are again permitting themselves forms like these:

Those two, no matter who spoke, or whom was addressed, looked at each other. (Dickens, *Our Mutual Friend*.)

It depends altogether on who I get. (May Sinclair, *Mr. Waddington of Wick*.)

If I were her. . . . (Middleton Murry, *The Things We Are*.)

Kitty and me were to spend the day there . . . (by the bye. Mrs. Forster and me are such friends!) (Jane Austen, *Pride and Prejudice*.)

Her towards whom it made / Soonest had to go. (Thomas Hardy, "In the Garden.")

Until very recently, histories of the English language usually ended with cheerful speculation on the outlook for it as a world language. There were several cogent arguments in favor of it. First, it was pointed out that it is a living language already spoken by a great number of persons all over the globe. Second, it has a comparatively simple grammar. It boasts of a rich and glorious literature which offers a strong inducement for any student to acquire mastery of it. It offers pleasure, in other words, as well as profit. And within the last few years a simplified form of it, Basic English, has been offered to beginners as a means of expediting communication through a vocabulary of 850 words, adequate for all practical purposes. By means of this list a student is able to express any ideas, and even achieve certain aesthetic values of simple poignancy, within a very short time. He learns to say "go in" for "penetrate" and "flow out" for "exude," and is thus able to meet any situation with an adequate periphrasis. (Whether he can understand the fluent replies of a native ignorant of Basic is a different question!) These are surely inducements towards the adoption of English. Mr. Ogden claimed too much when he stated that absence of an international language like Basic English is "the chief obstacle to international understanding, and consequently the chief underlying cause of war." Unhappily, much more will be needed than a single speech to end wars. Nevertheless, Basic has certain advantages that may have a practical value. At a later date they may be discussed for practical application.

But in the present rivalries among contending empires, it would appear foolhardy to make any arguments or prophecies. The advantages of English, aside from its archaic spelling, still stand. But it may be some considerable time, longer than many of us had hoped, before these matters are decided by such mild individuals as professional philologists. The appeal to reason, the argument from simple practicality for all mankind, may have to wait upon history for a long time. And by then it may be that another candidate among the languages of the world may have achieved the position of outstanding advantage. We can only wait and see.

9. Language and Poetic Creation

PLEASURABLE ASPECTS OF SPEECH

We may know very little about the origin of human speech, but it is probably safe to assume that men found pleasure as well as use in it from the very beginning. Like other means employed to make life increasingly bearable in a practical way, it was adapted also to aesthetic satisfactions. Pitch and stress, qualities of vowel and consonant, tempo and dynamics were present in spoken sentences and offered the raw material for artistic creation. We may assume that as long as men have been human they have been aware that one way of saying a thing might be more pleasing than another. We have no reason to suppose that they have ever been mere animated machines, content to enunciate a wishful statement with the utmost of curt efficiency. If the earliest pottery shows a striving for design, early sentences probably did too.

Language is different from the other media which may be used for artistic purposes. It has some noteworthy advantages—which upon closer examination turn out to be handicaps to the aspiring apprentice in the poetic art. Conversely, of course, there are media in which the initial difficulties may be subdued to downright advantage.

For one thing, the process of learning your mother tongue occurs early, and is performed by all normally functioning members of the community. It is a painless act when compared with the struggles over raw materials in the other arts. Everybody, so to speak, starts out as a potential artist in words. And an extraordinarily large number of children show at least some impulse towards this form of aesthetic expression if they are given encouragement. To put the situation simply: you have to be very good to rise above the average high level of achievement which is the rightful prerogative of every speaking human being, not to mention the occasional outstanding accomplishments of average citizens under emotional stress. This is one way in which your initial advantage turns against you.

WORDS AS SYMBOLS

For another thing, you are operating with a highly symbolic medium when you put words together. The word is not the thing, as we are frequently reminded. A pot may be a pot *plus* something more imponderable: an expression of aspiration, let us say, or of squat complacent solidity. But the word is *nothing but* that imponderable plus, the symbol. Like ambition (as described by Rosencrantz in *Hamlet*) the word is of so airy and light a quality that it is but a shadow's shadow. Its meaning, as we have observed repeatedly, is purely conventional and exists only by tacit consent on the part of the community as a whole. To elevate it to higher significance is a correspondingly difficult feat. There must be a second, added aura of symbolism to provide the aesthetic element. This is not meant to imply anything too pretentious. Perhaps a simple example will explain.

The single word "rain" is a sentence—a presentative sentence, as explained in the last chapter—insofar as it announces or presents the appearance of a familiar form of precipitation of moisture from the heavens. Yet there is nothing in the sounds of [ɹein] to compel their relationship in our minds with falling water. That is due to habitual association. An inflection of the voice may suggest pleasure in the rain, but still present it as an everyday experience. The individual sounds in the word, if pronounced by a pleasingly modulated voice, may have aesthetic quality, in and of themselves. But the symbol stands alone as a factual sign. There has been no organization of elements (sounds as parts of symbols) with the primary intent to convey aesthetic experience. And aesthetic experience requires meaningful organization of a medium, according to principles of unity, diversity, balance, imbalance (and so on), which have been found by experience to add effective elements of emotive power to ordinary experience.

The word "rain" as ordinarily used is a jaded symbol. It evokes no tactile memories of stinging impact, cool envelopment, or warm spraying diffusion; no lively visual memories of slanting silver wire; no auditory memories of dull thudding heavy drops or the sharp battering on slate roofs. If an artist wishes to make you relive the experience of rain by sharing in his word-stimuli, he must operate consciously on the medium and galvanize you into fresh awareness, the more powerfully since words are so much a part of your everyday experience. If he does this one thing alone he has conveyed a certain higher symbolic meaning to "rain" in merely causing you to relive it thus in terms of verbal symbols. He has put a frame about the image and thus heightened its meaning, for frames add to the sense of what they enclose merely by setting it off.

This may be worth doing for itself. The imagists were content with this accomplishment. But the word-artist may be engaged in a more exalted act of patterning his elements. He may be evoking the experience of rain as part of a much more complex creative effort in organization of the medium. The rain may contribute to a larger mood, and at the same time put forward the plot of a story by its effect on the characters. Finally it may itself suggest more elusive analogous meanings of an abstract order while it accomplishes the concrete re-creation of physical experience. It is thus that Joyce treats snow in "The Dead," the last story of his incomparable *Dubliners.* Here the verbal symbols are used in the erection of higher order symbolism, as is frequently the case in Dante.

LINGUISTICS AND POETRY

To investigate the methodology of all this would be to attempt a new handbook of poetics. But that is not the purpose of this chapter. Instead I wish merely to indicate briefly the uses of some practical linguistic knowledge in studying literature, particularly the work of modern poets reputed to be "difficult" for technical reasons. Philology may be a humble follower in the train of the Muses, but she is of some assistance in gaining you an introduction to the loftier handmaids of Apollo. The thorny path traveled in some of our earlier chapters may lead you direct to pleasures of the Pierean spring—or at least help to speed you on your way.

In the first place, certain concessions are necessary from the unpracticed and possibly impatient reader. Since the idiom of much contemporary writing (especially in verse) is special and alien, readers tend to assume over-hastily that it expresses nothing at all. They label it nonsense and so have done with it. To do so is to barricade comprehension effectively. A more fruitful attitude is to assume that something is actually being said. The comprehension of it may require several types of effort, including a fresh approach to language. In the end you may decide that the effort was not worth making. The content may not, in your opinion, justify the technical difficulties put in your way. But if it does, the effort of collaboration with the author will have intensified your eventual appreciation. The discovery must at least precede the judgment. Remembering the basic handicap of language as a medium, you are asked to consent to innovations which will help to surmount it. And among one of the most urgent demands put upon you is the obligation to look at words afresh.

The following are some of the most stimulating techniques to be observed in contemporary writing.

SEMANTIC REJUVENATION

We have seen in the discussion of compound words (chapter 4), that some of the most abstract terms in the language are really faded metaphors. On examination it turns out that an earlier meaning, now forgotten, is often lively in the extreme. Hence an obvious means of invigorating our jejune vocabulary is to fall back on those lively older meanings. True enough, the average speaker does not know that they ever existed. He is not *reminded* that "express" once meant, literally and physically, "to press out." But he can learn it instantaneously from a context. It may be that only the archaic literal sense is intended, or it may be that both the physical and the metaphorical are to be grasped simultaneously. In any event, the impact of the divergent use on an attentive reader forces him to a new experience of the word, without sacrificing comprehension. An example of the use of "express" in this revivified fashion will be found in Emily Dickinson:

> Essential oils are wrung;
> The attar from the rose
> Is not expressed by suns alone,
> It is the gift of screws.

In the age of Shakespeare, intensive classical education had shaped a reading public (among the few, of course) who could sense the older meaning with less effort than many feel today. The plays offer repeated vivid uses of etymological rejuvenation of words. Horatio's "Season thy admiration for a while with an attent ear" makes use of the Latin sense of *admirāri,* "to wonder at" something and of "attent" in the sense of "stretched." "Hast thou no *speculation* in those eyes?" recalls the literal meaning of *speculare,* "to gaze, look upon." "Occulted guilt" means guilt covered over, or hidden. When Troilus says "there's no maculation in thy heart" he reminds us of the concrete meaning of *macula,* namely "spot (of dirt)," and when he refers to his "sequent protestation" it is in the concrete sense of "my calling on witness, which now follows." Hamlet's injunction "Let it be tenable in your silence still" evokes the basic meaning of Latin *tenēre,* "to hold"—not merely "to maintain a theoretical position." So when Laertes warns his sister that "nature, crescent, does not grow alone in thews and bulk," the adjective reminds us that *crescrere* meant "to grow," to mature in a physical sense. In *Troilus and Cressida* Ulysses can speak of "deracinating" a political state and thus call upon us to think of *racine,* a root, so that the meaning of "uproot" is conveyed in an unaccustomed startling manner. The usual word having lost emphasis, the learned one infuses new life by causing us to share in the original metaphoric synthesis.

Sophisticated writers still impose the etymological task upon their readers as part of the aesthetic experience. It may be said, in fact, that etymology is one of the devices by which readers are now called upon to share in the creative act. The enormous influence of English metaphysical poets of the seventeenth century on modern writers—notably the influence of Donne—has accentuated this etymological awareness. The reason for a return to metaphysical poets as a source of inspiration is not our subject here. But a consequence of it is certainly a recourse to similar linguistic devices.

James Joyce, for instance, has evinced etymological preoccupations throughout his entire work. When he says that one pugilist's fist is "proposed" under the chin of another, he intends the word as Latin *proponere,* "to place under"; and he is capable of using "supplant" as "to plant under" in describing the Gracehoper (i.e., Grasshopper) of *Finnegans Wake:* "he had a partner pair of findlestilts to *supplant* him." T. S. Eliot expects the same etymological collaboration from his readers in his simile from "The Love Song of J. Alfred Prufrock":

> Streets that follow like a tedious argument
> Of insidious intent
> To lead you to an overwhelming question. . . .

Like Shakespeare, he wishes you to remember that "intent" means a thing that is taut and stretched for action, and that "insidious" (Latin *insidiae,* "sitting or lurking within") means "ambushed" against an enemy. At the same time the literal metaphor of warfare is merged in the image of a verbal argument. In "Preludes" there is another figure of the many he evokes from the streets of a city:

> The conscience of a blackened street
> Impatient to assume the world.

Here it is necessary to remember that "assume" means "to take on" (ad-sumere) and hence "to play the part of." In his epithet "maculate giraffe" ("Sweeny among the Nightingales") he is doing exactly as Shakespeare did: reminding us that our faded theological term "immaculate conception" contains a sharp visual image of literal, physical spots.

So C. D. Lewis makes use of both the literal and figurative senses of "derelict mills" in "You that love England." He means lonely and abandoned mills, of course, but also mills that have simply and unmetaphorically been "left behind" (de-linqui) by those who formerly worked in them. And W. H. Auden, speaking in "Sir, No Man's Enemy" of "the distortions of ingrown virginity," surely intends us to feel the root meaning of "twist, physical bending from the norm" under the abstract "distortion." When he uses the expression "trains that *fume* in the station" he evokes the literal visual image "to smoke" as well as the later extended meaning "to be impatient."

Hart Crane's strange vigor is in part derived from the reminder of root meanings. Here are a few examples. In a description of an airplane flying over Mount Hatteras, the pilot is thus addressed:

> Remember, Falcon-Ace,
> Thou hast there in thy wrist a Sanskrit charge
> To conjugate infinity's dim marge—
> Anew . . . !

If the general sense is the quasi-magic power of dominating the horizons of infinity, the root meaning of "conjugate" is still felt as "to put a yoke on," rather than "to inflect a verb." In "Garden Abstract" the opening lines are

> The apple on its bough is her desire,—
> Shining suspension, mimic of the sun.

The abstract word "suspension" is to be interpreted as "the thing which is hung." In the haunting phrase "the silken skilled transmemberment of song" there is an enormous heightening of effect when the trite word "trans-formation" (passing of one form into another) is replaced by "transmemberment" (passing of one member into another). This particular instance shows how readily an acquired skill in etymological rejuvenation will pass into creative independence in handling words. It is but a step to

WORD FORMATION

out of elements already known or guessed. There is less downright creation of words, even by the boldest innovators, than is popularly supposed. Hart Crane's "thunder is galvothermic" (from "The Tunnel") creates a word not registered in the dictionaries: but its component parts make clear the sense of "electrically warm." (The fuller form "galvanothermic" would have been more conventional.) Thomas Hardy subdues language to his purposes when he writes verbs like "to unbe," "unillude," or "unbloom," and nouns like "unease" and "lippings" (meaning "talk"). James Joyce has experimented in the creation of new word forms to meet special needs, especially adapted to the passages of interior monologue in *Ulysses*. In this he diverges conspicuously from the example of his predecessor Dujardin, whose novel of interior monologue, *Les Lauriers sont coupés*, does not contain any linguistic innovations and is written in conventional French.

Joyce tried to approximate the stuff of our flowing wakeful consciousness by reproducing in speech the leaps, combinations, and blurrings of word and image characteristic of our private thoughts. Only certain parts of the novel are composed in this fashion. Cutting across these are sharp word-images recording the sounds and sights of the objective world. Onomatopoeia shapes some of the new formations of words. A long-held note of a song, a "longindying call," is said to dissolve in "endlessnessnessness"; a woman's hair is "wavyavyeavyheavyeavyevyevy"; the sound of passing horses' hoofs becomes "steelhoofs ringhoof ring." The mundane sound of body gases accompanies the hero's solemn meditation: "Then, not till then, my eppripfftaph. Be pfrwritt." Disjointed meditation is indicated by clipped forms: "He saved the situa. Tight trow. Brilliant ide," for "He saved the situation. Tight trousers. Brilliant idea." But it is noteworthy that the most audacious coiners of verbal currency are limited to units capable of conveying sense—and therefore meaningful because they are in some degree familiar.

PUNNING

is a technique now being exploited once more in all seriousness after centuries of disrepute. It is made possible by the existence of homonyms in a language: words identical in spoken form but having different meanings, often different origins. The spelling may or may not differ. In French there are two words *louer:* one, meaning "to praise," from Latin *laudare;* the other meaning "to rent" from Latin *locāre.* The identity of forms today makes it possible to construct a witty compliment to a landlord in French, using a single phrase to indicate that a house is both praiseworthy and rentable. *"Je loue votre maison parceque je la loue!"* In Shakespeare's day this double use of homonyms was considered a legitimate adjunct of superbly serious style. It was not limited, although it was also applied, to joking frivolous discourse. In *Julius Caesar* the words of Mark Antony spoken alone over the dead body in the Senate—

> O world, thou wast the forest to this *hart,*
> And this indeed, O world, the very *heart* of three—

were not meant to elicit smiles. The conscious balancing of the two homonyms was felt to heighten the intensity of Antony's tribute because it offered an auditory bond, "hart: heart," for the linking of two very serious metaphors.

Among modern writers James Joyce is again the most conspicuous exploiter of the pun. He uses it as part of his general attempt to widen the scope of language. There are tentative trial instances in *Ulysses:* "She rose and closed her reading rose of Castille," or "With the greatest alacrity, Miss Douce agreed. With grace of alacrity . . . she turned herself." On the opening pages of *Finnegans Wake* we find the following double meanings:

> doublin = Dublin, doublin'
> retaled = retailed, re-taled (i.e., told again)
> erse solid man = Erse solid, arse-solid
> wills = wills (n.) and wills (vb., opposite to "won'ts")
> Finnegan = Finnegan, Finn again
> half = halve, have
> wan = wan, one
> lean on = lean on, lien on

If foreign words may be included the list may be lengthened:

> bygmester = big master, Danish *Byggmester* (master builder)
> violer d'amores = *viola d'amore,* violator of loves
> wallhall = wall hall, Walhalla
> one eyegonblack = *ein Augenblick;* a blackened eye
> fern = fern (the plant), *fern* (distant)
> far = far (adv.), Danish *Far* (father) (*cf.* p. 628)
> mere = only, *Meer* (ocean) (p. 628)

VERBAL AND PHRASAL DISTORTIONS

In many of the punning expressions of Joyce, there is use of words not strictly homonymous. Two words not precisely alike in sound are related to each other by a slight distortion of one of them which brings them closer together. This is employed far more widely than straight punning in *Finnegans Wake*.

The purpose is to extend the application of a single word or phrase by evoking simultaneously another one also pertinent to the occasion although in an entirely different fashion. The allusions are not limited to English. As with the simple puns, the phrases are so treated as to include references to other languages.

> dontelleries = *dentelleries* (French for lace-adorned objects); also discreet, intimate garments which "don't tell"
>
> erigenating = originating; also Erigena-ting (from Duns Scotus Erigena, the "Erin-born" philosopher)
>
> venissoon after = very soon after; venison after; Venus' son after
>
> eroscope = horoscope; Eros-scope; hero-scope
>
> Fiendish Park = Phoenix Park; Park of Fiends
>
> museyroom = museum; musing room
>
> Champ de Mors = Champ de Mars; Field of Death (Mors)
>
> herodotary = hereditary; hero-doter; Herodotus(?)
>
> pigmaid = made like a pig; pigmied

Whole phrases are made to evoke others at the same time, so that a simple statement is paralleled by another heard in overtones:

> and of course all chimed din width the eatmost boviality = and of course all chimed in with the utmost joviality (implications of noise, expansiveness, beefy appetite)
>
> honeys wore camelia paints = Honey swore Camelia paints; also *honi soit qui mal y pense*
>
> haloed be her eve, her singtime sung, her rill be run, unhemmed as it is uneven! = the Lord's prayer transferred to a mythological goddess-river
>
> when ginabawdy meadabawdy = gin-bawdy, mead-bawdy; also "gin a body meet a body"
>
> sware by all his lards porsenal = pig's fat; Lars Porsena

a king off duty and a jaw forever = a thing of beauty
and a joy forever; also a bore

Are you not danzzling on the age of a vulcano? = dancing on the edge; also, dazzled in a volcano-like age
(also, Vulcan-like).

POLYPHONIC SENTENCES

The purpose of Joyce is the achievement of the effects of
polyphonic music in verbal writing. Hitherto it has seemed
impossible for literature to approximate the advantage of
music: namely an ability to have the ear apprehend, simultaneously and yet distinctly, two or more themes being unfolded at once. Joyce substitutes for melodies polysemantic verbal patterns realized by means of distortions. The intonation
of the phrase is important in establishing the secondary motif.
This is not the place to discuss the value or aesthetic justifications for Joyce's experiment. It may be pointed out, however,
that the curious and ambiguous linguistic medium is employed
to treat a subject-matter derived largely from the subconscious:
a dream state.

There is an aptness in the occasion, at any rate. The material
of the "story" is the dream of a Dublin citizen, with lapses into
nightmare, interruptions, and starts into half-consciousness,
throughout a long night. The author tries to penetrate beneath
the most inclusive recordings of a flow of waking consciousness,
and to express in this new literary medium the flow of subconscious imagery in a dream. The attempt appears at first
sight to result in little more than a private, non-communicable
gibberish. A page of these multiple simultaneous themes, replete with unconventional punctuation and capitalization,
looks like strange nonsense to the uninitiated. But it does yield
to patient analysis.

To be sure a properly equipped reader is expected to be un-
precedentedly polyglot and widely read. Very few, presumably,
are in a position to decipher the text. And there are all sorts of
questions which may be legitimately raised about the ultimate
value of the significant content which may underlie all the

verbal distortions. Nevertheless the sheer virtuosity of Joyce's performance is beyond comparison. Even a slight experiment in interpretation of it will be found to be linguistically exhilarating. At the very least a reader will emerge newly alert to the resources of language as more ordinary people use it.

CONCRETES TO EXPRESS ABSTRACTIONS

There is another way of refreshing verbal concepts besides reminding readers of the component parts of abstract terms. It is to make bold substitution of entirely concrete simple terms for the vaguer abstract ones which are actually intended. "Protection" is a chilly, colorless word. It becomes more vivid if you are reminded that it means a covering-over *(tegere)* in behalf of *(pro)* someone. It becomes poignantly immediate if it is translated into the still more concrete image of *"roofing* over" *(tectum)*. The disadvantage is, however, that the implied abstraction, although still essential to the meaning, may be lost entirely from the image. Width of scope may be sacrificed to immediacy. "He gave me the roofing over me" is a heart-warming statement, but it may fail to convey the general and inclusive function of protection-in-general. It may be taken as a bald statement of a mere night's shelter—limited, literal, and unsymbolic.

Gerard Manley Hopkins is a master of the successful transposition of abstract into concrete. The implications of generality, even of universality, are never missed when he intends to suggest them through a tangible word. In "Felix Randall,' the priest speaks of the large and handsome body of the man who has just died—"his moult of man"—"pining, pining, till time when reason *rambled* in it." The errancy of thought during delirium is brought close by the concrete term. Of God it is said, "He *fathers-forth* whose beauty is past change," a vivid transmutation of theological terminology about divine creation. The acceptance of castigation is expressed:

> I did say yes
> O at lightning and lashed rod.

The grandeur and sweep of the adjoining images prevent any misunderstanding of the unpretentious first four words. Less skilfully placed they might have failed, because of over-simplicity, to convey the complex metaphysical act to be designated. This would have defeated half of the intent. Vigor would have been gained at the price of significance.

Gertrude Stein sacrifices more than most writers are willing to do in order to gain musical quality and immediacy. Most polysyllables go by the board in her effort to achieve concretion. Her consciously primitivistic vocabulary—a very different thing, by the way, from a primitive one!—is a perpetual challenge to the reader to create afresh the intended abstractions out of presented monosyllables. This one trick is in fact the summation of her style. A word portrait of a woman is an example:

Florence Descotes
Never to be restless
Never to be afraid
Never to ask will they come
Never to have made
Never to like having had
Little that is left then
She made it do
One and two
Thank her for everything.

Under the seemingly guileless statement you are supposed to perceive a sophisticated delineation, something like this: "She was a balanced, reconciled and courageous person; she did not harass herself and others about trifles. She never thought the thing done perfect nor did she seek possession. She was content with the residue of experience, great or little. She commands our gratitude."

In a recent novel, *Ida*, Miss Stein manages to convey the symbolical value of simple experiences by the use of this simplistic vocabulary. The heroine is in conversation with a young friend named Arthur:

He began to talk. He said. All the world is crying crying about it all. They all want a king.

She looked at him and then she did not. Everybody might want a king but anybody did not want a queen.

It looks, said Arthur, as if it was sudden but really it took some time, some months and even a couple of years, to understand how everybody wants a king.

He said. Do you know the last time I was anywhere I was with my mother and everybody was good enough to tell me to come again. That was all long ago. Everybody was crying because I went away, but I was not crying. That is what makes everybody a king that everybody cries but he does not.

Presumably the sense is this: "All persons are congenitally inclined to seek a ruler or a type of leader who will establish admirable patterns of conduct and live up to them. Curiously enough they do not usually look to a woman for this leadership. The last time Arthur had a significant experience of this was an occasion when he alone maintained self-control while others succumbed to emotion. This difference embodied the essential quality of the leadership which others seek."

The sentiment may be questionable but the purpose is fairly clear. In other writings Miss Stein is less lucid. In *Four Saints in Three Acts* the primitivistic material offered is so little organized that there is much wider scope to the reader's interpretation, and thus much less certainty about the themes being handled. Certain repeated juxtapositions seem to indicate that the two leading saints—Theresa and Ignatius—represent a cunningly planned contrast, let us say between the unratiocinating mystic (Theresa) and the analytical, intellectual saint (Ignatius). The unifying vision is repeatedly contrasted with the discriminating intellect which looks for distinctions. But this is merely suggested by fragmentary unsyntactical phrases and indirect allusions:

Saint Theresa seated and not surrounded. There are a great many persons and places near together.

There are a great many persons and places near together.

Saint Theresa once seated. There are a great many places and persons near together. Saint Theresa seated and not surrounded. There are a great many places and persons near together (p. 22).

A reader with patience and a lively imagination, trained in the verbal interchange of abstract and concrete, may paraphrase this to mean: "Saint Theresa, a brooding mystic, undelimited, passive and visionary, had the gift of perceiving things in juxtaposition which are conventionally regarded as separate. She annihilated space in her thought." (Mind you, I am not sure that this is precisely what was meant, but it can be *drawn out* of the text at will.) The description is amplified by a comparison with the inconscient fertility of the earth:

Saint Theresa with the land and laid. Not observing.
Saint Theresa coming to go.
Saint Theresa coming and lots of which it is not as soon as if when it can left to change change theirs in glass and yellowish at most most of this can be when it is that it is very necessary not to plant it green. Planting it green means that it is protected from the wind and they never knew about it. They never knew about it green and they never knew about it she never knew about it they never knew about it they never knew about it she never knew about it. Planting it green means it is necessary to protect it from the sun and from the wind and the sun and they never knew about it and she never knew about it and she never knew about it and they never knew about (p. 31 f.) .

The fundamental image contained in the first line compares the saint to tilled land, not "observing" in the sense, presumably, of not reflecting. This is embroidered by repetitious concrete statements in which an abstract term like "inconscience" or "awareness" is replaced by near-conjugation of the verb "to know" in a negative form.

Saint Ignatius, on the other hand, is linked repeatedly with concrete expressions implying intellectual preoccupations, as would be appropriate for the founder of the Jesuit order: "Saint Ignatius might be very well adapted to plans and a dis-

tance" (p. 32); "Saint Ignatius occurred Saint Ignatius withdrew occurred withdrew" (p. 44); "Saint Ignatius [says]. In
line and in in line please say it first in line" (p. 47). According
to his "friends" (the chorus), he is interested in things distant
as well as things close at hand: "the magpie in the sky" as well
as the "pigeons on the grass alas"! In fact, "he asked for a distant magpie as if they made a difference" (p. 47f.). "Was Saint
Ignatius able to tell the difference between palms and Euca-
lyptus trees?" (p. 33). Apparently he was, for he is described
as "A saint to be met by and by by and by continuing reading
read read readily" (p. 37). In the end the contrasted saints are
characterized in summary. To the question "who makes who
makes it do" the answer is, "Saint Theresa and Saint Theresa
too"—an affirmation of her creative or unifying role? To the
question "who makes it be what they had as porcelain" (i.e.,
fragile), the answer is: "Saint Ignatius and left right laterally
be lined"—a description of the analytical and demarking function of his intellect? These two definitions, if such they may be
called, conclude the "opera."

I do not know whether these proposed interpretations are
correct, that is, aesthetically justified or conformant to the
author's plan. Much of the Steinian text is constructed for
sound alone, and there is also much jocosity in the form of
puns, bizarre juxtapositions, and startling transitions, perhaps
unrelated to any central theme. Some of the puns are Joycean.
"An egg and add some. Some and sum. Add sum. Add some"
(p. 27) recalls Joyce's play on Latin *adsum*. There are many
such jests in Stein. Though decorative, they surely do not make
for clarity. But certain passages invite creative reinterpretation
by the reader; and it appears that we are invited to pursue some
method like the one here suggested.

The value of Miss Stein's innovation may be questioned, as
was Joyce's. My own criticism of her work is, not that it means
nothing, but that the rather snobbish pleasure derived from
collaborating with her in a quest for meaning is not great

enough to justify the effort and the slight results. The content of her verse is limited to truisms and facile antitheses after all. To a lesser degree than Joyce she does provide a kind of linguistic rejuvenation by a method of her own, but other poets give a heightened pleasure in language with far less sacrifice of propositional content.

ABSTRACTIONS TO EXPRESS THE CONCRETE

If the use of a limited concrete word heightens vivid immediacy, the use of an abstract one for a concrete situation will heighten the general sense of importance and significance in the situation. Much of the vague awe and reverence attendant upon the religious vocabulary in English is due to its formation out of Latin abstract nouns with no homely connotations in ordinary speech. In other languages with a more homogeneous vocabulary this may not be true. A German child learning the term *unbeflecktes Empfängnis* may recognize in the first word the humble word *Flecke*, "spot," which he first learned when he spattered mud or grease over his clothes. The correlation will help clarify the semantic situation for him, but it may somewhat reduce his sense of awe. An English-speaking child has no similar experience to fall back on when he learns the august phrase "immaculate conception." The vagueness of the connotations may therefore heighten his sense of mystery in dealing with the phrase. Emily Dickinson employs occasional abstractions in order to give transcendent value to poignant homely situations.

> Go not too near a house of rose,
> The *depredation* of a breeze
> Or *inundation* of a dew
> Alarm its walls away;
> Nor try to tie the butterfly;
> Nor climb the bars of *ecstasy*.
> In *insecurity* to lie
> Is *joy's* insuring *quality*.

Instances can be found in contemporary poets too. The shift from defined situation to an abstraction often marks the end of a poem. This is in line with the transmutation of significance implied in an abstract term. Robert Graves, concluding a brief sketch of a "Quayside," refers to the spaces at sea for contrast, where

> ships are few, each on its proper course,
> With no *occasion* for *approach* or *discourse.*

In a poem called "O Love in me," he presents first graphic images of the impact of existence, and then concludes:

> Take your delight in *momentariness,*
> Walk between dark and dark, a shining space
> With the grave's *narrowness,* though not its *peace.*

Two examples from Auden:

> You alone, alone, O imaginary song,
> Are unable to say an existence is wrong,
> And pour out your *forgiveness* like a wine.
> ("The Composer")

> May I, composed like them   [i.e., the Just]
> Of Eros and of dust,
> Beleaguered by the same
> *Negation* and *despair*
> Show an affirming flame.
> ("September 1, 1939")

The effect of abstractions is exploited in connection with the concrete theme of moonlight: "This lunar beauty has no history. . . ."

There is sustained use of abstractions implanted among particulars in the following stanza of Ben Belitt, describing "Battery Park: High Noon":

> Suddenly
> Between flint and glitter, the leant leaf
> The formal *blueness,* blooming over slate,
> Struck into glass and plate,

The public tulips, treading *meridian glare*
In bronze and whalebone by the statue bases
  Elude the Battery Square,
    Turn, with a southern gesture, in remembered air,
    And claim a loved *identity*, like faces. . . .

Hart Crane is as bold with abstractions as with their opposites. In fact it may be said that much of his verbal effect
comes from swift alternation of stingingly concrete images with
abstract terms. The illustrations are easy to find: "A boy runs
with a dog before the sun, straddling *Spontaneites* that form
their independent orbits. . . ." (p. 67); "Smutty wings flash
out *equivocations*" (p. 93); "from palms to the severe/Chilled
albatross's white *immutability*" (p. 105); "Infinite *consanguinity* it bears—This tendered theme of you. . . ." (p. 104); "Ex-
pose vaunted validities that yawn/Past *pleasantries*. . . ." (p.
130). To paraphrase these is to spoil the effect Crane deliberately strove for. Still, some periphrasis is required, since Crane
challenges the intellectual participation as much as sensuous
appreciation, quite in the manner of the complex metaphysical
poets. It will be noticed that in these quotations the effect of
the abstractions is heightened by emplacement near extremely
vivid words. "Smutty wings" and "equivocations" heighten
each other by contrast, as do "validities" and "yawning." This
leads to the general question of semantic enrichment by means
of another technique: juxtapositions.

JUXTAPOSITIONS

We have seen in the chapter on semantics that all words are
surrounded by an aura of connotations in addition to the precise denotations. When two words with similar connotative
spheres are put together they strengthen each other so far as
factual information is concerned, but they do not offer a challenge to the attention or a marked stimulus to the imagination.
It is otherwise when two words are juxtaposed out of different

connotative spheres. The element of conflict enriches the expression. A simple form of the usage has long been practiced by English poets. It consists in placing together two words belonging to two different realms of physical sense. Milton's "blind mouths" is an example. E. E. Cummings speaks of "eyes which mutter thickly" (*is 5*, Three, iv), of something "noisecolored" (*W*, or *Viva*, p. 3), and a "rolypoly voice" (*is 5*, One, i).

The general device is being widely employed today. T. S. Eliot is a past master of this technique, which harmonizes with his larger purpose of contrasting moods and cultures deliberately by way of satiric commentary. The technique is epitomized in the sentence from "Whispers of Immortality": ". . . her friendly bust/Gives promise of pneumatic bliss," where the derisive adjective conflicts with the traditionally "poetic" noun. In a more abstract way Gertrude Stein does the same thing: witness her titular expression "Tender Buttons." The satirical intent is lacking in such a pairing off; what you receive is rather a verbal shock producing an effect so diffuse that it can scarcely be used to serve a wider purpose. Eliot, of course, goes much farther than simple combinations of words. The balance may involve parts of a sentence. In

> I have measured out my life with coffee spoons.

the caesura of the line marks the break between the two antithetical elements. The same poem, "The Love Song of J. Alfred Prufrock," contains an extended example of phrasal juxtaposition.

> There will be time to murder and create,
> And time for all the works and days of hands
> That lift and drop a question on your plate;
> Time for you and time for me,
> And time yet for a hundred indecisions,
> And for a hundred visions and revisions,
> Before the taking of a toast and tea.

Here the first imposing line—held in suspense in your mind while you read the next five—is contrasted with the mundane ordinariness of the last. Within this enclosing envelope of juxtaposition there are smaller units: "murder" put beside "create," the abstract "question" beside the concrete "plate." And there is also a case of etymological rejuvenation. The juxtaposition of "revisions" beside "visions" reminds you that the word once meant "seeing for a second time." Here you are supposed to grasp both the literal and metaphorical meanings simultaneously.

"The Waste Land" is of course built on an elaborate pattern of contrasting juxtapositions. Echoes of Dante, *Parzival*, *Tristan*, Shakespeare, Verlaine, Baudelaire, and others of august connotation serve to enhance the bitter sordidness of contemporary allusions. Eliot demands recognition of these allusions for a full appreciation of his purpose.

> A crowd flowed over London Bridge, so many,
> I had not thought death had undone so many.
> Sighs, short and infrequent, were exhaled,
> And each man fixed his eyes before his feet.

Unless you perceive the use of Dante's *"io non avrei mai creduto / Che morte tanta n'avesse disfatta,"* you do not get the full effect. An elaborate and bizarre instance is given in the drab, furtive, meaningless seduction of a city typist by a small house agent's clerk, "carbuncular." The episode is opened with an echo of Sappho's beautiful distich on the evening star, which summons home to rest "all that the glittering morn hath driven afar," and is concluded with a sardonic modernization of Goldsmith's "When lovely woman stoops to folly." Insofar as the pleasure of recognizing literary allusion is at present limited to few out of the reading public, enjoyment of Eliot's technique remains snobbishly restricted. The necessary linguistic prowess is less exacting, however. The reasons for exclusiveness are special and different from the ones encountered in Joyce. They are based chiefly on ability to recognize allusions; much less on ability to manipulate linguistic elements.

LEVELS OF DISCOURSE

Comparable to the juxtaposition of words with conflicting connotations is the abrupt change from one level of discourse to another. It will be explained in the chapter on society and linguistic problems that languages like ours exist in several strata, according to the economic and cultural positions occupied by different speakers. To pass from one to another in the confines of a single poem is to give the reader another type of stimulating shock: a rhetorical one. John Dos Passos, interrupting lyrical passages in his novels with snatches of popular song, journalistic headlines, and colloquialisms, made sustained use of this variety in his novels. A German example, also in prose, is Alfred Döblin's *Berlin Alexanderplatz*. The alternation of styles may be found in poems like Horace Gregory's "Columbo Dominico" and "Longface Mahoney Discusses Heaven." Archibald MacLeish makes judicious use of the admixture of colloquial in lofty context in *Frescoes for Mr. Rockefeller's City*. Edgar Lee Masters tried the abrupt shift in some poems of his *Spoon River Anthology*, though here it was images rather than locutions which were put into bizarre juxtaposition.

Some contemporary poets are conducting experiments in the total use of substandard colloquial speech for lyrical purposes. John Weaver did so, some time ago, in his poems *In American*. Kenneth Fearing is exploring the possibilities today. E. E. Cummings sometimes produces a mystifying example of his own special type of "phonetic" writing on this level. Of course it is not phonetic. It takes liberties with the sounds really used on this level, presumably in order to satisfy the inner ear of Mr. Cummings, and it indulges in a curious vivisection of words to conform to his rhythmical desires. Here is an example:

> oil tel duh woil doi sez
> dooyuh unnurs tanmih eesez pullih hizmus tah oi
> dough un giv uh shid oi sez. . . .
>
> 　　　　　　　　　. . . Fur Croi saik
> ainnoughbudih gutnutntuhplai?

You may decipher this readily enough if you read it aloud without regarding the divisions of words.

EVOCATION OF THE UNSAID

Because we learn words and phrases in contexts, each fresh use of them tends to recall the original association. In expressions frequently employed, like proverbs, the initial word or two will be sufficient to recall the whole. An allusive and pregnant style results when discourse is made up of the minimum verbal signals necessary to recall an entire statement. No one is puzzled by the fragmentary "A word to the wise." The equivalent statement in Latin is even more pregnant, since it can be reduced to two words: *"Verbum sapienti."* Writers who attempt to record a stream of consciousness use fragmentary allusion generously, since it corresponds in some sort to the rapid short-cuts we make in thinking without elaborate verbalization, especially on the emotive level.

　Here again a considerable burden is placed on the reader. The difference between complete understanding and complete mystification may depend on knowledge of one incomplete allusion. So in the otherwise clear character sketch by E. E. Cummings:

> yonder deadfromtheneckupgraduate of a
> somewhat obscure to be sure university spends
> her time looking picturesque under
>
> the as it happens quite
> erroneous impression that he
>
> nascitur.

The task of supplying punctuation is not difficult, but the whole point of the sketch is lost if you fail to recall the Latin saying, *Poeta nascitur non fit,* "A poet is born, not trained." If you do remember, you will realize that "he" must be a poet. The self-conscious young lady graduate spends her time posturing for "him" under the illusion that he is a poet and will immortalize her. (The same proverb is alluded to in another of Cummings' lines: "Each dream nascitur, is not made. . . .") Without knowledge of the unsaid, that which is said usually conveys little or no meaning.

SHIFT OF GRAMMATICAL CATEGORY

Since the Renaissance, poets have been making use of the elasticity of English grammar. There is nothing to distinguish many verbs from the nouns derived from them; adverbs are often identical with adjectives or with prepositions in outward form. This being so, a creative writer is easily led to increase the elasticity of ordinary speech when he transforms it for his higher ends. Shakespeare uses an adjective as a verb when he says "*sicklied* o'er with the pale cast of thought" or "*violenteth* in a sense as strong"; a noun as a verb when he says "Lord Angelo dukes" it well. It is quite usual to hear "but me no buts" in ordinary speech; and most school children will recall Tennyson's "Diamond me no diamonds," and "Prize me no prizes" from the *Idylls of the King*.

The moderns furnish plenty of instances; in fact one is embarrassed by the multiplicity of them. Of course when writers abandon formal grammar temporarily it is hard to tell how much shifting is going on, and you are presumably at liberty to interpret the syntax (if any) as you please. This is only true, however, in the most esoteric passages of writers like Stein. Elsewhere a little reflection will clear up a seeming snarl of relationships.

Occasionally Gerard Manley Hopkins permits himself a daring shift in parts of speech. He refers to the ocean in "The Deutschland" as "widow-making unchilding unfathering deeps." Not only are two nouns here made into verbs, but they are provided with unprecedented negative forms. In the same poem an adverbial phrase becomes a noun: "dandled the to and fro." Joyce has made two similar adverbial expressions into verbs. "The hitherandthithering waters" of the Liffey River conveys the effect of currents and eddies; a dog "almosting" a bone indicates strain and frustrated effort better than the usual expression because it embodies the central transitive idea in the verb where it belongs. ("Get" has become as colorless as "is.") An adjective is treated the same way in the phrase "warm sunshine merrying over the sea." Here again the conventional expression "making merry" is ineffective because the verb—which should be important in a verbal idea—is lacking in color. A pronoun becomes a noun in Cummings's "the feline she with radish red legs." An adverb sprouts unorthodox suffixes in the phrase "hoop returns fasterishly." In Auden's

> Sir, no man's enemy, forgiving all
> But will his negative inversion, be prodigal,

the noun "inversion" appears to be used as a verb, with the object preceding. This is not certain, however. There is similar doubt about the construction of the sentence in his *Double Man*, lines 194-99, which hinge on the ambiguous words "frowns the young Rimbaud guilt demands." The hesitation engendered by such innovations may delay the current of the reader's attention in a salutary manner. But this is true only if the arrested flow serves to underscore a genuinely significant thought.

REARRANGEMENT OF SENTENCE UNITS

Normal English word order tends to carry the attention forward in a sequence Subject → Predicate → Complement. Modifiers are usually placed unobtrusively, where they will cause least interruption. Variations on the normal order are limited because of a lack of inflections to show syntactic relations. Still, poets and other writers take certain liberties with normal word order in order to gain for themselves some of the advantages of inflected languages. This too is nothing new in the history of English literature. The seventeenth-century prose writers imitated Latin ablative absolutes and other constructions which might not at first blush seem at all adapted to the genius of the English sentence. It is by inversions chiefly that modern writers try to approximate the values of Latin or German sentence structure. Whenever Joyce's hero of *Ulysses,* Mr. Bloom, pursues a reverie with any freedom, the sentences recording it become replete with inversions. The main image is put first, whether it is shaped in an adverb, a phrase, a verb (finite or non-finite) or any other part of speech. Whatever else is said becomes the predicate—that is, the thing predicated—no matter what its formal structure. Curiously enough, this unconventional handling of sentences corresponds to the theory of "segmented parts" elaborated by two French scholars, Ferdinand Brunot and Charles Bally, for the French language. Their books, by the way, are heartily recommended to any persons handicapped by too great regard for traditional grammar in the approach to contemporary literature.

This is how Joyce reorganizes sentences into "inverted parts" of image plus predication in *Ulysses:*

> God they believe she is: or goddess
> By went his eyes
> See me he might
> Glorious tone he has still
> Down she sat. All ousted looked

The scores of examples of this sort of usage in the novel simply illustrate what Bally calls *segmentation* in discussing the elasticity of sentence usage in colloquial speech. Ordinarily we use little tags and formulas in order to shift to the position of major "theme" (as he calls it) those parts not grammatically constituting a "subject" in the traditional sense. For instance, to give the desired stress we say: "So far as *the treaty* is concerned, they never intended to keep it," instead of merely

"They never intended to keep the treaty." Or in conversation we say: "That piece over there—if it's done give it to me." In the preceding discussion, the present author exemplified segmentation in the sentence beginning "It is by inversions chiefly that. . . ." French has its own formulas of segmentation like *quant à* ("so far as"); some appear cryptic to a foreign listener: *Ça alors—mais quand-même—par exemple!—je ne l'ai jamais su!* or *Cette fille là—vraiment je ne la connais pas.* A different intonation marks a segmented presentation from an ordinary sentence. In German the larger number of inflections makes rearrangement of parts possible in a sentence without modification of formal syntax. But in colloquial speech emphasis brings about sentences like: *Den Mann dort—den hab' ich nie vorher gesehen.*

All of this is by way of indicating that creative writers often make use of colloquial practices long since recognized by liberal grammarians. From Walt Whitman to Archibald MacLeish they have been giving us whole catalogues of nouns in verbless presentations. Cleanth Brooks has spoken of MacLeish as the poet of the noun, not of the verb. Other poets lean on verbs at the expense of nouns.

The poetic innovation, then, often consists in the mere heightening and exaggerating of a usage familiar to all of us. In an earlier day poets gained elasticity by a very different manner. They tried to impose alien structures on the English sentence. John Milton's opening lines of *Paradise Lost* also shift a predicate complement to the head of a sentence:

> Of man's first disobedience, and the fruit
> Of that forbidden tree whose mortal taste
> Brought death into the world, and all our woe
> With loss of Eden, till one greater Man
> Restore us, and regain the blissful seat,
> Sing, Heavenly Muse. . . .

The effect is far from the rhythms of colloquial speech. It is interesting to compare the difference in technique and effect.

REINFORCEMENT BY SOUND

This aspect of the poetic art might seem to be most simple and elementary. In all periods the phonological values of language have been exploited to heighten emotional effect. Euripides permits Medea to hiss her reproaches at Jason in a line full of sibilants (l. 476 of the play). Virgil imitates the sound of horses' hoofs or the clumping pace of a giant in the *Aeneid*. English poets have been attempting mimesis of droning bees, whistling wind, lumbering quadrupeds, and other natural phenomena for a long time. In this respect modern poetry has little new to offer. It still uses sibilants for hissing, gutturals for weight, liquids and nasals for languorous effects. These associations are lasting and appear to be quite fundamental.

For English readers in particular, however, a bit of technical knowledge is helpful towards an appreciation of the sound values of verse. Our spelling causes a discrepancy between what the eye sees and what the ear hears. If you are visual-minded you may be satisfied with the rhymes "flood: food" or "love: drove," but if you tend to hear internally what you are reading you will feel the discord. Wordsworth followed his ear in the rhyme "one: sun" [wʌn: sʌn] of "To a Child":

> Small service is true service while it lasts:
> Of humblest friends, bright creature! scorn not *one:*
> The daisy, by the shadow that it casts
> Protects the lingering dew-drop from the *sun.*

But he is led astray into a visual or "eye-rhyme" when he yokes together "one" with "stone" [wʌn: stoːn] in a stanza of the "Lucy" poems:

> A violet by a mossy *stone*
>   Half-hidden from the eye!
> —Fair as a star, when only *one*
>   Is shining in the sky.

You will find slips of this sort among the most admired of nine-teenth-century poets. That they were mistakes and not cunningly planned dissonances is indicated by the rigid perfection of all other rhymes in the poems concerned. Spelling alone appears to be the cause.

Moreover, spelling very probably restrains writers from using legitimate rhymes which look misleadingly different on paper. In Southern England and the Eastern United States "born: dawn" is an acceptable rhyme. Dialect influence plays a part here, however. A Scots poet or a Middle Western American would refrain from rhyming them because in their pronunciation a vowel difference really exists, besides the difference in the consonantal endings.

Many modern poets find perfect conventional rhymes monotonous, and are deliberately reverting to assonance and near-rhyme for variety. Assonance was the accepted ornament of Old French heroic poetry in the twelfth century. It consists in putting together final syllables in which the vowels are identical but the consonants can be anything at all (as opposed to rhyme, where they too must be identical). This is how Old French poets handled it:

> Tres vait la noit, et apert la clere albe
> Parmi cel host sovent e menu reguardet
> Li emperere; molt fierement chevalchet.
> "Seignors barons," dist li emperere Carles
> Veez les porz et les destreiz passages:
> Car me jugiez qui iert en la riere-guarde!"
>
> (*Chanson de Roland*, ll. 737 ff.)

Near-rhyme avoids identity of vowel, sometimes of consonant too, and yet uses sounds approaching perfect rhyme. In Auden's "Epilogue" there is sustained use of near-rhyme which occasionally becomes assonance. The paired words—"reader: rider," "midden: madden," "fearer: farer," "horror: hearer"— keep the consonants quite parallel but change the vowels in a manner suggesting vowel gradation (except of course that the paired words are not derived from identical roots). In the same poem there is one example of assonance: "path: pass." The vowels are identical but, as in Old French, the consonants differ. The two sounds [θ] and [s] are, to be sure, very close. Lispers confound them entirely. Here are some other near-rhymes employed by Auden:

result: guilt	add: god
all: prodigal	haunted: wanted
touch: itch	this: ease

When he puts together the verbs "lives" and "drives" he is not just slipping into a mistaken eye-rhyme, as we should suspect in the case of Wordsworth; he is consciously making use of the approximation of sounds not identical.

ENJOYMENT OF POETRY

The best heritage of poetry belongs, like the best of all the arts, to all the people who can enjoy it. Under more favorable circumstances I am convinced that this would include vast numbers who never hear about their heritage today. The chorus of snobs and cynics will say: "Ah, but the people as a whole are congenitally incapable of appreciating the work of those choice spirits known as poets. Such things are not for them. They *prefer* the cheap and vulgar sensations offered them by press, movies, and radio. Artists and critics must turn their backs on the profane herd to save themselves." Certain of the illuminati enjoy thinking this, as they are thus proved to be the rarer souls by contrast.

Such judgment is found in various forms, variously disguised. It involves sociology as well as literary criticism. Social attitudes are of course always closely related to literary dicta. If a critic believes that limits and stultification and indifference in the reading public have something to do with malnutrition, poverty, unemployment, and despair; with low vitality and the conscious commercial debauchery of literary taste, he will not conclude that innate human bestiality is the prime cause for a limited circulation of the classics. He will not echo Horace's *Odi profanum vulgus et arceo*. He may instead wonder optimistically how the barriers to culture may be broken down and the fertile tide released. Even the most "spiritual" of literary critics may have noted that he is himself temporarily disqualified to some degree from professional activity if he has allowed extreme hunger to bring on a headache. Conversely, he may therefore concede that food, light, air, and sleep may transform seeming dullards into alert people. It is no magic, only elemental human bio-chemistry. And it is a process which we now know is capable of realization. The conditions for doing so have been explored and tested.

How then, if in addition illiteracy were to be abolished, the specter of insecurity banished, and the arts of recreation so presented as to refine the public's sensibilities instead of corrupting them? The luminous possibilities can only be dimly imagined in our age of Hollywood films and venal journalism, not to speak of the actual bleak analphabetism of hundreds of thousands of our fellow-citizens. If deep-lying biological factors of inheritance have indeed worsened some part of our stock beyond repair, there is no need to assume that this is true of most of it, and certainly none to cause us to adjust all popular arts to the least talented of men and women among us.

All of this has some bearing on the material of this chapter. You will have noticed that I have expressed from time to time a certain doubt as to the enduring value of some of the authors cited. Naturally we cannot know which writings of today will earn the enduring affections of posterity. Even where great gifts indubitably exist, as with James Joyce, we have reason to doubt whether they have been applied to themes and techniques of perennial value. But one thing is sure: if the value *is* there, mere technical difficulty will not keep it alien to the reading public of the future. It is their heritage and they will enjoy it. Technical obscurities have a way of disappearing within the span of a generation. Some of us have the courage to hope that the first real age of human Enlightenment may succeed the contemporary horror. If science is at last permitted to serve the public's physical needs as it could do, art may minister to the spiritual solace of all as never before. For such readers of the future the technical devices of poetry here surveyed will no doubt appear much more transparent than now in our own day.

And even now there is no reason why they should mystify as many as they do. Within the limited circle of our own reading public, as it is called, there are many already waiting for the small amount of guidance needed towards the comprehension of beauties they vaguely surmise in the current offering of literature. It is a genuine pity, I think, that critical interpretation offers so little help. The radio alone, with its direct aural appeal, could be used to foster a tremendous renascence of poetry and the appreciation of poetry. Many of the appeals described in this chapter could better be explained by a speaking voice than by printed words.

An elementary knowledge of linguistics, then, could aid in the cultural enrichment of all our people. Even this forbidding science has its humane applications, too long neglected. I should like to see the study of language pursued, not only as an esoteric end in itself, but also as an auxiliary to aesthetic enjoyment. This chapter, an unconventional item in a book devoted primarily to linguistics, may indicate in a very sketchy way just how the assistance can be given.

10. Social Aspects: Class, Taboos, Politics

LANGUAGE LIKE CLOTHING

Speculating on the function of clothes in society, and what they have done to us, Carlyle at one point of *Sartor Resartus* asks us to imagine the functioning of "government, legislation, property, police, and civilized society" if all persons were abruptly forced to appear in public without any clothing whatsoever. We are so accustomed to reliance on badges, buttons, styles, and materials in judging our fellow-men, he argues, that august institutions would dissolve in "wails and howls" without them. These are the signs of rank and class; we deplore their artificiality, but we need them. "Lives the man," he asks, "that can figure a naked Duke of Windlestraw addressing a naked House of Lords? Imagination, choked as in mephitic air, recoils on itself, and will not forward with the picture. . . ." It is the wig, squirrel-skins, and plush gown that announce the judge; without them he would be no more by day than he is by night, only "a forked Radish with a head fantastically carved."

But Carlyle is wrong. Even with the badges and uniforms stripped away, something would remain as a guide, as sure if less ponderable, to the social position of each forked radish. Even a naked Duke of Windlestraw, upon opening his mouth, would speak the English language with a certain air, an accent and intonation inextricably associated with his rank and authority. An untrained impostor from the lower levels of society would be detected by his speech, although appearing as one nude radish among many. Of course, his speech could be faked for this occasion; but so could his clothes, for other occasions. Both types of deception have been practiced. It is a pity that Carlyle did not turn his attention to language as a metaphorical clothing of man in society.

CLASS DIALECTS

The existence of different manners of speech for persons in various ranks is a familiar fact. We are constantly sorting and classifying people according to them. A variation of any national language according to social levels is called a *class dialect*. Even within the class dialect there may be many variations and minor divisions. For instance, the younger members of a privileged class who attend special schools sometimes develop a special jargon among themselves which is almost incomprehensible to outsiders. Yet it is clearly an offshoot of the general "upper-class" dialect of their parents. Poorer youngsters also develop a kind of tribal school jargon as local and esoteric as the other. Even families and other restricted groups develop special jargons mystifying to an outsider. But these are even more clearly recognized and assigned to the general class dialects to which they belong.

When we talk, then, we tell much more about ourselves than the factual statements we are making. The sum total of small nuances will indicate much about our training, environment, economic position, and even profession. In conversation we are unconsciously providing a rich commentary about ourselves which supplements the clothing and outward possessions we gather.

COCKNEY ENGLISH

Not all European languages offer the same number of levels contrasted with equal sharpness. Within the English-speaking world the sharpest contrast is probably to be found between Cockney London dialect on the one hand and "upper-class" speech on the other. Londoners are not skittish about admitting this contrast; they are very frank about the existence of class levels in speech. The attitude of most observers is that Cockney is intrinsically humorous, and can be appreciated—at best—only by a condescending tolerance. Of course this is a result of the social connotations of the speech. In an early play, *Captain Brassbound's Conversion* (written before his better known *Pygmalion*), George Bernard Shaw experimented with the use of Cockney for dramatic purposes involving class distinctions. One of his problems was the difficult task of recording the vowel sounds of his low-class character, Drinkwater. This is what the attempt looked like on the printed page. Drinkwater, an engaging ne'er-do-well, finds himself entertaining Sir Howard Hallam, a judge before whom he once appeared as defendant:

Drinkwater (*placing the chair for Sir Howard*). Awskink yr pawdn for the libbety, Sr Ahrd.

Sir Howard (*looking at him*). I have seen you before somewhere.

Drinkwater. You ev, Sr Ahrd. But aw do assure yer it were hall a mistike.

Sir Howard. As usual. (*He sits down.*) Wrongfully convicted, of course.

Drinkwater (*with sly delight*). Naow, gavner. (*Half whispering, with an ineffable grin.*) Wrongfully hacquittid!

Sir Howard. Indeed! That's the first case of the kind I have ever met.

Drinkwater: Lawd, Sr Ahrd, wot jagginses them jurymen was! You an me knaowed it too, didn't we?

Sir Howard. I daresay we did. I am sorry to say I forget the exact nature of the difficulty you were in. Can you refresh my memory?

Drinkwater. Owny the aw [high] sperrits o youth, y'lawdship. Worterloo Rowd kice. Wot they calls Ooliganism. . . . Nime [name] giv huz pore thortless leds baw a gent on the Dily Chrorncile. . . . Awll eng [hang] abaht within ile [hail], gavner, hin kice aw should be wornted.

In this conversation, it will be observed, the only attempts at phonetic writing are limited to the speech of the Cockney.

Sir Howard Hallam's speech is given in conventional (that is, highly unphonetic) spelling. As Shaw admits, this procedure is quite inconsistent, but it has the merit of convenience. When educated persons, for instance professional people, read a printed page each assumes that the unreal orthography stands for his own special form of "acceptable" English. It would be too complicated for a dramatist to indicate every shading (even if he could) within that very inclusive territory. Shaw finds many attractive features in the Cockney dialect, and is particularly impatient with the snobbish contempt of outsiders for the so-called "misplaced aitch" which is one of its characteristics. "Roughly speaking, I should say that in England he who bothers about his *h*'s is a fool, and he who ridicules a dropped *h* a snob."

Yet persons with social ambitions have spent much time and suffered real distress in an effort to achieve conformity with their "betters" in details such as this. The matter has been treated with solemnity in a novel by May Sinclair, *The Divine Fire*, which was widely read about a generation ago. The hero was supposed to be a gifted poet born with the soul of ancient Greece lodged in a Cockney bosom: "The child of 'Ellas and 'Ollywell Street—innocent of—er—the rough breathing," [1] as one of the London literati puts it. Later his "innocence" of that minor phoneme when under emotional stress causes him the most excruciating social agonies. It is amusing to remember that at a certain time in ancient Rome it was considered very *chic* to insert unhistorical *h*-sounds before words normally beginning with vowels. It gave a fashionable Greekish flavor to ordinary everyday Latin. Catullus tells us in one of his poems that the fops of his day were saying *hinsidiae* for *insidiae* ("hambushes" for "ambushes"). It was the obverse of the Cockney poet's failing. So relative are the social connotations of a single sound!

---

[1] This is the term used in Greek grammars to designate initial [h].

VARIATIONS OF BRITISH "STANDARD" SPEECH

Rarely, for the reasons indicated by Shaw, has an author tried to record the peculiarities of a dialect of general upper-class speech. In one case, Mr. Thomas Wolfe's *Of Time and the River,* the attempt appears to be the result of bad temper. The hero of this novel is a young American writer, resident in Oxford during term time. He resents what he conceives to be the tight, complacent, exclusive atmosphere of those who "belong": the products of the cricket fields at accepted public schools. The exclusiveness, whether real or imagined, drives him to an extreme form of defiant provincialism, so that he flaunts his vulgarity and his special form of American speech self-consciously. And he falls into the fallacy of assuming that speech differing from his own is "affected." Naïve Americans visiting England have often expressed this astounding attitude towards any and all of the class dialects of the mother country. Wolfe attempts a phonetic rendering that is individual, if nothing else. "Year" is sometimes spelled as "yöh" and "there" as "thöh," though not always. The effort is inconsistent as well as inaccurate.

English writers themselves have sometimes jeered at certain details of "public school-Oxford" speech as being affected. One such detail is the tendency to change words like "dear, hear" [di:ə(ɹ), hi:ə (ɹ)] into "deah, heah" [dɪɑ, hɪɑ], even [djɑ:, hjɑ:]. Aldous Huxley records such variations with palpable distaste when he makes a character in *Point Counter-Point* say "ryahly fyahful" for "really fearful." He remarks of the speaker, Sidney Quarles: "His voice was resonant and full of those baa-ings with which the very Oxonian are accustomed to enrich the English language. . . . It was as though a flock of sheep had broken loose in his vocabulary."

LEVELS OF SPEECH

The existence of an accepted upper-class dialect associated with those who govern a country and man its professions has some amusing consequences. The sociological implications have never been adequately explored. For one thing, the levels will not be clearly preserved if historical change is moving rapidly, as at the time of the French Revolution. And even where change has been slow and barriers are clearly marked, the rise and fall of individuals brings about incongruities—a lack of harmony, let us say, between the physical clothing and the garment of speech.

It is only human for people in a stratified society to want to appear more smart and elegant than they are by birth and training. This is true if the society does leave some opportunities for personal advancement from the lower ranks. When people are over-eager to climb, they adopt a speech of uneasy and self-conscious gentility. One of its obvious characteristics is an excess of zeal for correctness: zeal to "talk good grammar," as it sometimes called. This solicitude produces what we call hypercorrect forms.

HYPERCORRECTNESS

For instance, a person may have been drilled in school to correct his native speech in the matter of present participles: to "pronounce the final *g*," as the unscientific saying is, in words like "ringing, singing, eating." The drill embarrasses him into self-consciousness, and he tends, for safety's sake, to substitute the syllable [ɪŋ] for *all* final [ɪn]'s in his speech. So he says "curting," "garding," "ruing" for "curtain," "garden," "ruin." Or it may be that in triumph at having corrected errors like "Him and me get along fine" into "He and I get along well," the rising individual produces sentences like "It's a secret between him (he) and I."

The *arriviste* in language is also apt to gloat in the use of perfect tenses and to overdo them. "It was a great pleasure *to have met you*." Excessive self-consciousness about adverbial endings produces "finely" or "fastly" if the speaker has recently learned to avoid "He works good." A preposition is doubled in sentences like "It's the man for whom I was wait-

ing for" when the speaker is just unlearning "who I was waiting for."

Another more refined vice of the self-consciously correct
person is the refusal to use unstressed forms of articles or
prepositions, as if they were always vulgar. He pronounces
"the man and the girl" with painful distinctness, as if he were
still in first grade struggling over individual words under a
teacher's strict eye. He says [ði: mæn ænd ði: gəɹl], pedan-
tically; and yet it is the best speakers, those at home in cultured English, who say: [ðə mæn ən ðə gəːl]. In accepted
English, too, there is a clear difference between "to" [tə] and
"too" [tu:]. The man at ease in society says: "I'm about to
come too" as [aɪm ə'baut tə 'kʌm 'tu:] not the hypercorrect
[aɪ 'æm ə'baut 'tu: 'kʌm 'tu:], which is in fact a bad self-betrayal.
A mistaken snobbishness prompts this schoolroom isolation of
words. Yet the most snobbish of snobs, the man poised with
inherited confidence, is the one who freely permits slurred
forms—provided, of course, they are the "right" slurred forms,
hallowed by general usage in his "set."

SNOBBISHNESS AND INFORMALITY

Class feeling in language is a huge and diverting subject, not
yet sufficiently studied by professional linguists. There is one
aspect of it which you can pursue for your own amusement as
you read even very light fiction, preferably of British make.
It has to do with the language of butlers and valets, as preserved in week-end novels and detective stories.

Thorstein Veblen and other observers of social behavior
have pointed out a phenomenon known as vicarious spending
or vicarious leisure. A man of wealth may not wish, or be able
to, consume the goods to which his income entitles him, or he
may not choose to avail himself of the idleness his money could
easily buy for him. Nevertheless he may feel that he must indicate to the world about him that he *could* dress in three or
four gold-braided suits at once, if he so desired, or he *could*

spend his day in conspicuous idleness. So he hires others to do this for him. He employs flunkeys, doormen, extra chauffeurs, often in quite dazzling costumes, and lets them advertise his resources to the world for him. Then he is free (the last word in snobbishness, this!) to go about in dark, inconspicuous clothes if he wishes, and to busy himself to his heart's content; even, conceivably, at a useful occupation.

Thus far the sociologist, observing the ways of the "leisure class." But notice the linguistic accompaniment in this transfer of function. Just as the heir of wealth may become bored with elaborate trappings and ostentatious leisure, he may wish to relax the formal speech traditionally associated with gold braid and buckles. So he relegates to the archaically clad menials the archaic speech of his class ancestors that has become irksome to him. So long as his butler pronounces rounded periods of eighteenth-century English in the style of Burke or Johnson, milord is free to be as slangy or as fatuous as he pleases. In fact, it becomes the swank thing to be both slangy and fatuous. Of course, it would never do for a man on a modest income to affect these lapses. It might appear (in the absence of a Johnsonian butler) that the speaker did not know any better.

Secure in the knowledge that Jeeves, his butler, is being Olympian for him, Mr. P. G. Wodehouse's hero permits himself the following type of discourse in describing a misadventure by one of his friends in America:

"This is a rotten country," said Cyril.

"Oh, I don't know, you know, don't you know!" I said.

"We do our best," said George. . . .

"Well, why don't the policemen in New York dress properly? . . . I mean to say, why don't they wear helmets like they do in London? Why do they look like postmen? It isn't fair on a fellow. Makes it dashed confusing. I was simply standing on the pavement, looking at things, when a fellow who looked like a postman prodded me in the ribs with a club. I didn't see why I should have postmen prodding me. Why the dickens should a fellow come three thousand miles to be prodded by postmen?"

"The point is well taken," said George. "What did you do?"

"I gave him a shove, you know. I've got a frightfully hasty temper, you know. All the Bassington-Bassingtons have got frightfully hasty tempers, don't you know! And then he biffed me in the eye and lugged me off to this beastly place!"

"I'll fix it, old son," I said.

While the Wodehousian hero and his cronies talk as the excerpt indicates, the Wodehousian butler Jeeves is delivering himself of remarks like these:

"Well, Sir, Spenser, Mrs. Gregson's butler who inadvertently chanced to overhear something of your conversation when you were lunching at the house, did mention certain of the details to me; and I confess that, though it may be a liberty to say so, I entertained hopes that something might occur to prevent the match. I doubt if the young lady was entirely suitable to you, Sir." . . .

"I hear nothing but excellent reports of the young lady, Sir. I think it is beyond question that she would be an admirable influence for Mr. Little, should the affair come to a happy conclusion. Such a union would also, I fancy, go far to restore Mr. Little to the good graces of his uncle, the young lady being well connected and possessing private means. In short, sir, I think that if there is anything that we can do we should do it."

Here by contrast we have, faithfully preserved, the tricks of eighteenth-century oratory which remind you of Edmund Burke in full flight. Jeeves uses complicated sentences, interrupted (as for breath) by "I fancy"; imitations of Latin constructions (as in the phrase about "the young lady *being* well connected"—the closest he can come to an ablative absolute), and the delicate periphrases ("should the affair come to a happy conclusion" for "if they get married") which recall the formal cadence of classical English. It is both Olympian and archaic, quite like butlers' formal dress.

UNDERWORLD SPEECH

There is another type of class dialect more baffling to the un-initiated: the argot of the underworld of great cities. Here the normal substandard speech is deliberately and frequently modified by slang periphrases to keep outsiders from under-standing. Thus it is that jewels become "ice," and stolen jewels, the object of police questing, become, quaintly enough, "hot ice." Drugs like heroin and cocaine become "snow." A whole vocabulary has developed around the use of the forbidden "reefers" of marihuana by "vipers" (addicts). It is interesting to note that American argot has had its influence on the under-world of foreign cities. Paris, rich in its own special language, shows in addition some loans from American gangster speech. In fact the word "gangster" has been taken over unchanged save for accent. Collaborated robbery is called "American robbery" or *vol à l'américaine*. If three work together they are called *le leveur* ("lifter"), *l'Américain* and *l'utilité* ("utility-man"). If there are two, one is designated by an American-English phrase, *le contact-man,* and the other is *le banquier* ("the banker"). Professions more or less related to a robber's life are also designated by picturesque English loans. The woman who works for a *souteneur* is called by many words, including an English one: *biftek* ("beefsteak"). A prostitute's work is called by another English term: *le bizness*. The under-world shows a certain measure of internationalism in its vocab-ulary. For the most part, however, it relies on metaphor and semantic shifts in native words.

COURTLY AND POLITE FORMS

In English we show our social levels primarily by choice of words and general style. One method used by other languages is unknown to us: the multiplication of personal pronouns to express various social attitudes towards the person addressed. We say "you" when talking to someone, whether he is a haughty superior, a friendly equal, or a subservient inferior.

In this one pronominal respect English may be said to be classless. Other European languages make differences which seem formal or exclusive or arrogant or groveling to us users of the simple "you." In addressing a child or an intimate or (strangely enough) one for whom he feels contempt, a German says *du*. In addressing a stranger, he uses *Sie*, which is identical in form as well as origin with the word for "they"—a tribute to the distance and importance (plurality) of the person addressed. If he wishes to be deferential he uses a third-person noun while he looks straight at the person addressed. Thus, "Did the lady (or the gracious lady) sleep well? Has the gentleman finished his coffee?" Other languages use the third person similarly for cautious and reserved address. A Dane will say *"Har Fruen tabt sin Bog?"* and a Frenchman *"Est-ce que Madame a perdu son livre?"* ("Has madam lost her book?") But both use such forms more sparingly, I think, than the polite German.

In courtly circles it was formerly quite customary to use (usually feminine) abstract nouns like "Excellency" or "Your Excellency" in speaking directly to a person of rank. The pronoun which might be substituted for this abstract noun, in languages with grammatical gender, was naturally "she." The contemporary Spanish word for "you" comes from a feminine noun with distinctly courtier-like connotations. *Usted* is a contraction of *vuestra merced*, which means "your mercy" or "your graciousness." A touch of the ancient formality of a sixteenth-century Spanish grandee hangs about the word.

Nothing in Europe, however, corresponds to the elaboration of pronominal snobbishness in some Eastern languages. In Malay a whole series of social levels are stratified in the pronouns of address. Nobody can simply and blithely say "you" without further reflection. He must stop to think: "How far is this man above or below me on the social ladder?" And according to the relative positions on that ladder, he will modify not only the "you" but also "I" and "we." The following table will indicate how many forms a Malay speaker must choose among, according to the social positions of the three possible persons to be designated. The choice involves not only words for "you" but *all* pronouns; and there are ten levels:

Person speaking	"I, we"	"thou, you"	"he, she, they"
Peasants to one another	*aku;* pl. *kita*	*ĕngkau*	*ia, dia*
Superior pointedly to inferior	*aku;* pl. *kita*	*ĕngkau*	*ia, dia*
Superior ordinarily to inferior	*sahaya,* pl. *kita*	*kamu, awak* [diff. dialect]	*ia, dia*
Superior with affected modesty to equals	*hamba (tuan)*	*tuan (hamba)*	*tuan (hamba)*
All classes to Europeans	*sahaya; kita*	*tuan*	*tuan*
Malay gentry to one another	*kami*	*ĕnche,' tuan*	*ĕnche,' tuan*
Commoner to chief	*hamba (dato') sahaya (dato')*	*dato'*	*dato'*
Commoner to rajah; lesser to greater rajahs	*patek*	*tĕngku; ĕngku*	*tĕngku; ĕngku raja*
Subject to sultan	*patek*	*tuan-ku*	*yam-tuan; tuan-ku*
Literary	*beta*	*sahabat beta*	[name and title]

In Japanese, according to Von der Gabelentz, politeness forbids a speaker to use the simple active voice in referring to high-class people, as if they were obliged to engage in activity themselves. So the speaker chooses the causative voice, giving them the role of persons acting mediately, by command—or the passive voice, as if the action were happening by itself. The Koreans are unequaled in this respect, since they express through the *verbal* form whether a higher personage is talking to a lower, a lower to a higher, or one equal to another; and, moreover, whether this is happening in a comparatively reverential, contemptuous, or indifferent manner. This would, properly speaking, yield 3x3x3 or 27 modal forms. Thus voice and other verbal inflections may also be determined by sociological relations—titles and income, in short. The Algonquian language is said to possess complex stratified forms of polite locution also.

REGIONAL DIALECTS

It is customary to distinguish class dialects from local or regional dialects. The latter include the ways of speech which mark people off according to the province, village, or region from which they come. "Everyone who does not speak a Regional dialect," says Henry Cecil Wyld, "speaks a Class dialect." Yet the matter is not quite so simple as that. The two dialect types cannot be so completely separated.

In America, for instance, we have several varieties of regional dialect. A citizen of Louisiana is said to speak Southern American; one from Massachusetts, New England American (English). A few tricks of pronunciation of vowels and many niceties of sentence tempo and intonation betray the regional origins of the two. The former will say "po'k" [po:k] for "pork"; the latter, [pɔ:k]. Each one, in fact, may tend to jeer at the other with entire good nature because of these perceptible differences, minor though they may be. But although the educated, traveled, and affluent Southerner may share some of these traits with poor cotton-pickers and mill workers, there are other ways of speech quite as marked which separate the two groups within the confines of the very same regional dialect. Comparative analyses are still lacking. It is probable, however, that the study of the levels *within* such a regional dialect would show two things: that the individual sounds were very much alike throughout the region, regardless of class, but that the syntax (grammatical structure) of sentences was different. In saying "He doesn't like me any more," speakers of all levels would agree on the vowel sounds in "like" [la:k] and "more" [mo:], and they might have the same deliberate and agreeable speech melody; but the mill worker would change the verbal agreement and use a double negative as Chaucer often did: "He don't like me no more." In this he would agree with many persons of the same class in other parts of the country.

DIALECT AND GOVERNMENTAL POWER

Where the governmental and economic power have been associated with one place and one dialect, the use of regional language may be a social or class handicap. The overlapping is clear in England, where the broad Lancashire dialect, for all its venerable history, is a label of class as well as region for a person wishing to rise in the social scale. According to English writers, the speech of the "better class" is heard with practically no variation all over the country: it is "Public School English," and all else—"the vulgar English of the towns, and the English of the Villager who has abandoned his native Regional Dialect"—is Modified Standard. In compiling his *English Pronouncing Dictionary* Daniel Jones tells us that he recorded what is "most usually heard in everyday speech in the families of Southern English persons who have been educated at the great public boarding schools. . . . The pronunciation may also be heard, to an extent which is considerable though difficult to specify, from educated people in the South of England who have not been educated at these schools." It is assumed, however, that the linguistic influence radiates from them. The Lancashire manufacturer may despair of changing his own speech, but he will probably see to it that his children learn Public School English. Even Scots dialect, with its distinguished literary history, has been regarded as a handicap. J. M. Barrie's play, *What Every Woman Knows*, presents the efforts of an ambitious politician who, with his wife's help, is at some pains to smooth out of his speech the local flavor which might hamper his career. In ancient Greece, the Attic dialect became the accepted "superior" language because it was used in the powerful city-state of Athens and particularly was employed in the writings of a splendid galaxy of writers in the fifth and fourth centuries B.C. As a consequence Attic speakers began to look down their noses at "countrymen" who used other local dialects. The only exception was perhaps Ionian, which also represented political power and had an early, distinguished literature. A politician hampered by a "countryman's" dialect has always been a subject of unkind jests by his enemies.

POLITICS AND AMERICAN "PROVINCIAL" SPEECH

In the early days of the American republic our ancestors were sensitive about the minor differences of pronunciation and vocabulary which already marked us off perceptibly from British speakers. Political independence seems to have converted the uneasy sense of inferiority into a truculent claim upon "superiority," as might be expected. Ardent patriots hoped that a new day had dawned for the English language in America. They wished to see differences recognized and accelerated. On the other hand, British writers tended to sharpen their attitude of disapproval towards American "provincialisms." Some of the Founding Fathers carried on a lively discussion on the desirability of showing the world by means of our language that we had become an independent, proudly republican state. English was supposed to be "purer" in the land of freedom, at the very time when British critics were making contemptuous remarks about it.

FRONTIER LIFE

As a matter of fact, some of the very "provincialisms" cited in early dictionaries of American speech, and condemned by British purists, give a lively picture of frontier life and struggles. They make up a colorful creation—an unconscious linguistic record of early American ways of living. Here are a few of them, classified according to the pioneers' occupations:

> *Farm Life*
> to make a bee-line
> to have a long row to hoe
> to fly off the handle

to sit on the fence
to have an ax to grind
to go haywire [origin in doubt]
to have a chip on the shoulder
to fork over
to have the wrong end of the stick

Hunting and Gunmanship
to make the fur fly
to knock the spots out of
to draw a bead [i.e., to take aim]
to bark up the wrong tree
to get on one's own hook
to be up a tree

Warfare (Indian style)
to scalp
to walk Indian file
to bury the hatchet
to put on war-paint
to go on the war path

Pioneering
to make tracks
to blaze a trail
to jump a claim
to pull up stakes
to peter out
to be as easy as rolling off a log
to clear out
to spark [to woo a girl]
to have the latchstring out
to be stumped
to swap horses in mid-stream

For all their vividness, however, it may be imagined that these expressions redolent of frontier life would be regarded as low barbarisms in the sophisticated coffee houses and drawing rooms of eighteenth-century London, and would therefore be a social handicap to the user of them.

LOWER-CLASS SPEECH IN EARLIER TIMES

The lower ranks of society had a dialect of their own in past ages too. Feudal England gives an especially clear case of linguistic division on class lines. For a certain period of time after 1066, as we have observed, government, courts, and local administration were in the hands of persons speaking a tongue foreign to the native English: French as opposed to Anglo-Saxon. The situation was solved more quickly, it now appears, than earlier historians supposed. But out of the original division came the tendency still noticeable in English to use Anglo-Saxon words for homely, intimate, and even ugly or indecent things, and to use French words for the loftier ideas (or to conceal the ugly ones).

With the development of town life and commerce, lower-class speech was further diversified. It was not merely the language of the peasant as opposed to that of the knight. It included the language of guildsmen and artisans, of retainers, clerks, and hangers-on of the aristocracy; of beggars, thieves, sharpers, and peddlers. Each trade had its own cant. Most diverting was the speech of the last group.

Robert Greene, Shakespeare's contemporary, wrote a series of satirical pamphlets describing the tricks of sharpers and cheats in the London underworld. They give us most valuable material on substandard urban locutions during the reign of Elizabeth. From dictionaries and other sources we can then trace the underworld language through the seventeenth and eighteenth centuries. Thievery created a list of metaphors which were not only esoteric—for trade use—but also poetic. Here are a few, taken from a dictionary compiled in the reign of William and Mary:

> *bacon:* skin; body. "He saved his bacon," meaning "he escaped."
> *bracket-face:* ugly, homely, ill-favored
> *briers:* trouble. "To be in the briers," to be in trouble.
> *bess:* an instrument to crack open a door

jenny: "an instrument to lift up a grate, and whip anything out of a shop-window."

dead men: empty bottles

dub: a pick-lock key

fork: a pickpocket. "Let's fork him" is thus glossed: "Let us Pick that man's Pocket, the newest and most dexterous way: It is, to thrust the Fingers, strait, stiff, open and very quick into the Pocket, and so closing them, hook what can be held between them."

green-bag: a lawyer

milch-kine: "a term us'd by Gaolers, when their Prisoners will bleed freely to have some Favor, or be at large."

mill: to rob, steal, break open. "Milling the Gig with a Betty, c[ant for] Breaking open the Door with an Iron-Crow, milling the Glaze, c. Breaking open the Window."

queer birds: "such as having got loose, return to their old Trade of Roguing and Thieving"

Spanish-money: "fair words and Compliments"

splitter-of-causes: a lawyer

unrig: to strip the clothes off someone—whether for stealing or amorous purposes.

METAPHORS OF SLANG

One fact emerges clearly from the study of disreputable slang, both past and present. No one impulse explains its creation and its peculiar qualities. It results from specialization, like any other trade dialect; also from a need for secrecy, for economy of expression; but certainly also from humor, delight in metaphor, and a quite uneconomic playfulness. Both conciseness and a pleasing contempt for conciseness will be found operative in the slang of the more respectable trades as well.

No occupation is more rushed, for example, than quick-lunch counter service at high noon. Hundreds of thousands of busy, nervous Americans besiege these dispensaries of pabulum every noon-time. Above the clamor of dishes and public conversation can be heard the cries of waiters and chefs calling and repeating orders for food in a language as special, mysterious, and playful as any thieves' cant. Surely here, you would suppose, the feverish tempo of service would make economy the paramount virtue of speech. And some expressions, like "B.T." for "bacon and tomato sandwich," are in fact a kind of spoken short-hand designed to clip a second or two off the necessary communication. Others are graphic as well as brief: *fizz* for "carbonated water"; *freezone* for "chocolate frosted milk"; *one-down* (referring to the electric toaster) for "an order of toast"; and *sparkle one* for "an order of Bromo-Seltzer." But what shall we say of the gay wastefulness of the following delightful expressions:

Adam's ale: Water
Clean up the kitchen: Hamburger; *also* hash
Coney Island bloodhounds: Frankfurters
Dough well done with cow to cover: Bread and butter
Draw one in the dark: Black coffee
Hudson River ale: Water
Noah's boy with Murphy carrying a wreath: Ham and potatoes with cabbage
Shot out of the blue bottle: Bromo-Seltzer
Slab of moo—let him chew it: Rare rump steak
Twelve alive in a shell: A dozen raw oysters
Yesterday, today, and forever: Hash

They ignore the requirements of economy but provide verbal entertainment.

Taboo on Death

Another social attitude reflected in our language is the existence of all sorts of forbidden subjects which must be avoided or carefully disguised when we speak. The reasons for fear in connection with certain words and names are deep-lying and complicated. The use of such words presumably gives the speaker an exposed and vulnerable feeling, due ultimately to the magic powers originally attributed to language. (See chapter 1.) To name death, disease, and wounds was felt, and indeed, is still felt, to be a way of inviting their presence. Hence elaborate phrases are to be found among many types of people, civilized and uncivilized, to avoid use of the simple words "die" or "be sick." We use them too. The very persons who protest that death is a fortunate release into a happier hereafter, or that disease is a negligible inconvenience easily conquered, are most wary about using the simple straightforward words to describe these aspects of our mortality. They use euphemisms like "passing on" or "passing away" or "being taken away." They also use noncommittal terms about someone who is seriously ill. Of course it is true that another element appears in the situation when politeness impells us to avoid direct reference to topics unpleasing to the listener. This may or may not be true among all peoples, but we certainly pride ourselves on this motive so far as we ourselves are concerned. Nevertheless it is very likely that some of the old fear of spirits and demons lurks within us still. Rational as we may think we are, we can still feel for the peasant of the fairy tales who cries out carelessly: "May the Devil take this stubborn mule of mine" —and at once beholds the Old Man himself at his elbow, smiling and saying "Always ready to oblige!" We still feel in some obscure way that to name is to summon.

TABOOS ON PHYSIOLOGY

The questions of decency and obscenity are still more complicated. The very nature of the subject makes it difficult for study. The words avoided because of a general feeling of "coarseness" in contemporary English cover a wide variety of topics: sex, physiological functions, diseases and their symptoms, parts of the body, odors, names of certain animals and insects. It will be noticed that fear and regard for decency overlap. References to blood, dirt, and disease can be classified in one category or the other depending on context. There is an element of primeval fear persisting even today, as we have seen, from the times when language was felt to have magic powers, and the mere naming of a disease might bring about a visitation of it upon the speaker. Drawing-room prudery has in addition some modern causes and connotations, no doubt.

But in recent years the wide economic independence of women, and also their advanced education, have contributed to the liberation of their speech. It is unreasonable to expect the word "legs" to evoke blushes on a young girl's cheeks (no matter how vigilantly she has been protected from "experience") when her scientific training has taught her to discourse glibly on genes, chromosomes, and monosexual reproduction in plants.

NATIONALISM

Language and politics offer a combination somewhat easier to investigate than language and indecency. Nevertheless we seldom stop to reflect upon the great import of language in political issues such as the conflict of nations. Many bloody struggles have centered about claims and oppressions which used languages as symbols. When a people engage in agitation for political independence, one very appealing issue is the demand to use a native tongue for official purposes, and to have it taught in the schools. It is usually felt by the most indifferent of observers that a real grievance is endured by any people when foreign officials, supported by a foreign army, take over a school system and suddenly forbid the use of a language hitherto officially accepted, as well as dear and familiar, to the children. Suppressed patriotism frequently centers about the determination of families to maintain the despised language within the home, no matter what may happen to it in the courts and schools.

A conspicuous example is the faithful preservation of Polish as a national language when the country had been divided by three empires in the eighteenth century. A language is also a rallying point for peoples who have never enjoyed the privileges of nationhood in the modern sense. In Ireland the Gaelic speech was consistently repressed for centuries, and a child who inadvertently slipped into native idiom in the (exclusively English) schools was severely punished, according to nineteenth-century reports. Parallel situations may be found all

over the world, especially in colonies and semi-colonial countries. Here the native peoples frequently have no access to any
schools except those founded and maintained by an outside
group, a linguistic minority who have established themselves
by military or commercial invasion.

Today, when conquest succeeds conquest with terrifying
rapidity, the shifts in official speech must be confusing in the
extreme to young students. If there were time in the midst of
world affairs, it would be very enlightening to have a study
by trained psychologists on the emotional and mental difficulties engendered in students by some of the recent political
shifts of territory. In some Central American countries the
situation is very complex for different reasons. The Indian
populations have quietly and faithfully retained the indigenous dialects as their primary speech; Spanish, the official
language, is still regarded as the imposed dialect of a conquering minority. But Spanish itself now finds competition in English, employed by resident company officials, higher paid
employees, wives, children, and teachers connected with the
small "colony" of American business enterprises. If Spanish
is still resented by many natives, it would be curious to know
what attitude is being built up towards English, the super-
language of rulers.

So strong is the feeling for language in relation to nationality
that it is quite possible to resurrect a language long since dead
and re-establish it among the living. Hebrew is an example in
point. The tongue of the Bible had become extinct so far as
everyday life is concerned, but the zeal of Jewish re-settlers in
Palestine has made it once more a living and expanding
medium.

In the conflict of nations, enthusiasts for one side or another
sometimes claim superiority for their special language. They
affirm that their cause must be right because their language is
"naturally" better than that of the opponent. Such statements
are based rather on emotion than scientific judgment. An over-
patriotic German will claim that his language is superior be-

cause it has such qualities as *Innerlichkeit* and *Tiefe*—and he will prove this to you triumphantly by pointing to idioms carefully chosen for the purpose. On the other hand the complacent Frenchman, sure that civilization and France are coextensive, will claim for his language a monopoly of lucidity: *"Tout ce qui est clair est français!"* It should be remembered, however, that the best scholars carefully avoid these extravagant and unscientific claims. The German *Literaturblatt* has frequently reproved linguistic flag-wavers for their excesses, with exemplary scientific honesty, and the French sins of a similar nature have been most devastatingly satirized by French-speaking scholars like Daniel Mornet, Charles Bally, and Ferdinand Brunot.

PURISM VERSUS INTERNATIONALISM

Patriotism is sometimes exhibited in exaggerated form in the attitudes adopted towards loan words. Since English is already very polyglot in its composition, for historical reasons, there is little resentment felt at the frequent additions made to it by way of direct borrowing. French and German are by contrast comparatively homogeneous (though only comparatively so). Loans in these languages stand out more sharply and are more often the subject of acrimonious discussion. The attitude to such words very neatly reflects some of the contradictions arising in modern society out of worldwide international trade. The modern industrial era opened up to European nations an international vocabulary of science and invention, more or less hospitably received by those who participated in the industrial revolution. Names of electrical units derived from inventors' names—the ampère, watt, volt, ohm, coulomb, farad —symbolize the collaboration of French, English, Italian, and German scientists in creating an international type of culture based on the use of electricity. With trade, invention, and communication accelerated, the current of words was accelerated too. But the fierce rivalries engendered by foreign trade gave rise to a countercurrent. With wars and other contests for commercial supremacy, there came self-conscious resistance to the language of national rivals, and a revulsion in many instances against the words that had accompanied actual benefits. Zealous spokesmen for national interests set about purging their vocabularies of alien contributions as a symbolic act meant to affirm national political superiority. When the German empire asserted its role in international affairs (latter nineteenth and early twentieth centuries) there was a systematic purgation of long-accepted French terms, even those connected with the arts and other amenities. Thus *Theater* yielded to *Spielhaus, Telephon* to *Fernsprecher, Billet* to *Fahrkarte,* and even the discreet *Toilette* to *Abort.* Solemn debate took place over the advisability of adopting terms which seem desirable to us as a matter of course, because of their universal currency in other European countries.

Racism and "Superiority" in Language

Chauvinism in language has recently been allied to a related subject: chauvinism in race. Political programs including suppression of minorities and foreign aggression have been justified on the plea that the ruling group are "racially superior" to those attacked. And often these claims have received support not only from politicians but also from interested or misled professors. They have used appeals to language as evidence. It has been claimed that a people using suffixed inflectional endings must be naturally superior to others using agglutinated prefixes. Both German and Italian apologists for their political systems have maintained that Indo-European languages in general (and their own in particular) are the best possible instruments of human thought, and that all others must yield before them. Hence, by implication, it must be right and even desirable to launch tanks, machine guns, flame throwers, and bombers against unfortunates who happen to use Hamito-Semitic or other vocabulary and sentence structure. The evidence, such as it is, is linguistic, but the divisions are called racial. One even hears the nonsensical term "Indo-European race." Plainly there is need for a little clarification.

The word "race" is a rather loose term referring to a group of people who share certain bodily characteristics through common inheritance. Among the tests used to establish unity of race are such simple, objective matters as color of the eyes, type of hair (straight, curly, "kinky"), stature, and shape of the skull. But within the confines of a single political nation you will often find all three types of skulls—long, round, and medium. Some American Indians are reported to have the narrowest skulls ever measured, and some the broadest. But there is no relationship whatsoever between the shape of people's skulls and their ability to think—or to learn one language more readily than another in infancy. When archaeologists dig up skulls of primitive men, dead for tens of thousands of years, they can only say: "These men were dolichocephalic (long-headed)" or "They were brachycephalic (round-headed)"; they cannot say "These men must have spoken a highly inflected language."

Only the extremely ignorant, or conscious demagogues, confuse the two categories. And what is true of cephalic size is also true of hair, pigmentation, eyes, and stature. There is no correlation between any of these and language—or the ability to learn a language as a child. A blond Scandinavian captured by a swarthy African tribe in extreme infancy will grow up speaking the indigenous language to which he was first exposed. The same would be true of a swarthy African baby kidnapped and reared in a Scandinavian village. Languages have spread by conquest and wholesale migration to peoples biologically quite unrelated to the original speakers. Sometimes the assimilation has been complete, and at other times only partial. But *that* depends on historical conditions which have nothing to do with "innate" intelligence or linguistic ability.

Americans, for instance, sometimes assume that there is an innate tendency on the part of Negroes to pronounce vowels in a certain way; to say [po:k] instead of [pɔːk] for "pork." It is assumed that when whites say the same thing their speech has been "corrupted" by that of Negroes. Actually, of course, the Negroes learned their English in the only possible way open to them: by imitating the special dialect of their owners. George Philip Krapp says: "The Negro pronunciation of *head, dead* to rhyme with *laid* has earlier historical justifications; even the so-called lazy or relaxed general tone of Southern speech, its slow tempo, its loose articulation of final consonants, often explained as the result of climate, is an inheritance from the general colonial English of the seventeenth century." In the West Indies the natives acquired British English (sometimes even the special form of it known as "public-school" English); in Haiti, French; elsewhere (as in Cuba) Spanish. The dialect differences within these groups are due to social distinctions, not to the amount of pigment in the skins of the speakers.

The foremost anthropologists are agreed that no evidence hitherto produced justifies any claim to superiority *in potential abilities* along lines of language or physical characteristics. It is very important to remember these things today, when brutal oppression is so often justified by appeal to grammar or somatic (bodily) traits. The confusions and persecutions associated with "Aryan" make one hesitate to use the word even in the justified sense (meaning the languages descended from Old Iranian and Old Indian). At the same time it is a salutary thing to recall that National Socialists and Italian Fascisti have had no monopoly on this cruel chicanery. Everywhere that there is abuse of subject peoples you are apt to find justification of it pretentiously expressed on grounds of racial superiority, with language dragged in as part of the proof.

UNDEVELOPED LANGUAGES

But, someone may urge, some languages *are* limited in one way or another. They may at this given moment have an inadequate vocabulary for modern needs, or their traditional syntax may be needlessly elaborate, or they may lack the use of simple common nouns like "tree" or "table" without which one cannot conceive of the philosophical "tree-in-general." Hence they can never rise to the abstractions of lofty Western European philosophy, with its tradition of abstract thought reaching back to Plato. If this is so, perhaps we are justified, after all, in thinking of such languages as really inferior, since they are handicapped by their very structure in comparison with our own.

We have touched on this question before, but it is so important that a bit of repetition is not out of place.

Let us grant that at this particular moment in world history some languages, remote from major currents of events, are less developed than others in the directions required by a dominant civilization based on industry and machines. The grammar may employ cumbersome, repetitious constructions to express simple relations. Nevertheless even these languages are dynamic, not static. Change is always going on, rapidly or slowly according to the stimulus of cultural change. The complex syntax may be simplified; the needed words borrowed or created by compounding (see chapter 4). Even sentence structure is modified with the ages. Useless distinctions are sloughed off when the need for them has died. If this has occurred unconsciously, for the most part, in the past, it is increasingly done with conscious direction today.

Under kindly tutelage directed towards the people's cultural advancement, a backward language can be speedily adapted, out of its own potential resources, to meet the requirements of modern civilization. Franz Boas reports how young Indian students can be introduced to the concept of Platonic universals even though their language traditionally lacks unmodified common nouns. They can easily be taught to isolate the term "house" out of expressions meaning "that-house-yonder," "my-house-here," and "the-house-made-of-wood." In the same way medieval scholastics created abstractions like "quiddity" when they felt the need for them. At first the natives may feel that they are doing violence to their language, since traditional syntax demands that every noun must have a modifier; but once they have been made to feel the intellectual need for the bare term "house," they will accept the usage—and thus push the language ahead a thousand years in one generation. A minority may first avail itself of the development, but there is no inherent reason why its use may not become general. The potentiality was always there; all that was needed was to elicit its application in a new situation.

Unfortunately people speaking undeveloped languages have hitherto encountered more developed idioms in a highly unpleasant manner. It was difficult to appreciate the virtues of a more economic speech when fellow-tribesmen had just been massacred in large numbers by those using it. The results may be quite different when a more fraternal spirit prevails. When the emissaries of a modern culture arrive with no intent to exploit or deceive or oppress, and without any arrogant assumption of superiority, they may obtain quite a different reception. There will be no sullen resistance to linguistic instruction, we may assume, when there is no resentment or fear. Under such happy circumstances a backward language can surmount structural handicaps in a very short time. Deficiencies in vocabulary have never presented serious difficulties. There is no reason why such adaptations should be left to slow and bungling processes as in the past. Conscious direction may be desirable in this situation as in others where an interchange occurs between one culture and another. Rarely, in fact, is the debt exclusively on one side when two languages meet on such a basis, even if one is more "advanced" than the other.

SEX DIVISIONS IN LANGUAGE

There is another social division which finds some reflection in language, namely the differentiation between women's interests and men's insofar as the activities of the two sexes are kept apart. In some civilizations there is a high degree of specialization along sex lines. Men may limit themselves to hunting and women may do all the agricultural work, with a resulting specialization in subjects for conversation. At times it is even forbidden for women to pronounce certain words connected with manly pursuits, or for men to intrude on the specialized vocabulary of the women. The discrimination may be so extensive, even, that it is possible to speak of a men's or a women's "secret" language.

The reason for sex taboo in language can easily be surmised. When women are forbidden to touch or approach or even name the weapons of men, one of the causes appears to be the idea that feminine debility (at the menstrual period) may affect the weapons adversely. The points might be blunted by the sympathetic influence from women, or women's speech. Fear of the magic power of blood may be present among people otherwise brave, with women otherwise husky. From such a simple taboo the restrictions on vocabulary might easily be extended to other terms separating the concerns of the two sexes. In our own society there is no sharp division in vocabulary between men and women. The only examples we can muster are a few expressions avoided by men because they are "sissy." Some of them are terms of approval, like "sweet," "darling," "ducky," and "divine." The opposite category of rough masculine words, formerly limited to bar rooms and exclusively male haunts, is shrinking under the incursions of women into all these realms. Swearing, like smoking, has been adopted by women with such enthusiasm that it may become in time a feminine trait abandoned by men in unspoken protest against the intrusion.

SLOGANS

Of course there is no aspect of man's social life which is not reflected in his language. Politics too offers material for the linguist. He may amuse himself by collecting the metaphors engendered in a lively campaign, or analyzing the special vocabulary of modern war, or tabulating the semantic shifts which accompany a change like the French Revolution. Upsetting movements like that of 1789 create a new terminology, elevating humble terms and hurling ancient ones into the discard, to the perturbation of conservatives. Back in 1799 an irate opponent of *Liberté, Egalité, Fraternité* expressed his disapproval of the new order by publishing anonymously in Venice a satirical Dictionary—really a political tract—called *Nuovo Vocabolario Filosofico-Democratico,* "indispensable," as the title page announces, "for all who wish to understand the new revolutionary language." Among the clichés the author denounced were: "ally, alliance," which, he said, "is used by Democrats only when they plan deceit"; "hypocrisy," a term applied to Napoleon and his followers for flirting with religion after denouncing it; "perfection, to perfect" an optimistic formula of Enlightenment expressing the hope of human progress, here stigmatized by the author as the immoral and irreligious slogan of assassins. Other expressions to be found in the alphabetical index are: "celibate," "civic guard," "gazette," "regeneration," "revolution," and "tribunal." Political slogans that have been cordially loved have also been cordially hated, until in many cases the intellectual content (if any) has been submerged by emotional inundations.

The linguistic aspect of demagogy and political spellbinding deserves more study than it has hitherto received. The Institute of Propaganda Analysis has done useful work in exposing the psychological devices employed. The rhetoric is just as interesting. For instance, archaisms are used, along with iteration, sound effects, epithets, and so forth, to play on the feelings of the listeners. A Biblical flavoring of seventeenth-century language will reinforce the appeal. Here it is still possible to use extinct pronouns like "ye, thou, thee" or verbal endings long since discarded, or constructions no longer understood like "Woe worth the day!" Such phrases affect people all the more because they are mysterious and unclear, with sacred connotations. Likewise the figures of speech are kept archaic when appeal is made to feeling rather than reason. Orators will speak of defending the gates or the walls of the city even when none exist, as everyone knows. Certain undefined terms like "free enterprise" or "rugged individualism" are used in a manner to suggest incantations more readily than reasoned exposition. Perhaps no department of human expression justifies more clearly the cynical statement that the chief function of language is to conceal thought.

SOCIAL VALUES OF CLARITY

Nevertheless we still use it, hopefully, to understand one another. By becoming aware of limitations we begin to circumvent them. Since language is so eminently social there is no end to the problems interrelating society and language. Amateurs may provide themselves with unending diversion if they wish to extend their original observation of language behavior into various special aspects of the subjects here indicated, and to others as well. In a living medium there are always new developments, significantly indicative to the trained listener. You will find that the correlation of social tendencies and language will deepen your understanding of both: what you say, and the milieu in which you say it.

In language as in many other things awareness is the first step towards intelligent adaptation and change. Laymen as well as professional linguists can have the fun and also the benefits of awareness. A pencil, a notebook, and an alert ear are all you need. You will learn much about yourself and your fellow man if you jot down striking phenomena connected with social concerns important for all of us: not only those here surveyed, but others. And you may very possibly be ready in a short time to make an original contribution concerning your discoveries. Language is the heritage of all of us, and so there is no reason why all of us may not be critical students of it—or even creators in the use of it.

11. Retrospect and Prospect

From the preceding cursory chapters it is to be hoped that the patient reader has by this time obtained some idea of the adventures to be enjoyed in language study. This has been an unconventional sort of survey, omitting or slurring over many technical matters that loom large in the usual book on linguistics, and including others which are generally avoided. The intricacies of grammar and syntax, for instance, are usually treated in elaborate detail, even in books which modestly proclaim themselves to be "Introductions" or "Handbooks" or "Manuals." For the general reader, however, it is probably sufficient to cite by way of example but a few of the adjustments in one's thinking which are necessary in adapting oneself to an alien syntax. It is the ability to make the adjustment which is important. It may constitute the humanistic value of the study. My purpose will have been achieved if my few scattered examples have pointed out the type of pleasure and profit which may be derived from a cultivation of the mental elasticity requisite in feeling one's way into another grammar. From this point on it is up to the reader to get the pleasure himself and savor it in true Epicurean fashion, by actually learning a few languages: not with traditional dull conformity, by sheer memory, but with alert awareness of all shaded differences from one idiom to another.

On the side of inclusiveness in this book there may be reckoned the discussion of poetry and poetics, a subject commonly left to literary critics. This is their domain, to be sure. Yet it may be gently suggested that the august critics as well as lowly laymen might gain by some measure of knowledge about the neighboring domain of language. I think the thesis is clearly defensible that poetry becomes more enjoyable as well as more intelligible (perhaps I should say *because* more intelligible?) when one knows something about language, its medium. Similarly the daily intercourse with our fellows becomes richer when our ears have been sharpened to the social implications of their speech. A knowledge of word compounding, of etymology, of semantic spheres will change the material of everyday speech into a cultural heritage of deepened significance.

Throughout the book it has been necessary to insist, perhaps to the point of wearisome repetition, on the essential dignity of all human speech. It is to be hoped that the need for such stress will soon pass away. In fact much that has been said on these pages arose from the need to counteract the widespread misunderstandings and prejudices, even hatreds, of our own era. It would be a happy thing if we could look forward to a speedy change, making these stressed passages in the present volume quickly outmoded. The sooner it becomes possible for readers to say "How old-fashioned! How unnecessary!" about such remarks on racial and linguistic minorities, the better it will be for the entire race. But, alas! that day seems far distant now. For the moment I presume I have little to fear in the way of readers' condescension in this regard.

It has not been my intention, of course, to deny differences of type or degrees of development in languages. From the point of view of the learner it is unquestionably true that some present a more cumbersome structure than others. Many are backward in vocabulary, because of isolation from major currents of world affairs. But all have a potentiality for development. Nor need that development be left to the slowest possible tempo, the result of accidental, usually sluggish evolution. Language, like other parts of human culture, is susceptible of change consciously directed by its creators. Certain types of simplification can be planned; provided intelligibility does not suffer, they do not have to wait upon centuries of slow evolution. Within narrow limits such conscious modifications have occasionally been tried. Bolder innovations may be attempted in the future. A new chapter will be written in the history of linguistic science when the recording of languages is supplemented by more creative direction of them. We have been slow in realizing that matters closest to us can also be shaped by us, if we so desire, instead of being "left to chance." Language may be one of the last institutions to be rescued from *laissez-faire* attitudes, simply because it is so close to us. When this happens, some of the principles assumed to be universal and necessary will turn out, as often happens, to be temporary compromises, products of a wasteful and roundabout procedure by trial and error.

The imperfections of ordinary speech have already attracted attention from some few independent spirits zealous for logic and symmetry. Their creative impetus has taken the form of elaborating perfect "artificial" languages, freed of the inconsistencies and anomalies marring even the most advanced of civilized languages. In intervals between world wars, attempts have been made to disseminate the study of Esperanto, Ido, Volapük, and other artificial languages as an aid to international communication. Those persons who expected to foster international amity by purely linguistic means have been repeatedly doomed to bitter disappointment as war after war has swept away the frail filaments of correspondence in these languages extending over national boundaries. We have seen more than once the demonstration of their insufficiency—taken alone —in promoting brotherhood among peoples. But they have served practical purposes creditably, within limits. They have facilitated the functioning of international congresses and the written communications of scientists. When the more basic problems of national fraternity have been solved, including such mundane matters as colonies, investments, and access to raw materials, then some type of international language can really begin to function in aid of an amity already established. Enthusiasts are convinced that an artificial language may one day replace all living ones and become the sole, universal means of communication for the entire world. The question is at this stage theoretical. For the present it is difficult to imagine exclusive reliance on a structure of speech so formally perfect. Put it into the hands of peoples still widely separated in their cultural development, and it will cease to be either logical or universal. It will be distorted in a thousand ways by local influences, and in a short time it will have broken down into dialects and even new separate languages. Still, it may be widely useful as an ancillary language supplementing a gradually diminishing number of national languages. In time of peace, this problem ought to be seriously discussed. Professional linguists may be little interested as scientists, since they conceive their study to be limited to a factual analysis of languages as they are; but they may be persuaded to consider the problem as citizens of the world.

Some readers may challenge the phrase about a "diminishing number of national languages." I admit it is merely a guess, and it deals with a highly problematical future. Nevertheless there is some reason for expecting diminution instead of increase in numbers.

Contemporary history has offered us a spectacle of two opposing tendencies in respect to national languages. A number of small independent states were created by the Treaty of Versailles (1919) out of the former Austrian, German, and Russian empires. These new or revived nations showed extreme awareness of their status. They properly regarded their recognized official languages as symbols of national integrity. Linguistic pride was sometimes permitted to degenerate into provincialism. Czechish citizens in the streets of Prague often went so far as to refuse to speak the language of Goethe with helpless tourists (though they knew it) because they wished to disassociate themselves completely from any knowledge of their late imperial masters. Nationalism was one of the dominant currents of European culture from 1919 to 1939 for reasons not at all mysterious to us now. In its wake came the multiplication of barriers—including languages. Not only were formerly suppressed languages recognized as official, but dying ones were rescued and given a new lease of life. Gaelic, Flemish, Polish, Finnish, and Czech were added to the list of languages represented on the maps. The more eagerly one wished to be a good European and a good internationalist, the more separate languages and dialects he was expected to master, in order to prove his international culture.

But during these fateful two decades technological advances were working in an entirely opposite direction. The radio and the speaking movies suddenly began to bring distant languages close to the ears of all nationals. Invention gave an enormous impetus to languages associated with the most important centers of radio diffusion and motion picture industry. In England, the British Broadcasting Corporation, popularly known as BBC, has been at some pains to adopt and disseminate a single version of standard English, which is thus brought to the ears of all hearers able to listen in on London. Aerial transmission thus offers a first powerful competitor to the many obstinate local dialects persisting in England, and it also brings the language to millions of other peoples who rarely heard it before the days of radio. American English is similarly extended, after a fashion, to populations hitherto cut off from all outside languages. So far there has been little effect, of course. But if radio and motion pictures were consistently directed towards the spread of several chosen languages, and above all if they were connected with universal and truly popular education in all countries (a dream yet to be realized), we should have a strong counter-tendency operative towards reduction in the number of dialects and languages. Even now, high school students of foreign languages—in certain favored communities —enjoy the enormous advantage of being able to see and hear movies acted in the languages they are studying. Students are able to aid their aural skill by playing phonograph records or tuning in on a foreign station of their radio. These last two methods are less effective than the first, since they fail to convey the important accompaniment of facial expression and gesture, but the newer art of television supplies both.

Before such unifying forces can be given fair scope, politics, economic organization, and technology will have to be brought into more harmonious accord than they show today. As it is, beneficent inventions are permitted to remain frustrated by the fierce rivalries of our times. We can only surmise how they may one day assist us when we permit them to do so. The conditions then prevalent will no doubt determine whether world communication will be more facilitated by adoption of an artificial auxiliary language in addition to the traditional ones still extant, or by the gradual spread of one living language, first as supplement to all the others and possibly, far in the future, as ultimate substitute for all of them.

And there is the still more remote and speculative possibility that spoken language itself, for all its advantages, may one day be replaced by some better means of communication from one intelligence to another. It is impossible to imagine now what that may be. No other organs of the body appear to be better adapted than the ones we now use in talking. Mr. H. G. Wells has suggested in one of his Utopian novels, *Men Like Gods,* that the human beings of the future may learn to communicate more directly by means of some sort of bio-physical process of thought activity in the brain cells. The medium is represented as being much subtler than the gross vibrations of air on which we now depend, but none the less purely physiological. This immediate transfer of thought would apparently reduce the possibility of lying, a factor which would alone do much to change human nature and human civilization.

At the moment, Utopian possibilities for language seem to be as little likely of realization as any other. The gloomier prophets of our day are inclined rather to point to deterioration if not extinction of what civilization we have. I do not think that linguists as a group tend to take the gloomy view. Insofar as they reflect at all on the general subject of their study, they must be impressed with the enormous value of the gift of speech and its power of service for humane ends. Let it be said again: it is language that has made us men. There is plenty of evidence that in time we will permit it to make us better men. Even now, in the shadow of threatened general slaughter, we may dare to hope for the day when language will collaborate with the other arts of peace to the adornment of a truly humane way of life. With the vision of such a day before us, we may the more easily take courage to continue living hopefully and cultivating the study of languages for the values they will yield in a more auspicious future.

APPENDIX

1. BIBLIOGRAPHY AND NOTES

NOTES TO CHAPTER 1

The sentence from Kant, quoted to illustrate abstractions, is from *The Critique of Pure Reason*, translated by F. Max Müller (New York, 1934), p. 339.

A good short history of earlier theories on the origin of speech is given by Otto Jespersen, *Language: Its Nature, Development and Origin* (New York, 1925). For an exposition of the theological point of view, which denies any kinship of human speech with expression in the lower animals, see the learned work of Wilhelm Schmidt, *Sprachfamilien und Sprachenkreise der Erde* (Heidelberg, 1926). The studies of R. L. Garner are presented in several books such as *The Speech of Monkeys* (London, 1892) and *Apes and Monkeys: Their Life and Language* (Boston, 1900). Rothman and Teuber correlated emotional expression of the chimpanzees with vowel quality in *Einzelausgabe aus der Anthropoidenstation auf Teneriffa* (Berlin: Presussische Akademie der Wissenschaften, 1915). The work of R. M. Yerkes is embodied in his *The Great Apes* (New Haven, 1929). For a survey of earlier studies see *ibid.*, 302 ff.

On the terminology "reference" and "referent" in linguistic communication see C. K. Ogden and I. A. Richards, *The Meaning of Meaning* (New York and London, 1923); also Willem Graff, *Language and Languages* (New York, 1932), chapter 2. On the general problem of communication see Karl Britton, *Communication: A Philosophical Study of Language* (London, 1939). Gustaf Stern elaborates the analysis of Ogden and Richards, emphasizing psychological factors and semantic applications, in his *Meaning and Change of Meaning with Special Reference to the English Language* (Göteborg, 1931: Göteborgs Hogskolas Aarskrift, XXXVIII, no. 1). There is a wealth of material on sympathetic magic in Sir James Frazer's *The Golden Bough* (London, 1911-26; one-volume edition 1926). See also J. W. E. Mannhardt, *Wald- und Feldkulte* (Berlin, 1875-77) and Edwin Sidney Hartland, *The Legend of Perseus* (London, 1894-96), Vol. II: *The Life Token*.

The curse from a Roman inscription is cited by Fr. Stolz, *Geschichte der lateinischen Sprache* (Leipzig: Sammlung Göschen, 1910), p. 121; the Quiché text is given by L. S. Schultze-Jena, *Indiana* (Jena, 1933), I, p. 186. The curse of Skirnir and Sigurd's conversation with the dragon are translated in Henry Bellows Adams's *The Poetic Edda* (New York: American Scandinavian Foundation, 1923), p. 115 ff. and 372.

NOTES TO CHAPTER 2

The phonetic characters used for transcribing English can be studied in more detail in any one of several excellent handbooks such as Walter Ripman's *English Phonetics* (New York: Dutton, 1931), or in the introduction to Daniel Jones's *An English Pronouncing Dictionary* (London and New York: Dutton, revised edition). The examples of ambiguity in spelling with the letter "a" are taken from Beulah Handler: *English the American Way* (New York: Barnes and Noble, 1940). Padre Ignacio de Paredes comments on the monotony of Aztec consonants in the Preface to the *Compendio del Arte de la Lengua Mexicana* of Padre Horacio Carochi (Puebla, Mexico, 1910 edition), p. 15. Ethel Aginsky's *A Grammar of the Mende Language* was published by the Linguistic Society of America (Philadelphia, 1935).

For an introduction to Egyptian hieroglyphs and grammar, see Alan H. Gardiner's fascinating *Egyptian Grammar* (Oxford, 1927). The article "Alphabet" by B. F. C. Atkinson in the *Encyclopædia Britannica* contains some instructive illustrations, as does Holger Pedersen's *Linguistic Science in the Nineteenth Century* (Cambridge: Harvard University Press, 1931). The graphical history of Princess Six Monkey is discussed by Herbert J. Spinden in "Indian Manuscripts of Southern Mexico," *Smithsonian Institution Reports* (1935), pp. 429-51. For additional examples of picture writing and alphabets, see Hans Jensen, *Geschichte der Schrift* (Hannover, 1925).

On runes and their history see *inter alia* the article by E. Sievers, "Runen und Runeninschriften" in Paul's *Grundriss der germanischen Philologie* (Berlin, 1891-93), I; Helmut Arntz, *Handbuch der Runenkunde* (Halle, 1935), including a survey of all theories concerning the origin of runes; Wolfgang Krause, *Runeninschriften im älteren Futhark* (Halle, 1937) with many examples with transliteration and commentary. The Old English runic poem is printed in C. W. M. Grein's *Bibliothek der angel-sächsischen Poesie* (Hamburg, 1921), I, 331. The similar passage in the *Elder Edda* is to be found in the Adams' translation, p. 391 ff. For an episode describing cure by runes see *Egil's Saga* in the translation by E. R. Eddison (Cambridge University Press, 1930), p. 174.

NOTES TO CHAPTER 3

There is a good brief survey of the world's languages, with an illustrative map, in Willem L. Graff's *Language and Languages* (New York, 1932), chapters 10 and 11. An elaborate survey is given by a group of specialists in *Les Langues du Monde,* edited by Antoine Meillet and Marcel Cohen (Paris, 1923). The maps in the appendix are most instructive. Much of the general information in this chapter is based on articles in this reference book. Father Wilhelm Schmidt's *Sprachfamilien und Sprachenkreise der Erde* (Heidelberg, 1926) is very informing, but some of the statements concerning wider relationships among groups must be regarded with extreme caution. The author avows his theological bias in the introduction and frankly reaffirms the validity of the story of the Garden of Eden as an explanation of human speech; therefore it is easy to understand his zeal to establish unities wherever possible, in order to facilitate a conclusion that all languages had a single origin.

The standard work on the culture of the parent Indo-European tribe is Hermann Hirt's *Die Indogermanen* (Strassburg, 1905). There is a brief discussion of the subject by William Dwight Whitney, *Language and the Study of Language* (New York, 7th edition, 1910), lecture 5. Much has been written since these two books appeared, but the general outlines of the problem remain the same. For the place of Indo-European among other cultures, see V. Gordon Childe, *The Dawn of European Civilization* (New York, 1925) and *The Aryans* (New York, 1926).

The article on Finno-Ugric by A. Sauvageot in *Les Langues du Monde* uses statistics which are now out of date (the last census under the Tsar, in 1897). For more recent information concerning the populations of various ethnic groups in Soviet territory, see a report by the Scientific Research Institute in Moscow: *Nationalities in the U.S.S.R., Results of the Solution of the National Question in the U.S.S.R.* (1936; published by "Vlast' Sovietov"), pp. 7 ff. It gives a table of some 168 items concerning language, nationality and literacy taken from the 1929 census. The Russian title is: *Natsional'nostei SSSR: Itogi Razresheniia natsional'nogo Voprosa v SSSR*, prepared by the Nauchno-Issledovatel'skii Institut. There is a special article on the Nentsy (Samoyeds) in the *Bol'shaia Sovietskaia Entsiklopediia*, volume XLI. The examples of Hungarian vowel harmony are taken from Robert J. Hall, *An Analytical Grammar of the Hungarian Language* (Language Monograph no. XVIII, Linguistic Society of America, Baltimore, 1940), which gives a clear exposition of the principles. The Semitic variations of the root of *qtl* come from Marcel Cohen's article in *Les Langues du Monde;* for the consonant change known as "lenition," exemplified in the root *mlχ*, see Carl Brockelmann, *Grundriss der vergleichenden Grammatik der semitischen Sprachen*, I (Berlin, 1908), p. 204. The Osmali examples come from J. Deny on Turkic, in Meillet and Cohen. For Bantu, see Sir Harry H. Johnston, *A Comparative Study of the Bantu and Semi-Bantu Languages* (Oxford, 1919), 2 vols. For American Indian languages the prime book of reference is by Franz Boas: *Handbook of American Indian Languages* (Washington, 1911 and 1922). Friedrich Müller's arguments for polygenesis appear in his *Grundriss der Sprachwissenschaft,* I (Vienna, 1876), p. 50 ff. Trombetti's arguments in refutation are presented in his *Elementi di Glottologia* (Bologna, 1922-23). The controversy is briefly surveyed by M. Schlauch, *Science and Society,* I (1936), 18-44.

NOTES TO CHAPTER 4

Any etymological dictionary of English will give information about the separate elements of our compound words and their original meanings. To get further information on Latin compounds taken over by us consult Alois Walde, *Lateinisches etymologisches Wörterbuch* (Heidelberg, 2nd ed., 1910). Otto Jespersen discusses Pidgin English in *Language* (New York, 1925), ch. 12. The examples of it—probably deliberately chosen if not edited for humorous effect —come from Charles G. Leland's *Pidgin-English Sing-Song* (London, 1900).

The humorous paraphrase by William James of a sentence in Herbert Spencer is quoted by Kenneth Burke, *Attitudes to History* (New York, 1937), I, p. 11 f. The quotation from Hegel will be found in his *Sämtliche Werke* (Leipzig, 1937), II, p. 68 and 71; the translation is the one by J. B. Baillie of the *Phenomenology of Mind* (New York, 1931), p. 137 and 140.

For loan words see Mary S. Serjeantson, *A History of Foreign Words in English* (New York, 1936) and the special studies listed in her bibliography (p. 301 f.). Especially interesting in connection with the linguistic situation in North America is H. W. Bentley's *A Dictionary of Spanish Terms in English* (New York and Oxford, 1932). The mystery story cited for Hawaiian loan words is Biggers's *House Without a Key*, ch. 11, *init.* The Finnish compounds have been lifted from M. Willewill, *Praktische Grammatik der Finnischen Sprache* (Vienna, 1906). For a systematic account of derivations see Knut Kannelin, *Finska Spraaket* (Helsingfors, 1932). The Malay compounds will be found in R. O. Winstedt's *Malay Grammar* (Oxford, 1927), p. 51 ff. The Chinese examples come from Georg von der Gabelentz, *Chinesische Grammatik* (Leipzig, 1881), p. 358. For the Cakchiquel, see the *Diccionario* by Saenz de Santa María (Guatemala, 1940).

NOTES TO CHAPTER 5

Semantic shift by way of metaphor is discussed by Hermann Paul, *Prinzipien*, p. 94 ff. See also von der Gabelentz, p. 232 ff. The chief types of semantic change are presented in Bloomfield's *Language*, ch. 24. Jost Trier propounds his theory of semantic fields in the introduction to *Der deutsche Wortschatz im Sinnbezirk des Verstandes*, I (Heidelberg, 1931). p. 1-26. Hans Sperber gives a general introduction in his *Einführung in die Bedeutungslehre* (Bonn and Leipzig, 1930). A very useful survey and critique of recent semantic (linguistic) studies is furnished by Otto Springer, "Probleme der Bedeutungslehre," *Germanic Review*, XIII (1938), 159 ff. For a simple introduction see Hugh Walpole, *Semantics: The Nature of Words and Their Meanings* (New York, 1941). An elaborate discussion is given by Gustaf Stern, *Meaning and Change of Meaning* (Göteborg, 1931).

P. W. Bridgman's *Logic of Modern Physics* appeared some years ago (New York, 1933); *The Intelligent Individual and Society*, more recently (New York, 1938). Alfred Korzybski's ambitious work is *Science and Sanity* (Lancaster, Pa., n.d.). The full diagram of "levels" and "labels" appears on p. 471. For brief popular statements of Korzybski's principles, with examples, see S. I. Hayakawa, *Language in Action* (New York, 1940) and Irving J. Lee, *Language Habits in Human Affairs* (New York, 1941). Thurman W. Arnold's analysis *The Symbols of Government* (New Haven, 1935) was followed by the more inclusive *Folklore of Capitalism* (New Haven, 1937). Stuart Chase, *The Tyranny of Words* (New York, 1938), embodies much of Bridgman, Korzybski, and Arnold.

NOTES TO CHAPTER 6

Charles Carpenter Fries has written a scientific, strictly inductive account of our speech in his *American English Grammar* (New York, 1940). See Chapter 5

Notes

for the discussion of our two living inflections. Margaret M. Bryant and Janet Rankin Aiken record examples of illogical syntax in their *Psychology of English* (New York, 1940). For the point of view of the logical positivist, see Rudolf Carnap, *The Logical Syntax of Language* (New York, 1937). On presentative sentences see Josephine M. Burnham, *University of Kansas Publications* (Humanistic Studies), VI, no. 4.

Hermann Hirt's discussion of gender inflections is quoted from his *Indogermanische Grammatik*, III: *Das Nomen* (Heidelberg, 1927), p. 85. The older theory about verbal endings and pronouns in Indo-European will be found in William Dwight Whitney, *Language*, ch. 7. The more recent theories and explanations will be found in H. Hirt, *op. cit.*, IV, *Das Verbum* (Heidelberg, 1928), p. 148, 153 *et passim*.

Wundt's claims in behalf of the Ewe language were made in his *Elemente der Völkerpsychologie*, p. 68 ff. For grammars see Diedrich Westermann, *A Study of the Ewe Language* (Oxford, 1930) and *Die Ewe-Sprache in Togo* (Berlin, 1939). The Malay examples come from the *opus* of R. O. Winstedt, previously cited. Mende, likewise referred to earlier, is analyzed by E. Aginsky; the tense aspect of pronouns is explained on p. 21 and 33. Von der Gabelentz, *Die Sprachwissenschaft*, has been cited for the syntactic function of Chinese word order (p. 117), and for the tense inflection of pronouns in Melanesian (Aneiteum) (p. 151). The "possessive" conjugation of Nenets (Samoyed) verbs is explained by A. Sauvageot in his article on Finno-Ugric, in A. Meillet and M. Cohen, *Les Langues du Monde*. For further examples of such usage see Louis H. Gray, *Foundations of Language* (New York, 1939), p. 152. Vestiges of it are to be found in Quiché: See Schultze-Jena, *Indiana*, I, p. 294 and 304 f. On the Manchu verb see Lucien Adam, *Grammaire de la Langue Mandchou* (Paris, 1873). The Nahuatl verbs are cited from Mariano Jacobo Rojas, *Estudios gramaticales del Idioma Mexicano* (Mexico, 1935). For Dravidian, see Robert Caldwell, *A Comparative Grammar of the Dravidian Languages* (London, 1913 ed.), p. 451. The complicated categories of noun classes in Chichewa are expounded by M. H. Watkins in his grammar before mentioned, p. 52 ff. On the relation of pitch, vowel position, and tense relations see Wundt, *op. cit.*, p. 67 f. and E. Prokosch, *A Comparative Germanic Grammar* (Philadelphia, 1939), p. 121 ff. and the references quoted. (D. Westermann gives interesting illustrations of semantic and grammatical functions of pitch in his Ewe grammar.) Prokosch discusses theories on origin of gender, *op. cit.*, p. 228-30. Gender in Potawatomi syntax is treated by Charles Hockett in *Language*, XV (1939), 235-48. Various theories of gender (comparing Indo-European and Algonquian dialects) are surveyed by J. P. B. de J. de Jong, *De Waarderingsonderscheiding van "Levend" en "Levenlos"* (Leiden, 1913). The Hawaiian examples are taken from Edward Tregear's dictionary. For the inclusive-exclusive forms of plural pronouns in Santal, see Wilhelm von Hevesy, *Finnisch-Ugrisches aus Indien* (Vienna, 1932).

NOTES TO CHAPTER 7

A trained ear and close attention to living speech are of greater aid than much reading of books when one is mastering the general types of sound change. Some technical books make valuable use of the phonetic approach in dealing with Indo-European philology: for instance, Joseph Schrijnen in his *Einführung in das Studium der indogermanischen Sprachwissenschaft* (translated from the Dutch, Heidelberg, 1921). Most of the examples in this chapter are taken from familiar words in familiar languages. The illustrations of Grimm's law may be augmented by referring to Hermann Hirt's *Handbuch des Urgermanischen*, I (Heidelberg, 1931), p. 80, and E. Prokosch, *A Comparative Germanic Grammar*, p. 47 ff. The examples of the Armenian consonant shift are taken from A. Meillet, *Esquisse d'une Grammaire Comparée de l'Arménien classique* (Vienna, 2nd ed., 1936), p. 24 ff. There is a clear and exhaustive account of ablaut (vowel gradation) in another of Meillet's books, *Introduction à l'Étude comparative des Langues indoeuropéennes* (Paris, 3rd ed., 1912), ch. 4. The greater part of the second volume of Hirt's *Indogerm. Gram.* is devoted to the intricacies of ablaut. For abundant illustrations of palatalization in the Romance languages, see any comparative study of them. Readily and cheaply accessible is Adolf Zauner's *Romanische Sprachwissenschaft* (Sammlung Göschen, nos. 128 and 250). See also E. Bourciez, *Éléments de Linguistique Romane* (Paris, 1930).

NOTES TO CHAPTER 8

For elaborate information on the Anglo-Saxons in England see Charles Oman, *England before the Norman Conquest* (London, 1910) and R. H. Hodgkin, *History of the Anglo-Saxons* (2 vols., Oxford, 1935). The literature is described by E. E. Wardale, *Chapters on Old English Literature* (London, 1935). To gain a quick insight into Old English grammar with simple readings, look at A. J. Wyatt's primer, *The Threshold of Anglo-Saxon* (New York, 1926). It presents the irreducible minimum of paradigms in 12 pages. There are more elaborate grammars by Milton Haight Turk, Marjorie Anderson and Blanche Coulton Williams, George T. Flom, Joseph Wright; the authoritative reference grammar is by Sievers, translated by A. S. Cook. Thomas Jefferson, who was interested in the study of Old English, drafted a simplified grammar based on modern English for practical purposes only. It has been used by Seltzer and Seltzer in their *Jefferson Anglo-Saxon Reader* (New York, 1938)—a practical short-cut not intended for specialists. The quotation from King Alfred is from his preface to Gregory's *Pastoral Care*, quoted by Charles Plummer in *The Life and Times of Alfred the Great* (Oxford, 1902). The passage about Moses in the bullrushes will be found in Wyatt's *Threshold*.

On the Danes in England, see Otto Jespersen, *Growth and Structure of the English Language* (Leipzig, 1919). For samples of Middle English, consult O. F. Emerson, *A Middle English Reader* (New York, 1915). For reading Chaucer—in the original, by all means!—use F. N. Robinson's Cambridge Edition (Boston, 1933). The quotation from "Poema Morale"—"Ich æm elder þen ic wes"—is from Emerson's *Reader;* "Wynter wakeneth al my care" is reprinted in *The Oxford Book of English Verse*, ed. Quiller-Couch (Oxford, 1939), p. 9.

Quotations from Pecock and Sidney are taken from George Philip Krapp's valuable *Rise of English Literary Prose* (New York, 1915). The passage from Jonson's *Poetaster* occurs in Act V, Scene iii, ed. Herbert S. Mallory (Yale

Studies in English, 1905), but the spelling has been modernized in this as in
other citations from the Elizabethans.

General studies of English since the Renaissance are to be found in George H.
McKnight, *Modern English in the Making* (New York, 1930) and Stuart Robertson, *The Development of Modern English* (New York, 1938).

For the general history of the language, in all periods, consult Albert C.
Baugh, *A History of the English Language* (New York, 1935). The bibliogra-
phies at the ends of chapters suggest additional reading in all periods. The
importance of Sanskrit for comparative philology is explained in Holger
Pedersen's *Linguistic Science in the Nineteenth Century* as translated by John
Spargo (Harvard University Press, 1931), ch. 1. Some of the examples of freer
grammatical usage today are taken from J. H. G. Grattan and P. Gurrey, *Our
Living Language* (New York and London, 1925). Reference grammars of modern English are fairly numerous. For the non-specialist Henry Sweet's *New English
Grammar* (Oxford, 1899) is still one of the most useful. See also Hans Kurath
and G. O. Curme, *A Grammar of the English Language* (Boston, 1931). On
Basic English, consult C. K. Ogden, *The System of Basic English* (New York,
1934). (The over-sanguine claims for international speech as an antidote to
war appear on p. 18.)

NOTES TO CHAPTER 9

The quotations and allusions in this chapter are to the following authors, in
the order in which they have been cited: Cleanth Brooks, *Modern Poetry and
the Tradition* (Chapel Hill, 1939); James Joyce, *Finnegans Wake* (New York:
Viking Press, 1939); T. S. Eliot, *Poems, 1909-1925* (New York: Harcourt Brace,
n.d.); Hart Crane, *Collected Poems* (New York: Liveright Publishing Corp.,
1933); James Joyce, *Ulysses* (New York: Random House, ed., 1934); Gertrude
Stein, *Lectures in America* (New York: Random House, 1935); Stein, *Ida* (New
York: Random House, 1941); Stein, *Four Saints in Three Acts* (New York:
Random House, 1934); W. H. Auden, *Poems* (New York: Random House,
1936); Auden, *The Double Man* (New York: Random House, 1941); E. E. Cummings, *is 5* (New York: Boni and Liveright, 1926); Cummings, *W (Viva)* (New
York: Horace Liveright Inc., 1931); John Weaver, *In American* (New York:
Knopf, 1926); Henri Delacroix, *Le Langage et la Pensée* (Paris, 1924) especially p.
384 ff.; Ferdinand Brunot, *La Pensée et la Langue* (Paris,1936)—Book I for "presentations" and "propositions"; Charles Bally, *Linguistique générale et Linguistique française* (Paris, 1932), p. 65 ff. Some of the poems cited will also be found in
contemporary anthologies such as George K. Anderson and Eda Lou Walton,
This Generation (New York: Scott, Foresman and Co., 1939) and the *Faber Book
of Modern Verse*, edited by Michael Roberts (London: Faber and Faber, 1936).
In discussing James Joyce the author has made use of an earlier study, "The Language of James Joyce," published by her in *Science and Society*, III (1939), 482 ff.

NOTES TO CHAPTER 10

The entertaining passage about clothes is taken from Carlyle's *Sartor Resartus*, Book I, ch. 9. "Captain Brassbound's Conversion" appears in Shaw's *Three*

Plays for Puritans, published by Brentano's (New York, 1912). The notes to the play are also interesting. May Sinclair's *The Divine Fire* was published by Henry Holt (New York, 1904). The animadversions of Thomas Wolfe on British English are to be found in *Of Time and the River* (New York: Harper & Brothers, 1935), Book V, ch. 48, p. 603 f.; those of Aldous Huxley in *Point Counter-Point* (Garden City, N. Y. : Doubleday, Doran, 1928) ch. 20.

On hypercorrect forms see Otto Jespersen, *Language,* p. 293 f. The most pertinent chapters of Thorstein Veblen's *Theory of the Leisure Class* (New York: B. W. Huebsch, 1918) are "Dress as an Expression of the Pecuniary Culture" and "The Conservation of Archaic Traits." The famous butler of P. G. Wodehouse—who so well illustrates Veblen's theories—is to be found in *Jeeves,* now readily available in an edition by Pocket Books, Inc. The quotations are taken from ch. 9, pages 80 and 87. The examples of French argot were taken from articles by Galtier-Boissière and Pierre Devaux in *Crapouillot* (1939). The table of Malay pronouns comes from R. O. Winstedt's grammar, p. 108. On Japanese forms of politeness see von der Gabelentz, *Sprachwissenschaft,* p. 246. Class dialects are discussed by Henry Cecil Wyld, *A Short History of English* (New York, 1929), p. 148 f. See also Daniel Jones, *English Pronouncing Dictionary* (New York, 1926), Introduction, especially p. vi f.

The works to consult first on American English are George Philip Krapp, *The English Language in America* (New York, 1925) and H. L. Mencken. *The American Language* (New York, 1936). For Krapp's statement on Negro pronunciation, see II, p. 34 f. Most of the American idioms and phrases quoted are taken from John Russell Bartlett's *A Glossary of Words and Phrases Usually Regarded as Peculiar to the United States* (New York, 1848). For others I am indebted to a course paper by one of my students, Miss Dorothy Hector. Greene's language of cony-catching is contained in his *Notable Discovery of Cosenage* (published 1591). The seventeenth century underworld slang is preserved in *A New Dictionary of the Terms Ancient and Modern of the Canting Crew* (London, n.d.) by a certain "B. E., Gent." The slang of lunch rooms is excerpted from Harold W. Bentley, "Linguistic Concoctions of the Soda Jerker," *American Speech,* XI (1936), 37-45. See also J. M. Steadman, Jr., "A Study of Verbal Taboos," *ibid.,* X (1935), 93. Mencken discusses taboos, *op. cit.,* p. 300-18.

On race and language in relation to politics, see Ruth Benedict, *Race: Science and Politics* (New York: Modern Age, 1940) and Julian Huxley and A. C. Haddon, *We Europeans* (London, 1935). Franz Boas, *The Mind of Primitive Man* (New York, 1911) is still very valuable—and more important today than ever before since it was written.

(These are offered as suggestions merely. The number
could be indefinitely increased.)

CHAPTER 1

1. To illustrate the power traditionally associated with the
   spoken word, make a collection of fairy tales in which the fate
   of the hero or heroine depends on knowledge of a name or a
   special word, or the asking of a question, or the solving of a
   riddle. In what stories must the hero or heroine remain nameless? In which stories is a wish like the building of a castle no
   sooner expressed than accomplished? You will find help in
   Mary Huse Eastman's *Index to Fairy Tales, Myths and
   Legends* (Boston, 1926; Supplement, 1937).
2. Observe the gestures of someone who speaks a foreign language. Note down the ones often repeated and define their conventional meaning.
3. By what terms do children refer to the persons or things they
   fear?
4. List the signals used in your school or place of work which
   convey messages without words. What verbal commands are
   most often used? How, if at all, could they be conveyed by
   gesture?
5. What signals does your cat or dog understand?
6. Take a hundred consecutive words at random in a dictionary
   which gives etymologies (e.g., the *Concise Oxford Dictionary*).
   How many of them are marked "imitative" or "onomatopoetic"? Compare your results with those of others trying the
   same experiment. What is the average percentage?
7. Do the words "hollow" and "horror" seem descriptive to you?
   Look them up in W. W. Skeat's *Etymological Dictionary of
   the English Language* and find out what they meant in earlier

times. Were they more or less descriptive then, according to your feeling for sounds?

8. Make a list of onomatopoetic words in English. Give equivalent words in French, German, or any other language you know. How do they compare in sound effects?

9. What are the learned terms for the following living creatures: whippoorwill, cricket, rattlesnake, hummingbird, wasp, bumblebee? What are the advantages of the popular terms over the learned? The learned over the popular?

10. Engage a group of children in pantomime games designed to express various types of statement. Begin with simple ones like "We want your toys," but include more abstract ones like "Our country has been insulted." Report how they expressed these ideas without words.

11. What was meant in ancient times by an "oracle"? Look up examples in Plutarch's *Lives* of Greek and Roman heroes. What circumstances enhanced the power of the spoken word in these situations?

Chapter 2

1. Make a record of the sounds substituted for the "correct" ones by a small child learning to talk. Present them systematically according to placement in the mouth: the sounds replacing labials, dentals, gutturals, etc.

2. Why are these substitutions made? Explain in terms of phonetics.

3. Make a record of the speech of a foreigner talking English. What sounds gave him trouble? If you know what sounds are present and which absent from his native tongue, explain his difficulty by comparison with the range of English sounds.

4. Record some sentences spoken by a person very tired or somewhat inebriated. What has happened to the standard sounds? Why?

5. Make a list of tongue-twisters like "She sells sea shells on the seashore." Introduce extra words to diversify the sounds. At what point do the sentences become readily pronounceable?

6. What sounds in French (or German, Spanish, Danish, Russian, etc.) are not represented in English? How would you explain their nature to a student?

7. What sounds in these languages resemble ours but are made with slight differences in position of the speech organs? Explain.

8. How are the normal sounds of your speech affected when you have a cold? Why?

9. Pronounce the following: [gʌn, gʊn, guːn], [tiːn, tɪn, taɪn], [kiː, ciː], [kuː, kau], [kuː, ciː], [kin, cin, tʃɪn], [iç, iχ], [ɑɣ, ɑχ,], [kirk, tʃəːtʃ], [sel, ʃel], [ɪm, ɪp, ɪŋ], [lɔː, loʊ], [θem, seɪn], [θen, fen], [væt, fæt], [jes, dʒest], [goʊ, ɣɔː].

10. How would you explain to an eighth-grade child the pronunciation of "singing": [sɪŋɪŋ] rather than [sɪŋɪn] or [sɪŋɪŋg]?

11. Prepare a list of other variations from standard pronunciation like this one, and describe them in phonetic terms.

12. How would you correct them?

13. What myths and fables do you know about the origins of the alphabet among various peoples? What attitudes do they reflect concerning the art of writing?

14. Look up the etymology of the following for the information implied concerning earlier forms of writing: "write, rune, alphabet, hieroglyph, pen, cuneiform." Look up *schreiben* and *Buchstabe* in Friedrich Kluge's *Etymologisches Wörterbuch der deutschen Sprache,* if you are interested in German.

15. What technical words do you know connected with the art of printing (e.g., "folio, quarto, colophon, incunabulum")? Find out their origin.

16. Were the *quipus*—knotted cords—of the Peruvian Indians a form of alphabet? See E. Nordenskiöld, *The Secret of the Peruvian Quipus* (Göteborg, 1925).

17. Translate the following sentences into picture writing:

> The hero killed the villain.
> The villain was killed by the hero.
> The enemy attacked us.
> We defended ourselves from the enemy.
> We kindled a fire.
> A fire broke loose.

Which shifts in grammatical relationship are most difficult to express by this method?

18. Study the examples of picture alphabets in Hans Jensen, *Geschichte der Schrift* (Hannover, 1925), and comment on their advantages and disadvantages.

19. Using a single unit of writing like a stylized man's figure walking for "to go," make up picture modifiers to change this into other verbs like "to hasten, to enter, to climb, to descend, to retreat," etc.

20. What similarities in sound caused students to make the following mistakes? Use phonetic symbols to explain.

Often when people are drowned you can *revise* them by punching their sides but not too hard.

In Christianity a man can have only one wife. This is called *monotony*.

The bottom of the sea is composed of clay and fine *sentiments*.

Geometry teaches us to *bisex* angels.

"Land where our fathers died, Land where the pilgrims *pried* . . ."

The dog came bounding down the path emitting *whelps* at every bound.

A *Soviet* is a cloth used by waiters in hotels.

(From *The Pocket Book of Boners*, New York, 1941.)

Chapter 3

1. Make lists of the words for numbers one to ten in several languages you know to be related. Try the same experiment with languages in a group you have never studied, such as the Polynesian languages. (Use Edward Tregear's *Maori-Polynesian Comparative Dictionary*.) How close are the words for the same numbers?

2. Read Sir Harry Johnston's description of Parent Bantu (including reconstructed forms for numbers, pronouns, etc.) in his *Comparative Study of the Bantu and Semi-Bantu Languages* (Oxford, 1919), I, p. 29ff. Can you perceive the method he used to arrive at his description of the lost ancestor-language?

3. Explain the differences between the Polynesian forms in phonetic terms. How close are the resemblances? Which forms appear to be most archaic and which the most developed?

4. Look up population tables for the world in the *World's Almanac*. Estimate what proportionate part is composed of persons speaking languages of the major groups such as Indo-European, Semitic, Hamitic, etc.

5. Study the linguistic maps of the world in the appendix to Meillet and Cohen's *Les Langues du Monde*. What are the chief territorial shifts in language groups that have occurred since 1500?

6. Find out the importance of the following for our knowledge of languages and their relations: Rosetta Stone, Oscan-Umbrian, Ogham script, Darius the Great and his inscriptions, Hittite, Old Turkish runes, Dvenos inscription. (You will find most of the information in Holger Pedersen's *Linguistic Science in the Nineteenth Century*, translated by John Spargo.)

7. What did the Greeks have to say about the relation of their language to others? The ancient Hebrews?

8. Study the place-names in your locality. How many are Indian? After a conquest, are the terms borrowed from a conquered people more apt to be common or proper nouns? Why?

9. If you have lived in a bilingual or trilingual country like Belgium or Switzerland, try to recall which types of words were most likely to be borrowed from one language to another. Do you know of any similar contact of languages in America?

10. Here is the opening sentence of the Lord's Prayer, "Our Father which art in Heaven, hallowed be Thy name," in several Indo-European languages. Can you detect resemblances which would lead you to deduce that they are related?

> Latin: *Pater noster qui es in coelis, sanctificetur nomen tuum.*
> Greek: *Páter hēmôn ho en toîs ouranoîs, hagiasthḗtō tò ónoma soû.*
> Irish: *Ar n-athair a·ta air neamh, gu naomhaichear t'ainm.*
> Old Slavic: *Otĭče našĭ, iže jesi na nebesexŭ, da svetiti sę imę tvoje.*
> Gothic: *Atta unsar, þu in himinam, weihnai namō þein.*

(From Hermann Hirt, *Indogermanische Grammatik*, I, p. 71 f.)

CHAPTER 4

1. Make a study of the headlines in your newspaper for several consecutive days. What words are used in place of others in order to save space? To what extent is this technological necessity affecting ordinary speech? Where in journalistic writing do you find an approximation to clipped style of telegrams?

2. Look up the following words in an etymological dictionary. What metaphors do you find in them?

transcendent	exoneration	impugn
infringement	expense	devastation
convince	disastrous	posthumous
transgression	intervention	erosion

3. Consult a thesaurus (for instance, Roget's) of the English language for the words connected with the general subjects of heat and light. Which words are usually limited to these subjects in a physical sense? Which are used figuratively as well?

4. Make a list of names of jewels and find out their origins.

5. Compose a miniature dictionary of words connected with some specific article of trade such as cosmetics or delicatessen. Are they chiefly loan words or native compounds? Common or proper (geographical) nouns?

6. Try restating theorems in geometry exclusively with words of Anglo-Saxon origin. Analyze the effect.

7. What is the stylistic effect of the Anglo-Saxon vocabulary used by Edna St. Vincent Millay in her opera libretto, *The King's Henchman?*

8. Jot down in a notebook any words you see that look like new formations. How many of them have been registered in dictionaries?

9. By what process did these words originate:

burgle (vb.)	gas	chowder
outrage	simony	*Blitzkrieg*
gargle	mob	paranoia
knockout	interloper	bus

10. What is the relationship between the following pairs of words:

treasury: thesaurus	alms: eleemosynary
frail: fragile	aid: adjutant
intrigue: intricate	gym: gymnasium

11. Make a study of the technical vocabulary of one of the fine arts. What does it reveal about the indebtedness of English to other cultures?

12. Examine the use of classical compounds in the vocabulary of one of the sciences. (Special word-lists exist for some: e.g., Frank Fenner, Jr., *A Glossary for Photography,* Chicago, 1939; A. L. Melander, *Source Book of Biological Terms,* New York, 1937.)

13. Every language has words which are difficult to render in another. German *gemütlich* is an example. What words of this sort have you encountered in the foreign languages you have studied? How do you convey the sense of them in English explanations?

14. What types of English words have you noticed being borrowed into other European languages? To what extent have they been modified in being transferred?

15. Here are some noun phrases used to designate familiar places: "bus stop, beauty parlor, flying field, box office, race track." Extend the list, including slang expressions such as "clip joint, hot-dog stand, spaghetti joint." Can you create single words out of learned classical elements to designate the same places?

16. Explain how these compounds came to be misunderstood by young students:

The plural of monocle is binnacle.
Amphibia lead a double life.
Parallelepipeds are animals with parallel feet.

A philanderer is a person who gives money freely to charitable and needy institutions.

An octogenarian is an animal which has eight young at a birth.

An optimist is a man who looks after your eyes, a pessimist looks after your feet.

Polycarp is a rare, many-sided fish. (*Pocket Book of Boners.*)

17. How does W. H. Auden achieve satiric effect by bizarre use of loan words? (See especially his *Double Man*, New York, 1941.) Compare Heine's use of the same device in poems like *Sie sassen und tranken am Teetisch,* from *Das Buch der Lieder.*

18. Can you cite an example from literature where excessive use of loan words gives an effect of snobbishness or artificiality?

19. Look up the examples of English with and without the use of polysyllabic fused compounds in C. K. Ogden's *The System of Basic English* (New York, 1934), p. 142 ff. Does the simplified version limit the sense?

20. Next time you undertake to answer a child's question like "Why do things fall down instead of up?" notice what simple words you substitute for terms like "gravitation."

Chapter 5

1. What changes of meaning occur in the use of "book" in these phrases: "to bring to book, bookkeeping, booking office [British], Book of Books, Book of Fate"?

2. Jot down as rapidly as you can the words associated in your mind with these: "recess, monitor, fire-drill, assembly, blackboard, chalk."

3. What words do you know, otherwise colorless, which take on an unpleasant connotation in certain special uses? An example is "detention" in "detention room." Military and legal vocabulary will furnish others.

4. What is the literal meaning of "protective custody"? What are its connotations?

5. What theological terms have arisen by giving august significance to simple words?

6. Single out the key words of newspaper editorials which cause semantic difficulty, and explain why. Here is a specimen for analysis:

> We would probably be exceeding the duties and functions of the United States were we trying to AMERICANIZE the world.
> But the New Deal is NOT trying to Americanize the world.
> It is trying to COMMUNIZE the world.
> It is not trying to sow the seeds of American individualism and consti-

tutional liberty, and freedom of thought and speech and publication, and equality before the law, and opportunity for all men throughout the world.

Most assuredly NOT, since the New Deal has discarded these essential and elemental freedoms here at home.

Have not our most distinguished New Deal leaders repudiated the Constitution as belonging to the ox-cart era?

Have they not rejected the Bill of Rights as an outmoded survival of the horse and buggy period? Have they not substituted for American independence and rugged individualism the regimentation and confiscatory taxation of Communism?

This is an editorial from the New York *Journal-American,* August 15, 1941.

7. Make a list of political terms which need clarification in ordinary discourse. Ask non-specialists to give you definitions on the spur of the moment. Then consult books of reference like the *Encyclopedia of the Social Sciences* for explanations. Can you construct simple, workable definitions which will facilitate coherent and good-natured discussion?

8. Try the same procedure with a list of religious terms. Use J. Hastings, *Encyclopedia of Religion and Ethics* for reference.

9. What tools do you know which are named from their resemblance to other objects? From their function alone? From the sound they make?

10. Arrange the following words in the order of their ambiguity, from most clear to most doubtful in meaning:

gravity	kilogram
pound	seriousness
specific gravity	heaviness
weight	frivolity

11. Mention some words whose meaning has become more solemn as they became more archaic. More narrow. More extended. (You will find examples of all tendencies in the King James translation of the Bible.)

12. Consult the *New English Dictionary* for an historical record of the uses of these words, and point out how they have changed meaning since 1600:

commonwealth	evolution
juror	fancy
wit	communism
non-resistance	democracy
leveller	(third) estate

13. Suggest situations in which each of these sentences might have various meanings:

> How very sweet it is!
> He advocated communism.
> We got rid of the louse.
> It was a womanly thing to do.
> This race is superior to that.
> It's a tragedy.
> We are blood-brothers.
> This will undermine American institutions.
> It's a question of relativity.

14. Find out how "definition" is defined in textbooks of logic. Read the chapter on "Definition" in Hugh Walpole's *Semantics* (New York, 1941), and try to apply the 25 "routes" to some of the key words in the quotation under question 6.

15. Compare Walpole's "routes" to the Categories of Aristotle.

16. What does "invaluable" mean: value-less or precious? Explain the shift.

17. Analyze the key words and phrases in famous political speeches of the past, such as the funeral oration of Pericles (Thucydides, Book II) and Lincoln's "Gettysburg Address."

18. Study the examples of semantic nonsense in the appendix to Stuart Chase's *Tyranny of Words*. Collect further examples of your own. How would you undertake to clarify them?

19. What names of animals are used as epithets of abuse? Why the pejorative transfer?

20. Look up the analysis of propaganda, with examples, given in Violet Edwards's *Group Leaders' Guide to Propaganda Analysis* (New York: Institute of Propaganda Analysis, 130 Morningside Drive, 1938). Work out some of the group projects suggested together with some of your friends. Comment on the semantic aspects of the language problem.

21. Read "The Disorderly Conduct of Words" by Zechariah Chaffee, Jr., in *Columbia Law Review*, XLI (1941), pp. 381-404. List cases of comparable ambiguity in the language of other professions.

Chapter 6

1. Compose sentences in which "it" is used as a noun; "book" as a verb; "pretty" as a verb; "mass" as an adjective; "drive" as a noun.

2. By what means do we indicate plurality in English nouns besides adding *-s* to the singular?

3. What verbal forms resemble nouns in their use in a sentence? Adjectives?

4. Do you consider the use of apostrophes in possessive forms a help? Why?

5. Which verb forms would you choose in these sentences:

> The United States (is) (are) a strong nation.
> The government (is) (are) of divided opinion concerning the proposal.
> The committee (is) (are) unanimous in the decision.
> One-half of the men (has) (have) been lost.

(See Otto Jespersen, *A Modern English Grammar*, London, 1928, Part II, Vol. I, chapters 5-7.)

6. How do we indicate that an adjective once applied to a person or thing, but does so no longer? Can you imagine doing this by an inflection of the adjective itself?

7. How do you explain the relation of the italicized words to the rest of the sentence in

> *To be frank with you,* I don't like it.
> I want *to be frank with you.*
> He knew it *to be him.*
> *To continue:* the cause of the present situation is clear.
> We are beginning *to understand.*

8. In an inflected language like German or Russian, word order permits almost any part of the sentence to be placed first for emphasis. In spoken English we sometimes break the construction for the same purpose: for instance, "This brother of yours—I don't like him!" What other methods are used to shift sentence structure for emphasis?

9. Which do you say: "I couldn't think of him being there alone" or "I couldn't think of his being there alone"? Consult a reference grammar to find out the usage of recognized writers in this matter. How do you interpret the function of "being"?

10. Compare the English tense system with that of Russian or Greek (or some other showing differences from ours). What relations are present in one but lacking in the other?

11. Try using English prepositions as if they were inflectional endings of nouns: "I sat the house-in, gave him a piece bread-of, butter-with." Does this usage help you to understand how to handle the endings of highly inflected languages? Would you prefer it to prepositions?

12. In Danish, definite articles are placed after nouns, as if one were to say "house-the," except in cases where an adjective precedes ("the big house"). Try the effect in English.

13. If English had a feminine suffix for all nouns denoting feminine creatures, what ending would be practicable for all nouns?

Could it be suffixed to verbs with "she" as subject? (Try the effect.) Would the sentences be clearer with such suffixes?

14. It is possible to express plurality by reduplication. That is, if "house" is singular, "house-house" would be a reduplicated plural. What other grammatical categories can you suggest that might be expressed in this way?

15. Try the effect of showing change in tense merely by a change in musical pitch: "I eat" (high) for present, and "I eat" (low) for past. Do you find it more satisfactory to use the low for present and high for past? Which seems most appropriate for lowest pitch: "I can" or "I could" or "I could have . . ."?

16. Do these sentences mean what the verb forms imply ?

> I do not doubt but that you would do it.
> Sorry, but I couldn't say.
> He is sure to turn up missing.
> Who's ringing?— That will be the postman, Sir.
> This would be the eminent critic Mr. X.
> I admit having done it.

17. Are there any advantages in having a verb agree with its subject in person and number? Disadvantages?

18. Look up Otto Jespersen's presentation of the verb as an "adjunct" of the subject in a sentence (*Modern English Grammar*, Part II, Vol. I, chapter 1, par. 41ff.). How does sentence stress bear out the assumption that the subject is primary and the verb secondary? What does Jespersen mean by "verbids"?

19. What does Jespersen mean by "principal," "adjunct" and "subjunct" as the three ranks in grammar (*ibid.*, par. 21)?

20. Make a clear statement on English conventions on the sequence of tenses. (Consult Henry Sweet, *A New English Grammar*, Oxford, 1892-98.)

CHAPTER 7

1. What general tendencies in sound change explain these occasional slips in pronunciation?

sec'etary for	secretary		nomilate for	nominate
gov'ment "	government		don'tcha "	don't you
pardy "	party		lily-rike "	lily-like
shill "	skill		awmost "	almost
folly "	follow		crudle "	curdle
asteriks "	asterisk		canditure "	candidature

2. Assimilation of the last sound of one word to the first of the next word is called *sandhi-* assimilation. (The term comes from

Sanskrit grammar. Look it up in an unabridged dictionary.)
Explain how the sounds are affected in sandhi position when
these words are spoken rapidly

saved today	long curtains
forget me	breeze sank
let go	win prizes

3. Notice how words that end with a written r are pronounced in
the speech around you (a) before words beginning with a vowel
(b) before words beginning with a consonant. Is the [ɹ] ever
heard? Always? Never?

4. Make a list of words that exist in two forms, stressed and unstressed, like "the." Transcribe the two pronunciations in
phonetic characters.

5. Explain the following sound changes taken from the history of
other languages:

> Vulgar Latin *fixare became Italian fissare, "to fix."
> Vulgar Latin *ausare became French oser, "to dare."
> English "beefsteak" (loan word) became French biftek.
> English "euphuism" (loan word) became Russian evfuizm
> Vulgar Latin *vita(m) became Spanish vida, "life."
> Vulgar Latin *forte(m) became Spanish fuerte, "strong."
> Vulgar Latin *periculo became Spanish peligro, "danger."
> Germanic *dōmjan became English "deem."

6. Using phonetic characters, explain what happens to the vowels
in the following pairs of words which show moving accent:
"finite, infinite; fragile, fragility; injure, injurious."

7. Explain what happens to the stressed vowels when dissyll-
lables are made into polysyllables without shift of accent in
pairs like: "severe, severity; austere, austerity; serene, serenity;
opaque, opacity."

8. Why are the vowels shortened in the second of each of these
pairs of words: "keep, kept; clean, cleanly; dream, dreamt"?

9. Compare your pronunciation of the vowels in "me, mead,
meet." Describe the differences in quantity. What changes of
quality (specifically, in tenseness) accompany the changes in
length?

10. Do you tend to lengthen accented vowels more readily in final
open position or in a closed syllable? Do you notice a tendency
to diphthongize when you lengthen these vowels?

11. According to a theory of sounds put forward by Sir Richard
Paget in Human Speech (London, 1930), certain sounds are
used to designate certain acts because the tongue, lips, etc.,

behave in an imitative way when making them. Read the discussion for yourself (p. 139ff.). Test it by commonly used words, in relation to their meanings. Do you find such a correlation?

12. What exclamations do you prefer when you are in a state of excitement? Of lassitude? Do you vary the same exclamations according to your mood? How?

13. Can you explain how these sound changes have occurred:

> Early Germanic *water* became Modern German *Wasser*.
>
> Latin *pipa*, borrowed in Early Germanic, became Modern German *Pfeife* [pfaifǝ].
>
> Early Germanic *tō* became Modern German *zu* [tsu:].

14. What foreign language known to you has the greatest variety of vowel sounds? The least?

15. Why does Modern Italian pronounce *c* before *e, i* as [tʃ], and only before *u, a, o* as [k]? (The *k*-sound was original in all positions.)

CHAPTER 8

1. Paraphrase this comment by Chaucer on changes in language:

> Ye knowe ek 1 that in form of speche is chaunge   [1 also
> Withinne a thousand yeer, and wordes tho 2   [2 then
> That hadden pris 3, now wonder nyce and straunge   [3 value
> Us thinketh hem, and yet thei spake hem so,
> And spedde as wel in love as men now do.
>
> *Troilus and Cressida*, II, 22ff.

2. Study the selections from Middle English given in the appendix to Baugh's *History of the English Language*. Translations are given also. Can you see evidence that they represent different regional dialects?

3. What is the meaning of these archaic words: "fain, eftsoons, forlorn, tarn, scathe, lea, glaive, quoth, wot"?

4. What did these words mean in Old English contexts: "thrall, brand, byrnie, thane, earl, churl, knight, wight, scop, moot"?

5. Compare these translations of a line (Mark 10: 14) from the Gospels, in respect to vocabulary. Can you see similarities of Gothic and German to the English versions?

> Gothic: *Letiþ þo barna gaggan du mis, yah ni waryiþ þo, unte þize ist biudan-gardi Guþs.*
>
> German: *Lasset die Kindlein zu mir kommen, und wehret ihnen nicht, denn solcher ist das Reich Gottes.*
>
> Old Eng.: *Lǣtaþ đa lytlingas to me cuman, and ne forbēode ge him, sōþlīce swylcera is heofona rīce.*

Wycliffe: Suffre ȝe litle children for to come to me, and for-bede ȝe hem not, forsoth of such is the kyngdom of God.

Tyndale: Suffre the children to come vnto me, and forbid them not, for vnto suche belongeth the kingdom of God.

King James: Suffer the little children to come unto me, and forbid them not: for of such is the kingdom of God.

Modern English: Allow the little children to come to me, and do not prevent them; for of such is the Kingdom of God.

6. For a study of the treatment of abstract words at various periods, look up John, 17:1; for the treatment of an absolute construction, see Mark 8:23. The texts may be found in: Joseph Bosworth, *The Gothic and Anglo-Saxon Gospels in Parallel Columns with the Versions of Wycliffe and Tyndale* (London, 1888); Ferrar Fenton, *The Holy Bible in Modern English* (London, 1913), and the widely used Lutheran and King James translations, most familiar in German and English respectively.

7. Compare this example of sixteenth-century English with the instances of Latinized English of the same period cited in chapter 8:

> This last summer, I was in a gentleman's house where a young child, somewhat past four year old, could in no wise frame his tongue to say a little short grace; and yet he could roundly rap out so many ugly oaths, and those of the newest fashion, as some good man of fourscore year old hath never heard name before: and that which was most detestable of all, his father and mother would laugh at it.—Roger Ascham, *The Schoolmaster* (spelling modernized).

8. William Bullokar, an Elizabethan, tried to lay down a scientific orthography for English. Look up his *Book at Large for the Amendment of Orthography for English Speech* and make a criticism of his system from the point of view of consistency and practicability.

9. What were the historical circumstances under which the following words were borrowed into English: "trek, gnu, punch [a drink], tamales, luftwaffe, dungarees, kindergarten, pogrom, material, matériel, boudoir, divan, vezir, kosher?" (Consult the *New English Dictionary*.)

10. How have these words changed in meaning since Anglo-Saxon times: "wench, buxom, quean, with, speedy, dizzy, starve, knave, owe, shall, bury"?

11. Make a list of legal phrases like "notary public" and "fee simple" which preserve French word order.

12. What do you think of modified English spelling known as "Anglic," proposed by R. E. Zachrisson (*Anglic*, Uppsala, 1932)? There is a specimen in Baugh's *History of the English Language,* p. 401.

13. Study the list of American English words which have different equivalents in British English. H. L. Mencken, *The American Language* (ed. 1936), p. 233ff. What types of difference are involved?

14. Make a similar study of some other regional variation of English, outside the United States (e.g., C. Pettman's *Africanderisms*).

15. Which surviving inflections in English seem to you most likely to be eliminated in the future? Why?

CHAPTER 9

1. In his *Seven Types of Ambiguity* (New York: Harcourt Brace, 1921) William Empson quotes examples of verse in which the effect of emotional intensity is heightened by doubt as to the exact meaning or grammatical construction. An example (used on p. 66) is Shakespeare's Sonnet 42:

> Thou dost love her, because thou know'st I love her;
> And for my sake even so doth she abuse me,
> *Suffering* my friend for my sake to approve her.
> If I lose thee, my loss is my love's gain,
> And losing her, my friend hath found that loss. . . .

The meaning changes according to the construction of "suffering," which might be read with what follows instead of what precedes. Can you cite other examples in which syntactic ambiguity heightens emotional effect? (Robert Browning used the device deliberately.)

2. Cite examples of startling juxtapositions from W. H. Auden's *The Double Man.*

3. Collect examples of assonance in Emily Dickinson. Of experimentation in compounding words in Thomas Hardy, *The Dynasts.*

4. Collect examples of alliteration in Swinburne.

5. Quote lines in Shakespeare using simple Germanic words; polysyllabic Latin ones.

6. What words in William Butler Yeats are used most frequently as symbols implying more than the ordinary word-symbolism of prose?

7. **What usages in these lines of verse differentiate them from ordinary prose?**

                    everyone
          that's been there knows what
          i mean a god damned lot of
          people don't and never
          never will know
          they don't want
          to

          no

                    E. E. Cummings, *is* 5

Maculate speculations of personal prowess
Are forgotten in foyers of Moscow: the drama too absorbing,
The protagonists real.

          Norman Macleod, "A Russian Letter"

And twelve o'clock arrived just once too often,
     just the same he wore one grey tweed suit, bought
     one straw hat, drank one straight Scotch,
     walked one short step, took one long look,
     drew one deep breath,
     just one too many.

          Kenneth Fearing, "Dirge"

Tell me not in mournful numbers
     Life is but an empty dream,
For the soul is dead that slumbers,
     And things are not what they seem.

          H. W. Longfellow, "The Psalm of Life"

Now do I grow indignant at the fate
Which made me so imperfect to compare
With your degree of noble and of fair;
Our elements are the farthest skies apart;
And I enjoin you, ere it is too late,
To stamp your superscription on my heart.

          Elinor Wylie, "One Person," V

Forget not yet the tried intent
Of such a truth as I have meant;
My great travail so gladly spent,
     Forget not yet!

Forget not yet when first began
The weary life ye know, since whan
The suit, the service none tell can,
     Forget not yet!

          Sir Thomas Wyatt (1503-42)

Presentiment is that long shadow on the lawn
Indicative that suns go down;
The notice to the startled grass
That darkness is about to pass.

Emily Dickinson

You also, laughing one,
Tosser of balls in the sun,
Will pillow your bright head
By the incurious dead.

Babette Deutsch, "A Girl"

With little here to do or see
Of things that in the great world be,
Sweet Daisy! Oft I think of thee,
   For thou art worthy.

W. Wordsworth, "To the Daisy"

'Mid pleasures and palaces though we may roam,
Be it ever so humble, there's no place like home . . .

J. Howard Payne

8. Paraphrase these quotations. If there is doubt as to the sense, point to the cause of ambiguity.

9. Criticize the appropriateness of deviations from prose vocabulary.

10. What archaic words are associated with "poetic diction"? Quote examples. What do you think of the use of such words by contemporary writers?

CHAPTER 10

1. Why are a considerable number of French loan words employed in connection with dressmaking, restaurant dining, cosmetics?

2. Look up the etymologies of "boycott, strike, exploit, proletariat, propaganda." Which of these were used before the industrial era with other meanings?

3. Look up the following words in Helen Eaton's *Semantic Frequency List for English, French, German and Spanish* (Chicago: University of Chicago Press, 1940): "strike, bath, sin, virgin, democracy, business, examination." Does the comparative frequency of usage throw any light on the cultures represented?

4. Make up a list of terms of reproach used (a) in labor struggles (b) in politics (c) among students. Can you explain their pejorative significance?

5. Make a list of slogans for which men have died, like *Senatus populusque Romanus, Liberté egalité fraternité, Volk und Vaterland,* "Democracy," "Freedom of the Seas." What semantic problems do they represent?

6. Can you cite instances in literature where a character impersonating someone from another rank of society was betrayed by his speech? Instances of successful impersonation?

7. Using Eric Partridge's *Slang Today and Yesterday* (London, 1935), investigate the expressions connected with modern equivalents of cony-catching. Augment the list from your own recording of such phrases.

8. Study the use of Negro dialect in Carson McCullers's *The Heart Is a Lonely Hunter* (Boston: Houghton Mifflin, 1941). What characteristics—phonological and syntactical—point to regional dialect merely? Which indicate class dialect as well? Here is a sample:

> "It don't take words to make a quarrel. It look to me like us is always arguing even when we sitting perfectly quiet like this. It just this here feeling I haves. I tell you the truth—ever time I come to see you it mighty near wears me out. So less try not to quarrel in any way no more. . . .
> "Take Willie and me. Us aren't all the way colored. Our mama was real light and both of us haves a good deal of white folks' blood in us. And Highboy—he Indian. He got a good part Indian in him. None of us is pure colored and the word you all the time using haves a way of hurting peoples' feelings. . . . Everybody haves feelings—no matter who they is—and nobody is going to walk in no house where they certain their feelings will be hurt. You the same way. I seen your feelings injured too many times by white peoples not to know that" (p. 74 and 77).

9. Compare the preceding treatment of Negro dialect with the one by Richard Wright in *Native Son* (New York: Harper & Brothers, 1940), especially in the character of the preacher. Here phonology is emphasized. How consistent is the recording in the following extract?

> "Son, yuh know whut tha' tree wuz? It wuz the tree of knowledge. It wuzn't enuff fer man t' be like Gawd, he wanted t' know *why.* 'N' all Gawd wanted 'im t' do wuz bloom like the flowers in the fiel's, live as chillun. Man wanted t' know why 'n' he fell from light t' darkness, from love t' damnation, from blessedness t' shame. 'N' Gawd cast 'em outa the garden 'n' tol' the man he had t' git his bread by the sweat of his brow 'n' tol' the woman she had t' bring fo'th her chillun in pain 'n' sorrow. The worl' turned ergin 'em 'n' they had t' fight the worl' fer life . . ." (p. 242).

10. Point out the peculiarities of this poem which mark it as Scots dialect. Is it in any way humorous?

An' noo ance mair the Lomon'
  Has donn'd his mantle green,
An' we may gang a-roamin'
  Thro' the fields at e'en. . . .

An' juist the ither nicht, man,
  Twa barefit Mays were seen
(It maun hae been a sicht, man!)
  Dancin' on the green. . . .

Sae mild's the weather, Dauvit,
  That was but late sae bauld,
We gang withoot a grauvit
  Careless o' the cauld.

The auld mune to her ruin
  Gangs rowin' doon the sky,
When, swith, a braw bran new ane
  Cocks her horn on high! . . .

This is taken from James Logie Robertson's "Hughie's Advice to Dauvit to Enjoy the Fine Weather," as quoted in *A Book of Scottish Verse* (The World's Classics, Oxford University Press). For words unfamiliar to you, consult Joseph Wright, *English Dialect Dictionary*.

11. Contrast the effect of this use of regional dialect by James Russell Lowell. To what extent is it produced by purely orthographic and linguistic means, and to what extent by subject matter and treatment?

> We were gittin' on nicely up here to our village,
>   With good old idees o' wut's right an' wut ain't.
> We kind o' thought Christ went agin war an' pillage,
>   An' that eppyletts worn't the best mark of a saint.
>   But John P.
>   Robinson he
> Sez this kind o' thing's an exploded idee. . . .

The stanza comes from "What Mr. Robinson Thinks."

12. Read George Philip Krapp's discussion of regional dialect as opposed to general colloquial speech, in his *The English Language in America* (New York, 1925), I, p. 229 ff. Apply the distinction to the quotations given above under questions 8 and 9.

13. In the following passage, make separate lists of the dialect characteristics which fall under: sound (phonology), vocabulary, grammatical usage (syntax):

> "Yas, suh! dere warn't no stoppin' dem bones. Dey jus' gone whoopin' right t'rough dat jail, a-pullin' me after 'em. And den, on de las' day, de big buckra guard hear 'bout it, an' he come an' say I gots to gib up de bones. But I been seein' um roll wid de jailer in de watch house, an' I know he weakness. I ask dat buckra if he ain't likes me to teach um how to sing lucky to de bones 'fore I gib' dem up, an' 'fore he get 'way I done gone t'rough um for t'ree dollar an' seben cent an' dis shirt."

The selection is from *Porgy* by Dorothy and Dubose Heyward (New York: published for the Theater Guild by Doubleday, Page, 1927), Act IV.

14. When you next see a "gangster" film at the movies, jot down on slips of paper the slang expressions of the underworld used

in it. Can you judge of the accuracy and inclusiveness of the vocabulary?

15. What designations for articles of clothing appear to you to arise from false modesty? From a form of provocativeness? From a desire to imply associations of luxury and refinement?

16. Find out the equivalents for these objects in French, German, or any other foreign language you may know: brassieres, panties, dress shields, water closets, menstruation, venereal diseases. Which are the most factual designations? Which the most delicate? (Some of the terms are not registered in dictionaries. You may have to consult a native speaker.)

17. How many popular terms do you know for a state of inebriation? What metaphors are involved in them?

18. Make a vocabulary of special terms used in a boys' or girls' club.

19. What types of persons would you expect to use these sentences?

"Certainly, Madam. May I suggest that, as his lordship is greatly fatigued, he would be better able to assist you after he has slept."—Dorothy Sayers, *Lord Peter Views the Body*.

"Depend upon it, it is me."—Jane Austen, *Mansfield Park*.

"Mr. James MacPherson: I received your foolish and impudent letter. Any violence offered me I shall do my best to repel; and what I cannot do for myself the law shall do for me. I hope I shall never be deterred from detecting what I think is a cheat, by the menaces of a ruffian."—Samuel Johnson, Letter of 1775.

"They was the time when we was on the lan'. They was a boundary to us then. Ol' folks died off, an' little fellas come, an' we was always one thing—we was the fambly—kinda whole an' clear. An' now we ain't clear no more. I can't get straight. They ain't nothin' keeps us clear. . . . There ain't no fambly now."—John Steinbeck, *Grapes of Wrath*.

"Nothing's what it used to be. It's the restlessness after the war. It's going to take quite a while before we get over the dislocations. Take the income tax. I never imagined that I should live to see the day when some Government whippersnapper could walk into my office and pry into my private affairs. I never thought I should live to see the time when radicals were organizing labor or when a sentimentalist in the White House could almost get us into a League of Nations. I suppose war is disturbing."—John P. Marquand, *H. M. Pulham, Esquire*.

"Wot aggrawates me, Samivel, is to see 'em a-wastin' all their time and labor in making clothes for copper-colored people as don't want 'em, and takin' no notice of the flesh-colored Christians as do. If I'd my vay, Samivel, I'd just stick some o' these here lazy shepherds behind a heavy wheel-barrow, and run 'em up and down a fourteen-inch-wide plank all day. That 'ud shake the nonsense out of 'em, if anythin' vould."—Charles Dickens, *Pickwick Papers*.

"The divisions into classes, my lord, are not artificial. They are the natural outcome of a civilised society. There must always be a master and servants in civilised communities, my lady, for it is natural, and whatever is natural is right. . . . My lady, I am the son of a butler and a lady's maid—perhaps the happiest of all combinations; and to me the most beautiful thing in the world is a haughty, aristocratic English house, with every one kept in his place. Though I were equal to your ladyship, where would be the pleasure to me? It would be counter-balanced by the pain of feeling that Thomas and John were equal to me."—J. M. Barrie, *The Admirable Crichton*, Act I.

20. Comment on the linguistic methods used by these authors to indicate social levels of speech.

3. ENGLISH WORDS DISCUSSED IN THIS BOOK

Index